The Notebooks of
F. SCOTT FITZGERALD

The Notebooks of

F. SCOTT

FITZGERALD

Edited by MATTHEW J. BRUCCOLI

A Harvest Book
HARCOURT BRACE JOVANOVICH / BRUCCOLI CLARK
New York and London

Copyright © 1945 by New Directions Publishing Corporation

Copyright © 1972, 1978 by Frances Scott Fitzgerald Smith

Portions of this book reprinted by permission of New Directions

All rights reserved. No part of this publication may be reproduced or transmitted in any form or by any means, electronic or mechanical, including photocopy, recording, or any information storage and retrieval system, without permission in writing from the publisher.

Printed in the United States of America

Library of Congress Cataloging in Publication Data
Fitzgerald, Francis Scott Key, 1896-1940.
The notebooks of F. Scott Fitzgerald.
(A Harvest book)
I. Bruccoli, Matthew Joseph, 1931-   II. Title.
[PS3511.I9N6   1980]   818'.5'203   79-18490
ISBN 0-15-667362-2

First Harvest edition 1980
A B C D E F G H I J

Contents

Introduction

We know more about F. Scott Fitzgerald than about any other American writer of this century because he was a compulsive self-historiographer. More than authorial ego compelled him to document himself so fully and so painfully. These *Notebooks* were his workshop and chronicle. They were his literary bankroll. They were also his confessional.

Fitzgerald had a keen awareness of history—and of himself as the product of history. He understood that he was an exemplary figure (serving as a pattern; serving as a warning; serving as a type). Perhaps he even sensed what the mytho-historical process would later make of him. The *Notebooks* were assembled not during the Twenties when Fitzgerald seemed to have the Midas touch, but during the Thirties when everything that he touched crumbled. They document three periods: the writing of *Tender Is the Night* (1932-1934), the Crack-Up (1935-1937), and the Hollywood exile with the comeback of *The Last Tycoon* (1937-1940). This was a time of self-assessment for Fitzgerald—a time of endings. The concept of "lastness" echoes through Fitzgerald's life and work. He wrote about "The Last of the Belles" and *The Last Tycoon*. In the *Notebooks* he observed, "I am the last of the novelists for a long time now." This designation may be understood in terms of his allegiances to older American values. Fitzgerald may have been the last novelist committed to belief in the promises and possibilities of American life. He saw himself as coming at the end of a complex American historical process and identified with it. Malcolm Cowley has noted that it was as though Fitzgerald wrote in a room full of clocks and calendars. (He did, in fact, have an historical chart on his study wall.) Moreover, Fitzgerald accepted the symbolic roles that were assigned to him. He was fortune's darling in the Jazz Age—which he named. He was the shell-shocked casualty of the Depression.

The term "fragile" has often been applied to Fitzgerald. But, as these *Notebooks* show, his talent had tensile strength. It may have been the strength of weakness, but his talent did not break. At the end of his life Fitzgerald was writing as well as ever, and *The Last Tycoon* endures as the most heart-breaking fragment in American literature.

There are many impressive qualities in the *Notebooks*—wit, pathos, imagination, sensitivity—yet the dominant impression is of Fitzgerald's literary intelligence. One of his stereotyped images is that he was an ignorant genius who did not understand his gift. His *Notebooks* correct that sloppy assumption. Although he bitterly regretted that he had been an indifferent custodian of his genius, he understood profoundly well the claims of his craft. F. Scott Fitzgerald on the subject of writing merits close attention. As James Dickey has testified, "These *Notebooks* make writers of us all."

As a Princeton undergraduate F. Scott Fitzgerald acquired a copy of *The Note-Books of Samuel Butler** on 14 April 1917. At this time he had formed the ambition to become one of the greatest writers who ever lived and was seeking models for literary conduct. On 19 September 1919 Fitzgerald inscribed his copy: "The most interesting human document ever written." This testimonial was written the day after Fitzgerald received Maxwell Perkins's letter accepting *This Side of Paradise* for publication by Scribners— indicating that he had returned to Butler's *Note-Books* for guidance.

It is not known when Fitzgerald began assembling his Notebooks. The evidence suggests that it was after May 1932, when he moved to "La Paix" outside of Baltimore. One of the binders was purchased from Meyer & Thalheimer, a Baltimore stationer. At "La Paix" Fitzgerald hired his first secretary, one of whose duties was to type the entries for the Notebooks. Fitzgerald did not

---

*New York: Dutton, [1917].

type; all the entries were typed by his secretaries. Although he added to them for the rest of his life, Fitzgerald does not seem to have been compulsive about maintaining his Notebooks—as the miscellaneous late notes appended here indicate. The Notebooks were probably regarded as something to occupy his secretaries whenever there was no pressing work.

Fitzgerald began keeping his Notebooks with a special purpose in mind. He needed a place in which to bank the strippings from his short stories—as well as to record ideas or observations. When Fitzgerald determined that one of his stories was not to be reprinted, he culled from it the passages he regarded as worth using in a novel. These passages were preserved in his Notebooks. One of the main functions of the editorial material in this edition is to identify the story strippings. Some are from abandoned stories and cannot be identified. Others have no doubt eluded the editor.

Edmund Wilson included sixty percent of the Notebooks entries in *The Crack-Up* (New York: New Directions, 1945), with alterations. The present edition publishes the complete *Notebooks*, to which is appended a selection from the loose notes that are now with *The Last Tycoon* manuscripts at the Princeton University Library. Most of these loose notes—typed or in Fitzgerald's hand— are related to the work-in-progress on the unfinished Hollywood novel, but some are of a general nature. The editor has made a selection from these miscellaneous notes, restricting himself to those which do not seem to bear directly on *The Last Tycoon*.

The *Notebooks of F. Scott Fitzgerald* is not "The most interesting human document ever written"; but it is one of the most interesting and usable documents we have from a writer from whom we can never have too much.

Editorial Note

F. Scott Fitzgerald's Notebooks at the Princeton University Library are in two spring binders with alphabetized index separators. The pages are typed on 8½" x 11" white paper—except for yellow sheets 1-17 inserted after Z. The white sheets are unnumbered, and it is possible that they are not now in their original order.

Fitzgerald did not number the entries in his Notebooks. The identification numbers have been supplied by the editor to facilitate reference.

This volume publishes the complete Notebooks from the two binders with a selection of miscellaneous notes. The notes are printed without emendation—except for obvious typewriter spacing problems and strike-overs ("inthe" is printed as "in the"; "t he is printed as "the"). Spaced hyphens are treated as dashes. All brackets are Fitzgerald's brackets. Notes that he deleted have been omitted. Because the Notebooks were typed by secretaries from batches of Fitzgerald's holograph notes and magazine tearsheets, a number of entries were repeated. This edition of the *Notebooks* does not include repeated entries—except in cases where the repetition may have been intended for use in different contexts: see entries 348 and 1179, 512 and 1903. Notes that Fitzgerald marked for transfer to other sections have been moved. The "Supplementary Notes" include Fitzgerald's letter designations indicating the Notebooks sections into which he intended to insert each entry. When Fitzgerald corrected a typed entry in holograph, it has been printed as he corrected it. The significance of Fitzgerald's starred notes has not been determined, but his stars have been retained. Check marks have been omitted.†

The following people helped me: Alexander Clark, Glenda Fedricci, Michael Havener, Carol Johnston, Laura Myers, Harriet Oglesbee, Mardel Pacheco, Jean Rhyne, Peter Shepherd, Agnes Sherman, Willard Starks, Susan Walker, Joyce Werner, and Cara White. I owe a great debt to the Department of Special Collections at the Princeton University Library: this volume could not have been published without the generous assistance of Richard Ludwig and his efficient staff. And I am especially obligated to Karen Rood, who collaborated with me on the explanatory notes.

---

†Andrew Turnbull added circles or zeros in the margins of the Notebooks to indicate entries that were not included in *The Crack-Up*. These marks have not been retained.

Anecdotes

1   Rene had never before searched for a colored man in the
     Negro residential quarter of an American city. As time
     passed, he had more and more a sense that he was
     pursuing a phantom; it began to shame him to ask the
     whereabouts of such ghostly, blatantly immaterial
     lodgings as the house of Aquilla's brother.

2   But he came back because the herd (society) is all we
     have and we cannot stray without shortly finding that
     the wolves have to eat us too. He preached his special
     gospel to the herd. They (let us assume) liked it or half
     liked it. It worked.

3   Versailles fourth class (enlarge)

4   Story about Rose Marie's husband (Geneva) and his
     sleeping upstairs instead of working.

5   Isn't it too bad that the cow stepped on Eleanor's pencil.

6   Eleanor and the shot gun.

7   B.D.'s first frightening experience.   ★

8   Paris, Sept. 22nd, 1926.
     Dear Charles: —I send you a copy of your wire as it came to
     me
          Mrs. Hose Mattison
          Happ Birdy From Gunch and Me
                         Charles
     These French!

9   Then there's Emily. You know what happened to her; one night her husband came home and told her she was acting cold to him, but that he'd fix that up. So he built a bonfire under her bed, made up of shoes and things, and set fire to it. And if the leather hadn't smelled so terrible she'd have been burned to death.

10   Mutiny in the army.

11   The drowning

12   Sgt. Este

13   The absent minded gentleman on the train started to get off at the wrong station. As he walked back to his seat he assumed a mirthless smile and said aloud as though he were talking to himself;
"I thought this was Great Neck."
But he couldn't smooth over his mistake—we all knew that he had made a fool of himself and looked upon him with distaste and contempt.

14   A man wrapped up some domestic rate in small blankets cut from an old carpet, lest they should spread germs. A few months after he had turned them loose he found young rats around the house with carpet patterns on their fur.
     "How peculiar!" he exclaimed, "I didn't suspect it would turn out that way when I wrapped up those rats."
     But it did.

15   Story of the ugly aunt in album
Jimmy the 95 pd. center
The girl who fell off the shelf   ★

16   Once there was a whole lot of bird seed around the room because an author had adopted a chicken. It was impossible to explain to anyone just why he had adopted the chicken but still more impossible to know why he had bought the bird seed for the chicken. The chicken was later broiled and the bird seed thrown out,

but the question of whether the man was an author or a lunatic was still unsolved in the minds of the hotel servants who had to deal with the situation. The hotel servants didn't understand it. They didn't understand how months later the author could write a story about it but they all bought the magazine.

17   A man in the next room started a fire. The fire burned all through the mattress. Maybe it would have been better if the fire had burned through him but it missed him by a few inches. The mattress was carried out with great ceremony.

18   . . . would become a literary man and wrote an imitation of Ivanhoe called Elavoe. (I guess I wasn't alone in such phenomena for my daughter tells me about a composition of a friend at school concerning a certain Sir Tonsidor—who got his name, I gather, from some tonsilitis operation combined with some fragmentary memory of el toreadoro—I never heard any of the effusions about Sir Tonsidor but the name will stay with me forever. What did he look like? Would he break through doors with the facility of Mickey Mouse or were his tonsils always swollen?

19   Levan was a paralysis case. It was doubtful if he'd ever walk again. When he reached Lawrenceville he was placed on the team in the important position of Headguard, then considered the keystone post.
      Few of these people will get to the Rose Bowl, but if they do, we'll all be back of them. And few will be farther back than I will.

Bright Clippings

20   Snowladen evergreens will decorate the stairway   ★
and foyer leading to the ballroom, where a reproduction
of the boat in which the Viking princes, at the invitation
of the Russians, came to rule Russia in the ninth century,
will be arranged against a mirrored background. Its huge
golden sails will bear the imperial insignia, the double-
headed eagle, and Joss Moss and his orchestra, in
Russian garb will be seated in the craft.

Flags of old Russia will recall the imperial regime.
The ancient Russian custom of welcoming guests will be
invoked by six young Russian girls, in costume, who will
serve to those arriving, at a table near the ballroom
entrance, tiny squares of black bread dipped in salt and
small tumblers of vodka.

Prince Alexis Obolensky will sing during the
midnight supper in the oval restaurant and will present the
Siberian Singers, a male ensemble on their first
appearance in New York, in a selection of Russian folk
songs. Several dance numbers will feature the entertainment.

21   "Blossom Time" —the greatest musical romance ever
written. Cleveland: *One of the best musical sows written
in modern times.*

22   "Men of Genius are great as certain ethereal
Chemicals operating on the Mass of neutral intellect—
but they have not any individuality, and determined
Character." —————Keats.

23   Egyptian Proverb: The worst things:
      To be in bed and sleep not,
      To want for one who comes not,
      To try to please and please not.

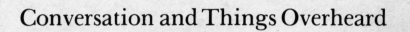

Conversation and Things Overheard

24   "I'm having them all psychoanalyzed," he said. "I got a
guy down from Zurich, and he's doing one a day. I
never saw such a gloomy bunch of women; always
bellyaching wherever I take 'em. A man I knew told me
he had his wife psychoanalyzed and she was easier to be
with afterward."

25   "When I hear people bragging about their social
position and who they are, and all that, I just sit back
and laugh. Because I happen to be descended directly
from Charlemagne. What do you think of that?"
Josephine blushed for him.

26   "I like poetry and music better than anything in the
world," she said. "They're wonderful."
He believed her, knowing that she spoke of her
liking for him.

27   "Yes, he has a position with the Dolleh Line, has a   ★
position with the Dolleh Line."
"Sweetie, he just scratched and scratched and   ★
scratched all night. Scratched and scratched and—"

28   From the yard next door a small boy shouted
mysteriously: "Who let that barrier through on me?"

29   "They claim you insulted one of the girls."
"That's nonsense, I only told her I'd like to bite her

neck. I wish all you ladies had one neck so I could bite it all at once. I'm a glutton for ladies' necks."

30   Rosalind's advice as to changing places with Zelda.

31   "Of course I'm afraid of horses. They try to bite me."
        "I've never met a horse—socially, that is—who didn't try to bite me. They used to do it when I put the bridle on; then, when I gave up putting the bridle on, they began reaching their heads around trying to get at my calves."
        "When I went to Southampton, I was—thrown at him."
        "Thrown from a horse?"

32   "She's really radiunt," she said, "really radiunt."   ★

33   You meig me sick to my stomach.

34   S'Chris' Watisis—a ship?

35   "Perfectly respectable girl but only been drinking that   ★
day. No matter how long she lives she'll always know she's killed somebody."

36   "Well, isn't it true? I told him how American education was terrible and you thought mine ought to be different."
        "Oh-h-h! And then to finish it off you slapped him?"
        "Well, I thought the best thing was to be partly American and slap him."

37   I think if one is V. W. M. you know (woman interrupts)
Yes I know curious, amazing, extraordinary, what I mean I think are—I mean to say—preferred
I don't know

38   "There's no use looking at things, because you don't like   ★
things," remarked Raines, in answer to his polite interest.
        "No," said Charlie frankly, "I don't."
        "You like only rhythms, with things marking the beats, and now your rhythm is broken."

39   "You believe in something," he said, after a long time.
"I don't know yet what it is. You're lucky to believe in
something."
"I believe in nothing."
"Yes, you do. You believe that's crouching in this room
very near you now—something that you tried to do
without and couldn't do without. And now it's gradually
taking form again and you're afraid."
Charlie sprang to his feet, his mouth quivering. "No!" he
cried. "I'm—I'm—"
"Sit down," said Raines quietly. He looked at his watch.
"We have all night; it's only eleven."
Charlie gave a quick glance around and sat down,
covering his face for a minute with his hands.

40   "What nice words," she teased him. "If you keep on I'm   ★
going to throw myself under the wheels of the cab."

41   "Call me Micky Mouse," she said suddenly.
"Why?"
"I don't know—it was fun when you called me Micky
Mouse."

42   "What do you think I ought to have?" Mary groaned.
"God what a mess!
Did you pay that man for his hat?"

43   Mr. Melarky wants to see the villa because he's here
studying human nature.

44   Man on pier pronouncing dessert as *des*ert.

45   I am willing to die with my boots on—I just want to be
sure that they are my own boots and that they're all the
on.

46   "Showing off."
"Well, then, so was Christ showing off."

47   "Prowling the rattlers" = robbing freight cars

48   Beginning of a story "Incorrigible"
        Father: Who do you admire?

Son: Andy Gump. Who do you think I admire—
George Washington? Grow up!

49   With a piquant face and all the chic in the world. This
is because I was educated in Paris and this in turn I owe
to someone's chance remark to Cousin Arletta that she
had a nice big daughter who was only twenty-two or
three at the time. It took three bromides to calm Cousin
Arletta and I started for the Convent of the Sacree Coeur
next day.

50   Somebody might have thought of bringing the jug of
water ashore. If I don't do anything it isn't done in this
house—I mean this family.

51   Kitty, if you write on that pillow with my lipstick

52   People's homes—a lovely home

53   Have you a wadder closet?

54   "Am I right or wrong?" he asked the head waiter. The   ★
answer was obvious—he was right—gloriously and
everlasttingly right. Interesting too.

55   "The French Riviera."
"But surely not now," objected Mrs. Woodle. "It's—it's
closed."
"How do you mean closed. We're not going hunting."

56   "I'm giving a dinner tonight, some very fine cultivated
people. I want you to come. I sent a note to your cabin."
"For God's sake," Lew groaned, "I don't want to meet
any people. I know some people."

57   "Look me up in the Social Register"

58   Movie conversation about Anne of Austria

59   You hate people, don't you?
Yes, and you do too.
I hate them like hell.
What are you going to do about it?

I don't know. But not that anyhow. If I'm cold I'm not going to always use it to learn their secrets by finding them off guard and vulnerable. And I'm not going around saying I'm fond of people when I mean I'm so damned used to their reactions to my personal charm that I can't do without it. Getting emptier and enptier. Love is shy. I thought from the first that no one who thought about it like you did ever had it.

60   "Or have you got an engagement with your drug-taking friend in Monte Carlo?"

He sat down and began putting on his shoes.

"I shouldn't have told you that. I suppose you think he'll convert me to the habit."

"I certainly don't think it's a very profitable association."

"Oh, yes it is. It's not everybody who can get the dope habit from a prominent moving picture director. In fact, it's begun already. At this very moment I'm full of dope. He started me on cocaine, and we're working slowly up to heroin."

"That isn't really funny, Francis."

"Excuse me. I was trying to be funny and I know you don't like my way of being funny."

She countered his growing bitterness by adopting a tone of calm patience.

61   In Virginia the Italian children say:

"Lincoln threw blacks out; now they're back"

"The white people fit the Yankees"

"Yankees *are* white people"   Statement.

"Not I ever hear tell of."   Ans.

62   I really loved him, but of course it wore out like a love affair. The fairies have spoiled all that.

63   "Just a couple of old drunks, just a couple of ol-l-ld circus clowns."

64   SCRATCHING: "Any particular place?"
                "Yes."
                "Where?"
                "All over."

65   Mr. So and So went on a spree and lost his position.

66   "Some people are just naturally uxorious—I love
      Katherine but if she died I'd marry again in a year—and
      I'd say that in front of her."
      "Not I," Cass thought. "When I married Jill I didn't
      want to and I had every reason not to. But afterwards I
      had eight perfect years—eight perfect years with never a
      night of going to sleep in anger and never a morning
      when we didn't think first of each other."
      He tried the usual specifics for sorrow—endless work, an
      expedition into drink, almost everything except women.
      And he said aloud a few times without striving for effect
      "That's over—my heart's in the grave."
      Now when a man of thirty-four, successful and well-
      liked, with no extra flesh around his middle and no pink
      spot in his hair lets it be known that his affections are
      underground there are a certain number of women who
      will think "Maybe" and wonder.

67   I'm in a hurry
                I'm in a hurry. I'm in a hurry
      What are you in a hurry about?
                I can't explain I'm in a hurry

68   This is a tough girl and I'm taking her to tough place.

69   300 a day die in auto accidents in the U. S. A.

70   Man looking at aeroplane. "That's one of them new   ★
      gyropractors."

71   Bijou, regarding her cigarette fingers:
                "Oh, Trevah! Get me the pumice stone."

72   His life was a sort of dream, as are most lives with the
      mainspring left out.

73   Suddenly her face resumed that expression which can
only come from studying moving picture magazines over
and over, and only described as one long blond wish
toward something—a wish that you'd have a wedlock
with the youth of Shirley Temple, the earning power of
Clark Gable; the love of Clark Gable and the talent of
Charles Laughton—and with a bright smile the girl was
gone.

74   Feel wide awake—no but at least I feel born, which is   ★
more than I did the first time I woke up.

75   The cartoon cat licked the cartoon kitten and a girl
behind me said, "Isn't that sweet?"

76   In utter weariness he asked her once in different
words, "Then where do you go from here—where do you
turn?"
    "Toward life," she said "Toward life," and turned
toward him.

77   We can't just let our worlds crash around us like a lot of   ★
dropped trays.

78   Q: What did he die of? A: He died of jus' sheer die-
ability.

79   Mother saying she went over to Baltimore "right after
the funeral."

80   "Hello, Sam." When you were a good guest you knew
the name of the servants, the smallest babies, and the
oldest aunts. "Is Bonny in?"

81   "You're now talking to Mr. Brugerol's second.
Anything you say will be used against you. My client
demands an apology."
    "My client refuses to apoligize."
    "Well, my client says unless he gets an apology and a
good one, he wants to kill your client."
    "Well, he's got to catch him first." We all laughed
noiselessly; then with sudden compunction Francis
added, "Is that old bloodhound serious about this?"

82   At Laundry Convention. First he vomited on my car, then he vomited on my dogs. Then I got the hose etc. Was I right?

83   That's Mr. Woodles—he had a vurry, vurry low cephalic index.

84   "Oh, all we sickies used to smoke in Switzerland, sort of disinfectant don't you know."

85   I like writers. If you speak to a writer you often get an answer.   ★

86   Woman says about husband that he keeps bringing whole great masses of dogs back from the pound

87   "We haven't got any more gin," he said. "Will you have a bromide?" he added hopefully.

88   A Beach. The nurses. Passing through a phrase, "Nothink, didn't I, Mummy?"

89   "Our typical remark is a very doubtful. Well, I don't know" (This was one of Seth's un-American days.) "For the British it's 'Extraordinary'—a stupefaction toward something not understood—but it disposed of, for their ends at least."
      "For the French i 's 'Eh, voila!' " said Abe.
      "Exactly. A point proved, an exposition made."
      This doesn't sound real, but I'm sure that's what we said—
      I talk in a rather cracked bookish voice, for instance, with really quite well balanced sentences.

90   Long engagements, nothing to do but to marry or quarrel so I decided to quarrel.   ★

91   *I* didn't do it," he said, using the scented "I"

92   They get thrown together so much. They have to kiss each other so much. That's the danger of the stage. They get thrown together.

93   Remember you're physically repulsive to me

94   By opposing to them a tensity such as a quarterback
opposes to a big tackle coming down to take him out.
All right—into this smaller compass between my muscle
I will interpose a (something—look up) of tissue that
will stand you—but something more, big boy, I will
wear you out psychologically until you give me the
game, until I fascinate you like whatever beasts of prey
go in for fascination.

95   Just suppose you tried to put over a point by main   ★
strength. Look here, I'd take this fixture, this lamp,
anything, and crack you with it." ˙

96   Learn young about hard work and good manners—and
you'll be through the whole dirty mess and nicely dead
again before you know it.

97   Now it's all as useless as repeating a dream.

98   The Caux Count's Bricks.

99   "There seems to be some man named Jack that all the
waiters want to see," he remarked seriously.
"That means money."
"Oh Jack means money. Oh yes, oh yes, oh yes I see—
jack."

100   Will you be long in Naples? That sounds like Hugo's
All you want to know in German. Don't you know the
questions? Are all your rooms taken and is attendance
included?
Do not shut the windows entirely.
We will finish up with black coffee cigars and liqueurs.
I always like that one.
I used one of those pamphlets once in Italy—confessed.

101   I'm going to break that stubborn stupid part of you that
thinks that any American woman who has met
Brancuse is automatically genius and entitled ever after
to leave the dishes and walk around with her head in
the clouds.

102   They read a couple of books and see a few pictures   ★
      because they haven't got anything else to do, and then
      they say they're finer in grain than you are, and to
      prove it they take the bit in their teeth and tear off for a
      fare-you-well just about as sensitive as a fire horse.

103   You look to me like a very ordinary three piece suit

104   I still don't understand why we're not only the boat—
      why we're on the rocking house.

105   "This here nigger's my boy Hugo."
          "Your son!" The girl stared from one to the other in
      wild fascination.
          "No, he's my body-servant. I guess you'd call it.
      We call a nigger a boy down yonder."

106   Man to Woman "You look as if you wanted
      excitement—is that true?"

107   Go and sleep with a cheap skate—go on—it'd do you
      good. It would take another little tuck in your soul and
      you'd fit better, be more comfortable.

108   I'm sore—I'm going home and read fine print.

109   Francis says he wants to go away and try his
      personality on a lot of new people.

110   He drew himself up with a dignified hiccup.
      "That was before repeal," he said, "I am now tryin to
      stand behind the President."
      "But you're not standing behind the President,"
      objected Georgy, "You're—teetering."

111   "You went out of your way to make a preposterous
      attack on an old gentlewoman who had given you
      nothing but courtesy and consideration."

112   "I have decided that the office cannot continue to hold
      both you and me. One of us must go—which shall it
      be?"

"Well, Mr. Wrackham, your name is painted on the doors—I suppose it would be simpler if you stayed."

113   "My last husband was thrown from his horse. You must learn to ride." He takes one look around uneasily for a horse..

114   "We throw in one of these flowers. You know how frails are—if a stone sails in they put up a yelp—if it's a rose they think there's the Prince of Wales at last."

115   That one about the four girls named Meg who fall down the rabbit hole

116   He wants to make a goddess out of me and I want to be ★ Mickey Mouse.

117   Sara's remark "Can't they get along with anybody?"

118   Third class passengers (Archie on boat)

119   No, there is no one here. Pay attention. No one I say, or if there is one like another. Pay attention.

120   "Everytime some debutante decides to dazzle the world there's another flop due on Broadway.

121   Mr. Powell by a circular motion of his finger sped Hugo on the designated mission. Then he seated himself gingerly in a rocking-chair and began revolving his thatched straw hat rapidly in his hands.

122   "Yes mamn, if necessary. Look here, you take a girl and she goes into some cafe where she's got no business to go. Well then her escort he gets a little too much to drink an' he goes to sleep an' then some other fella comes up and says 'Hello, sweet mamma' or whatever one of those mashers says up here. What does she do? She can't scream, on accout of no real lady'll scream nowadays—no—she just reaches down in her pocket and slips her fingers into a pair of Powell's defensive brassknuckles, debutante's size, executes what I call the

Scoeity Hook, and Wham! that big fella's on his way to the cellar.

123   "Well—what—what's the guitar for?" whispered the awed Amanthis. Do they have to knock somebody over with the guitar?"

"No, mamn! exclaimed Jim in horror. "No mamn. In my course no lady would be taught to raise a guitar against anybody. I teach 'em to play. Shucks! you ought to hear 'em. Why when I've given 'em two lessons you'd think some of 'em was colored.

124   "What are they doing?" whispered Amanthis to Jim.

"That there's a course in southern accent. Lot of young men up here want to learn southern accent—so we teach it— Georgia, Florida, Alabama, Eastern Shore, Ole Virginian. Some of 'em even want straight nigger—for song purpose."

125   Why aren't you at Captain's table?

126   Dinah's "you'll spoil everything."

127   Don't you think you're sort of hogging your son, Mrs. So and So?

128   "Nothing and nothing make nothing."

"What was that Mrs. X said?"

"What was it you said, Mrs. X? Let us listen and next time we'll hear her. She says priceless things. What was it you said, Mrs. X?"

"I said 'Nothing and nothing make nothing.' "

129   To Bertram Russell:

"Well, for Christ's sake, I'm not keeping you."

"Thanks for your polite curses. I have nothing against you. In fact I etc. and had meant to etc. I do believe there is a certain class of Englishmen who profit by a good peck in my backside occasionally. And there is a certain section of my countrymen who take pleasure in giving it very much as to make it clear, it was once considered a good rag at Eton to kick physically the

bottom of the current candidates for the kingdoms of
Abysinnia and Spain.''
> Your Lordship's Most Obediant Servant

130   "Oh last month they had pictures of a lot of girls, only
under mine it said that it was Miss Somebody Curtis
from Philadelphia who was visiting in the city." She
groaned, "That was the last straw."

131   Biggest laugh of the seasing.

132   Adjust my strap.

133   Hey, set still. Doan get so excited. You'd think you was
the firs guy ever got boined.

134   Frances' "Terribly Aryan looking"

135   Girl on train who said "So bigoted"

136   Bud Murray's inferior complex.

137   Ogden and Jesus

138   The Bowes children: "I blame it on the door," and "I didn't ★
push her—she didn't break her leg—see, it's on."

139   "The time I fell off a closet shelf.
"You what?"
"I fell off a shelf—and he put it in the paper."
"Well, what were you doing?"
"I just happened to be up on a shelf and I fell off."
"Oh, don't say it."
"I've stopped giving any further explanations. Anyhow
father said it was news."

140   "I feel panicky," she confessed. "Last Christmas I thought I
was through with boys and then one night in May up at
New Haven the orchestra kept playing Poor Butterfly
over and over again and lots of them were in uniform
already and they all got touching and romantic like they
used to be. I began thinking suppose the war lasts five
or ten years more and they all get killed. Every day I

wait I'll have less men to choose from—and if I wait till
I fall in love again I'll just wait forever.''

Description of Things and Atmosphere

141   The wind shivered over the leaves, over the white
casements—then as if it was beauty it could not stand,
jumped out the window and climbed down from the
cornice on the corner.

Then it came to ground. All that had happened was
that green had blown through the wind and back and
returned to settle on the same red walls, waving it
forever after as a green flag, a heavy, ever bearded, ever
un-shaven flag, like water when you drop a petal in it,
like a woman's dress and then the little trickles that
wound about the casements—faint, somnescent and gone.

After that silence—the wind blowing the curtains.
The cross child you had to scold. The moment had gone.
The moment had come and existed for a minute. A lacy
light played once more—a scherzo, no a new prelude to
ever blooming, ever greening and he was sorry for what
he had ever said or thought.

Once more the wind was dead. There was only one
leaf flickering against the white casement. Perhaps there
was someone back of it being happy.

142   *The pleasant, ostentatious boulevard was lined at
prosperous intervals with New England Colonial
houses—without ship models in the hall. When the
inhabitants moved out here the ship models had at last
been given to the children. The next street was a
complete exhibit of the Spanish-bungalow phase of

West Coast architecture; while two streets over, the cylindrical windows and round towers of 1897—melancholy antiques which sheltered swamis, yogis, fortune tellers, dressmakers, dancing teachers, art academies and chiropractors—looked down now upon brisk busses and trolley cars. A little walk around the block could, if you were feeling old that day be a discouraging affair.

On the green flanks of the modern boulevard children, with their knees marked by the red stains of the mercurochrome era, played with toys with a purpose—beams that taught engineering, soldiers that taught manliness, and dolls that taught motherhood. When the dolls were so banged up that they stopped looking like real babies and began to look like dolls, the children developed affection for them. Everything in the vicinity—even the March sunlight—was new, fresh, hopeful and thin, as you would expect in a city that had tripled its population in fifteen years.

143   Days of this February were white and magical, the nights were starry and crystalline. The town lay under a cold glory.

144   Dyed Siberian horse.

145   As thin as a repeated dream.

146   The sea was coming up in little intimidating rushes.

147   The island floated, a boat becalmed, upon the almost perceptible curve of the world.

148   Lost in the immensity of surfaceless blue sky like air piled on air.   ★

149   A sudden gust of rain blew over them and then another—as if small liquid clouds were bouncing along the land. Lightening entered the sea far off and the air blew full of crackling thunder.   ★
                    to]

150   The table cloths blew around the pillars. They blew and blew and blew. The flags twisted around the red   ★

chairs like live things, the banners were ragged, the
corners of the tables tore off through the burbling,
billowing ends of the cloths.] There was Pat O'Mara, his
hands, adequate enough smoothing hair. Blow, banners,
blow. You in ermine slow down you, slow, whip, no
snap, only whip wind in the corners of the tables. Can I
have a flower if they don't want one.

151 On the great swell of the Blue Danube, the summer ball
rocked into motion.

152 A circus ring for ponies in country houses.

153 The tense, sunny room seemed romantic to Becky, with
its odor of esoteric gases, the faint perfumes of future
knowledge, the low electric sizz in the glass cells.

154 A rambling frame structure that had been a residence in
the 80's, the country poorhouse in the 1900's, and now
was a residence again.

155 The groans of moribund plumbing.

156 The silvery "Hey!" of a telephone.

157 The curious juxtapositions made him feel the profound ★
waves of change that had already washing this
country—the desperate war that had rendered the
plantation house absolete, the industrialization that had
spoiled the easy-going life centuring around the old
court house. And then the years yielding up eventually
in the backwater those curious young products who
were neither peasants, nor bourgeois, nor scamps, but a
little of all three, gathered there in front of the store.

158 New York's flashing, dynamic good looks, its tall man's
quick-step.

159 Afterward they would drive around until they found the ★
center of the summer night and park there while the
enchanted silence spread over them like leaves over the
babes in the wood.

160   Stevedores appeared momentarily against the lighted hold of a barge and jerked quickly out of sight down an invisible incline.

161   Whining, tinkling hoochie-coochie show.

162   The first lights of the evening were springing into pale existence. The Ferris wheel, pricked out now in lights, revolved leisurely through the dusk; a few empty cars of the roller coaster rattled overhead.

163   Metropolitan days and nights that were tense as singing wires.

164   The late sun glinted on the Mississippi flats a mile away.

165   When the stars were bright enough to compete with the bright lamps.

166   The limousine crawled crackling down the pebbled drive.   ★

167   Three frail dock lights glittered dimly upon innumerable fishing boats heaped like shells along the beach. Farther out in the water there were other lights where a fleet of slender yachts rode the tide with slow dignity, and farther still a full ripe moon made the water bosom into a polished dancing floor.

168   That stream of silver that waved like a wide strand of curly hair toward the moon.

169   The club lay in a little valley, almost roofed over by willows, and down through their black silhouettes, in irregular blobs and patches, dripped the light of a huge harvest moon. As they parked the car, Basil's tune of tunes, Chinatown drifted from the windows and dissolved into its notes which thronged like elves through the glade.

170   Deep autumn had set in, with a crackling wind from the west.

171   Next door they were scrubbing a building upon a lit-up platform. It was fun to see it come out all bright and new.

172   The hotel we selected—*The Hotel de la Morgue*—was small and silent enough to suit even the most refined taste.

173   The droning of frogs in the Aislette Valley covered the sound of the bringing up of our artillery.

174   In the afternoon they came to a lake. It was a cup of a lake with lily pads for dregs and a smooth surface of green cream.

175   You can order it in four sizes; demi (half a litre), distingue (one litre), formidable (three litres), and catastrophe (five litres).

176   In the deep locker-room of the earth.

177   The rear wall was formed by a wide flag of water, falling from a seam in the rock ceiling, and afterwards draining into some lower level cave beyond.

178   *SEEN IN A JUNK YARD*

Dogs, chickens with few claws, brass fittings, T's elbow, rust everywhere, bales of metal 1800 lbs., plumbing fixtures, bathtubs, sinks, water pumps, wheels, Fordson tractor, Acetylene lamps for tractors, sewing machine, bell on dingy, box of bolts, No. 1 van, stove, auto stuff (No. 2), army trucks, cast iron, body hot dog stand, dinky engines, sprockets like watch parts, hinge all taken apart on building side, motorcycle radiators, George on the high army truck.

179   Across the street from me in Hendersonville, N.C. is a movie sign, usually with a few bulbs out in the center. It reads tonight: The Crusades: the Flaming Passion of a Woman Torn Between Two Camps.
        This is the right idea and to aid in the campaign to prove that a woman (not *women* mind you—that point

is granted) is at the tiller in every storm, I submit the following suggestions to draw in the elder gadgets and their tokens.

Huckleberry Finn—how a girl changed the life of a ★ Missouri boy.

180   A strip of straw, half-braided, that fell across another desk.

181   A region of those monotonous apartment rows that embody the true depths of the city—darkly mysterious at night, drab in the afternoon.

182   Memory of coming into Washington.

183   All of a sudden the room struck like a clock.

184   For a while the big liner, so sure and proud in the open sea, was shoved ignominiously around by the tugs like a helpless old woman.

185   There were Roman legionaries with short, bright swords and helmets and shields shining with gilt, a conqueror in his chariot with six horses, and an entourage of sparkling, plumed Roman knights, captured Gauls in chains, Greeks in buskins and tunics of Ionian blue, black Egyptians in flashing desert reds with images of Isis and Osiris, a catapult and, in person Hannibal, Caesar, Rameses and Alexander.

186   The evening gem play of New York was already taking place outside the window. But as Charlie gazed at it, it seemd to him tawdry and theatrical, a great keeping up of appearances after the reality was gone. Each new tower was something erected in defiance of obvious and imminent disaster; each beam of light a final despairing attempt to pretend that all was well.

"But they had their time. For a while they represented a reality. These things are scarcely built; not a single generation saw them and passed away before we ceased to believe."

187   The rhythm of the weekend with its birth, its planned gaieties and its announced end, followed the rhythm of life and was a substitute for it.

188   The blurred world seen from a merry-go-round settled into place; the merry-go-round suddenly stopped.

189   The city's quick metropolitan rhythm of love and birth and death that supplied dreams to the unimaginative, pageantry and drama to the drab.

190   Spring came sliding up the mountain in wedges and spear points of green.

191   Far out past the breakers he could survey the green-and-brown line of the Old Dominion with the pleasant impersonality of a porpoise. The burden of his wretched marriage fell away with the buoyant tumble of his body among the swells, and he would begin to move in a child's dream of space. Sometimes remembered playmates of his youth swam with him; sometimes, with his two sons beside him, he seemed to be setting off along the bright pathway to the moon. Americans, he liked to say, should be born with fins, and perhaps they were—perhaps money was a form of fin. In England property begot a strong place sense, but Americans, restless and with shallow roots, needed fins and wings. There was even a recurrent idea in America about an education that would leave out history and the past, that should be a sort of equipment for aerial adventure, weighed down by none of the stowaways of inheritance or tradition.

192   The nineteen wild green eyes of a bus were coming up   ★
         to them through the dark.

193   The mingling and contrast of the silver lines of car   ★
         track and the gold of the lamps, the streams of light
         rippling on the old road and the lamps on the bridge,
         and then when the rain had stopped the shadows of the
         maple leaves on the picket fence.

194   The train gave out a gurgle and a forlorn burst of false noise, and with a clicking strain of couplers pulled forward a few hundred yards.

195   When the freight stopped next the stars were out, so sudden that Chris was dazzled. The train was on a rise. About three miles ahead he saw a cluster of lights fainter and more yellow than the stars, that he figured would be Dallas.

196   The music indoors was strange in the summer; it lay uneasily upon the pulsing heat, disturbed by the loud whir of the fans.

197   There were only the colleges and the country clubs. The parks were cheerless, without beer and mostly without music. They ended at the monkey house or at some imitation French vista. They were for children—for adults there was nothing.

198   A half-displayed packet of innocuous post cards warranted to be very dirty indeed.

199   Against the bar a group of ushers was being photographed, and the flash-light surged through the room in a stifling cloud.

200   In one corner of the ballroon an arrangement of screens like a moving-picture stage had been set up and photographers were taking official pictures of the bridal party. The bridal party, still as death and pale as wax under the bright lights, appeared, to the dancers circling the modulated semidarkness of the ballroom, like those jovial or sinister groups that one comes upon in The Old Mill at an amusement park.

201   She thought of electric fans in little restaurants with ★ lobsters on ice in the windows, and of pearly signs glittering and revolving against the obscure, urban sky, the hot, dark sky. And pervading everything, a terribly strange, brooding mystery of roof tops and empty apartments, of white dresses in the paths of parks, and

fingers for stars and faces instead of moons, and people
with strange people scarcely knowing one another's
names.

202 Drawing away from the little valley, past pink pines and ★
fresh, diamond-strewn snow.

203 A sound of clinking waiters.

204 The music started again. Under the trees the wooden
floor was red in the sun.

205 Phonograph roared new German tangoes into the smoke
and clatter.

206 Cannes in the season—he was filling the cafe, the light
which blazed against the white poplar bark and green
leaves with sprightlier motes of his own creation—he
saw it vivid with dresses just down from Paris and
giving off a sweet pungent odor of flowers and
chartreuse and fresh black coffee and cigarettes, and
mingled with these another scent, the mysterious
thrilling scent of love. Hands touched jeweled hands
over the white tables; the vivid gowns and the shirt
fronts swayed together and matches were held, trembling
a little, for slow lighting cigarettes.

207 Parts of New Jersay, as you know, are under water, and
other parts are under continual surveillance by the
authorities. But here and there lie patches of garden
country dotted with old-fashioned frame mansions,
which have wide shady porches and a red swing on the
lawn. And perhaps, on the widest and shadiest of the
porches there is even a hammock left over from the
hammock days, stirring gently in a Victorian wind.

208 The battered hacks waiting at the station; the snow- ★
covered campus, the big open fires in the club houses.

209 Not long after noon—he could tell by the thin shadow
of the shutter.

210 Duty, Honor, Country, West Point—the faded banners
on the chapel walls.

211   But while the crowd surged into the bright stadium like lava coming down a volcano from the craters of the runways.

212   No one has even seen Richerees, near Asheville because the windows fog with smoke just before you get there.

213   The — Hotel was planned to give rest and quiet to tired and overworked business men and overwrought and over societied women.

214   When opened up the fish smelled like a very stuffy room.

215   Trolley running on the crack of dawn

216   An old style flivver crushed the obliterated borders of the path.

217   It was a not at all the remodelled type of farmhouse favored by the wealthy, it was pristine. No wires, and one was sure no pipes led to it.

218   Occasionally two yellow disks would top a rise ahead of them and take shape as a late-returning automobile. Except for that they were alone in a continual rushing dark. The moon had gone down.

219   The decks were bright and restless, but bow and stern were in darkness so the boat had no more outline than an accidental cluster of stars. Francis took the trip one lonely evening.

220   One of those places they used to call somebody's "Folly." Already for a whole slew of people who weren't there—hopeful little shops built into the hotel, some open and some closed.

221   There was rosy light still on that big mountain, the Pic de Something of the Dent de Something, because the world was round or for some such reason. Bundled up children were splattering in for tea as if the outdoors were tired of them and wanted to change its dress in

quiet dignity. Down in the valley there were already bright windows and misty glows from the houses and hotels of the town.

222   The sun was already waving gold, green and white flags on the Wildstrubel.

223   Its familiar light and books and last night's games always pushed just out of sight under something, the piano with last night's songs still open on it.

224   A toiling sweating sun stoked the sky overhead.   ★

225   Green jars and white magnolias

226   Clairmont Avenue

227   Shallows in the Lake of day

228   Colors at Oregon: gold, dark green, little white buoys on safety rope, background white figures, grey underpinnings—all seen thru foliage dark and light green.

229   Bird call: Weecha, weecha, weecha, weecha *eat*?

230   Suddenly the room rang like a diamond in all four corners.

231   Josephine picked them out presently below a fringe by their well-known feet—Travis de Coppet's deft, dramatic feet; Ed Bement's stern and uncompromising feet; the high, button shoes of some impossible girl.

232   He passed an apartment house that jolted his memory. It was on the outskirts of town, a pink horror built to represent something, somewhere, so cheaply and sketchily that whatever it copied the architect must have long since forgotten.

233   The two orchestras moaned in pergolas lit with fireflies, and many-colored spotlights swept the floor, touching a buffet where dark bottles gleamed.

234   Abruptly it became full summer. After the last April storm someone came along the street one night, blew up the trees like balloons, scattered bulbs and shrubs like confetti, opened a cage full of robins and, after a quick look around, signaled up the curtain upon a new backdrop of summer sky.

235   White chestnut blossoms slanted down across the tables and dropped impudently into the butter and the wine. Julia Ross ate a few with her bread.

236   The stench of cigars in small houses. (Remember it with old mill.)

237   Zelda's worn places in yard and hammock.

238   The river flowed in a thin scarlet gleam between the public baths and the massed tracks upon the other side. Booming, whistling, far-away railroad sounds reached them from down there; the voices of children playing tennis in Prospect Park sailed fraily overhead.

239   God's whitest whiskers dissolved before a roaring plane bound for Corsica.

240   The corpses of million blue fish.

241   Bryn Mawr coverlet.

242   Her face flushed with cold, etc. (more to this)

243   It was a crisp cold night with frost shooting along the grass.

244   the familiar, unforgotten atmosphere of many Negroes and voices pleading-calm and girls painted bright as savages to stand out against the tropical summer.

245   The Grand Duc had just begun its slow rattling gasp for life in the inertness of the weakest hour.

246   Out the window, the snow on the pine trees had gone lilac in the early dusk.

247   The lights of many battleships drifting like water jewels upon the dark Hudson.

248   We looked out at the port where the rocking masts of boats pointed at the multitudinous stars.

249   The wind searched the walls for old dust.

250   cluster of murky brown doors so alike that to be identified it seemed that hers must be counted off from abutting blackness of an alley.

251   listless disorder

252   on the sky-blue sky, the clouds low above the prairie, the grand canyonesque architecture of the cliffs, the cactus penguins extending conciliatory arms

253   the new trees, the new quivering life, the new shadows that designed new terrain on the old

254   The main room, for which no adequate name has yet been found in the Republic.

255   Hot Springs:

    In a Spring vacation hotel the rain is bad news indeed. The hundred French windows of the great galleries led the eye out to ink-and-water pines snivelling listlessly on to raw brown tennis courts, to desolate hills against soiled white sky. There was "nothing to do" for hotel and resort were one and the same and no indoor activity was promised on the bulletin board until the concert of the Princeton Glee Club Easter Monday. Women who had come to breakfast in riding clothes rushed to the hairdresser instead; at eleven the tap-k'tap of ping-pong balls was the only sound of life in the enormous half empty hotel.

    The girl was one of a pair in white skirts and yellow sweaters who walked down the long gallery after breakfast. Her face reflected the discontent of the weather, reflected darkly and resentfully. Looking at her Deforrest Colman thought: "Bored and fierce," and then

as his eyes continued to follow her, "No, proud and
impatient. Not that either, but what a face—vitality and
hand cuffs—where's this getting me—liver and bacon,
Damon and Pythias, Laurel and Hardy.

256   The German band started to play on deck but the
sweeping majesty of the city made the march trivial and
tinkling; after a moment it died away.

257   The gaunt scaffolding of Coney Island slid by.

258   Save for two Russian priests playing chess their party
was alone in the smoking room.

259   Everybody in the room was hot. There was a faint flavor
of starch on the air that leaked out to the lovely garden.

260   One of those huge spreading hotels of the capital, built
to shelter politicians, retired officers suddenly
discovering themselves (homeless, of ginless in their
retirements, foreigners with axes to grind)
without a native town, legation staffs, and women
fascinated by one of the outer rings of officialdom—
everyone could have their Congressman or Minister, if
not their Senator or Ambassador—

261   The terrible way the train had seemed to foreshorten and
hurry as it got into motion.

262   It was already eight o'clock when they drove off into a
windy twilight. The sun had gone behind Naples,
leaving a sky of pigeon's blood and gold, and as they
rounded the bay and climbed slowly toward Torredell
Annunziata, the Mediterranean momentarily toasted the
fading splendor in pink wine. Above them loomed
Vesuvius and from its crater a small persistent fountain
of smoke contributed darkness to the gathering night.
"We ought to reach our destination about twleve," said
Nosby. No one answered. The city had disappeared
behind a rise of ground and now they were alone, where
the Maffia sprang out of rank human weeds and the
Black Hand rose to throw its ominous shadow across

two continents. There was something eerie in the sound of the wind over these gray mountains, crowned with decayed castles. Hallie suddenly shivered.

263   Motor boat like clock tick.

264   The sky that looks like smoke on Charles Street

265   Feeling at Francis Fox like cat-house.

266   Orange in Province

267   He heard them singing and looked down toward the lights. There was a trembling of the leaves before they passed.

268   *Night at Fair*—Eyes awakening.

269   *March*—The crepe myrtle was under corn stalks

270   "I'm glad I'm American," she said. "Here in Italy I feel that everybody's dead. Carthaginians and old Romans and Moorish pirates and medieval princes with poisoned rings—"
The solemn gloom of the countryside communicated itself to all of them.
The wind had come up stronger and was groaning through the dark-massed trees along the way.

271   White and inky night

272   A soft bell hummed midnight

273   In children's books forests are sometimes made out of all-day suckers, boulders out of peppermints and rivers out of gently flowing, rippling molasses taffy. Such books are less fantastic than they sound for such localities exist, and one day a girl, herself little more than a child, sat dejected in the middle of one. It was all hers, she owned it; she owned Candy Town.

274   The red dusk was nearly gone but she had advanced into the last patch of it

275   Yellow and lavender filled her eyes, yellow for the sun
through yellow shades and lavender for the quilt,
swollen as a cloud and drifting in soft billows over the
bed. Suddenly she remembered her appointment and
uncovering her arms she squirmed into a violet negligee,
flipped back her hair with a circular movement of her
head and melted into the color of the room.

276   Lying awake in bed that night he listened endlessly to
the long caravan of a circus moving through the street
from one Paris fair to another. When the last van had
rumbled out of hearing and the corners of the furniture
was pastel blue with the dawn, he was still thinking.

277   The road was lined sparsely by a row of battered houses,
some of them repainted a pale unhealthy blue and all of
them repainted far back in large plots of shaggy and
unkempt land.

278   It was a collapsed house, a retired house, set far back
from the road and sunned and washed to the dull color
of old wood.
One glance told him it was no longer a dwelling. The
shutters that remained were closed tight, and from the
tangled vines arose, as a single chord, a rich shrill sound
of a hundred birds. John Jackson left the road and
stalked across the yard knee-deep in abandoned grass.

279   Stifling as curtain dust

280   The pavements grew sloppier and the snow in the
gutters melted into dirty sherbet.

281   The sea was dingy grey and swept with rain. Canvas
sheltered all the open portions of the promenade deck,
even the ping-pong table was wet.

282   It was the Europa—a moving island of light. It grew
larger minute by minute, swelled into a harmonious
fairyland with music from its deck and searchlights
playing on its own length. Through field-glasses they
could discern figures lining the rail and Evelyn spun out

the personal history of a man who was pressing his own pants in a cabin. Charmed they watched its sure matchless speed.

"Oh, Daddy, buy me that!" Evelyn cried.

283   She climbed a network of steel, concrete and glass, walked under a high echoing dome and came out into New York.

284   hammock was of the particularly hideous yellow peculiar to hammocks.

285   adorned in front by an enormous but defunct motometer and behind by a mangy pennant bearing the legend "Tarleton, Ga." In the dim past someone had begun to paint the hood yellow but unfortunately had been called away when but half through the task.

286   On all sides faintly irregular fields stretched away to a faintly irregular unpopulated horizon.

287   In the light of four strong pocket flash lights, borne by four sailors in spotless white, a gentleman was shaving himself, standing clad only in athletic underwear upon the sand. Before his eyes an irreproachable valet held a silver mirror which gave back the soapy reflection of his face. To right and left stood two additional menservants, one with a dinner coat and trousers hanging from his arm and the other bearing a white stiff shirt whose studs glistened in the glow of the electric lamps. There was not a sound except the dull scrape of the razoe along its wielder's face and the intermittent groaning sound that blew in out of the sea.

288   But here beside the warm friendly rain that tumbled from his eaves onto the familiar lawn

289   Next morning, walking with Knowleton under starry frosted bushes in one of the bare gardens, she grew quite light-hearted.

290   "Ballroom," for want of a better word. It was that room, filled by day with wicker furniture, which was always

connotated in the phrase "Let's go in and dance." It was referred to as "inside" or "downstairs." It was that nameless chamber wherein occur the principal transactions of all the country clubs in America.

291   They were there. The Cherbourg breakwater, a white stone snake, glittered along the sea at dawn; behind it red roofs and steeples and then small, neat hills traced with a warm orderly pattern of toy farms. "Do you like this French arrangement?" it seemed to say. "It's considered very charming, but if you don't agree just shift it about—set this road here, this steeple there. It's been done before, and it always comes out lovely in the end."
It was Sunday morning, and Cherbourg was in flaring collars and high lace hats. Donkey carts and diminutive automobiles moved to the sound of incessant bells.

292   Those were the dog days. Out at the lake there was a thin green scum upon the water and in the city a last battering exhausting heat wave softened the asphalt till it retained the ghastly prints of human feet. In those days there was one auto for every 200 inhabitants so in the evening

293   A large but quick restaurant.

294   Aeolian or Wind-built Islands

295   They all went to the porch, where the children silhouetted themselves in silent balance on the railing and unrecognizable people called greeting as they passed along the dark dusty street.

296   The first lights of the evening were springing into pale existence

297   At three o'clock in the morning, grey broken old women scrub the floors of the great New York Hotels.

298   (Missed) re great flatness of American life when everything had the same value—
the cook's complaint etc. etc.

299   The run to the purple mountains and back.

300   Spring had come early to the Eastern seaboard—
thousands of tiny black surprise berries on every tree
were shining with anticipation and a fresh breeze wafted
them south all day.

301   Is there anything more soothing than the quiet whir of
a lawnmower on a summer afternoon?

302   A Mid-Victorian wind.   ★

303   This restaurant with a haunted corner.

304   Lunar Rainbow

305   New Jersey village where even Sunday is only a restless
lull between the crash of trains.

306   Elevators look like two big filing cabinets.

307   Out in the suburbs, chalk white windows looked down   ★
indifferently at them in sleeping roads.

308   The abundent waiters at Dartmouth seemed to me rather
comedy characters—I mean not in themselves but in their
roles. They go all out of character and begin to talk to the
guests just like the man who hires himself out to do that.

309   St. Paul in 1855 (or '66)—The rude town was like a great
fish just hauled out of the Mississippi and still leaping
and squirming on its bank.

310   The lobby of the Hotel Roi d'Angleterre was as desolate
as a school house after school. In the huge, scarcely
completed palace a few servants scurried about like
rabbits, a few guests sidled up to the concierge, spoke in
whispers and vanished with a single awed look around
at the devastating emptiness. They were mostly women
escaped from the deep melancholy at home, and finding
that the torture chamber was preferable to the tomb.

311   Passing the building which housed the negro wards.
The patients were singing as always. Among the voices

that lay suspended in sweet melancholy on the August air in the early summer night, Owen recognized the deep base of Doofus who had been there two years—an interne on that ward had told him that Doofus was due to die; his place in the chorus would be hard to fill.

312   Red and yellow villas, called Fleur des Bois, Mon Nid, or Sans-Souci.

Epigrams, Wise Cracks and Jokes

313 A man says to another man: "I'd certainly like to steal your girl. Second man: "I'd give her to you, but she's part of a set."

314 Has D.P. injured you anyway. No, but don't remind her. Maybe she hasn't done her bad deed for the day.

315 The movies are the only court where the judge goes to the lawyer for advice.

316 Show me a hero and I will write you a tragedy.

317 Not a word in the Roosevelt inaugural was as logical as Zangara saying he shot at Roosevelt because he had a stomach ache.

318 Agility (vitality)—pleasing people you perversely shouldn't please and can't reach.

319 Her unselfishness came in pretty small packages well   ★
     wrapped.

320 After all the portrait of an old shoe by Van Gogh hangs in the Louvre, but where is there a portrait of Van Gogh by an old shoe.

321 Berry Wall. He doesn't dare go back. He was drafted for the Civil War and he doesn't know it's over.

322 Optimism is the content of small men in high places.

323   Send up a fat bell boy and a whip.

324   She's bashful. She has small pox. She stumbles so she couldn't get up.

325   Wouldn't a girl rather have half of *him* than a whole Spic with a jar of pomade thrown in? Life was so badly arranged—better no women at all than only one woman.

326   One of those tragic efforts like repainting your half of a delapidated double house.

327   Bryan to Darrow. Fellow Apes of the Scopes trial.

328   Trying to support a large and constantly increasing French family who jokingly referred to themselves as "our servants."

329   Sent a girl flowers on Mother's Day.

330   You don't write because you want to say something; you write because you've got something to say.

331   The cleft palate (crested parrot): "Bring it along." "Can't very well leave it home."

332   Genius is the ability to put into effect what is in your mind. There's no other definition of it.

333   Get a man for Elspeth, a man for Elspeth, was the cry. This was difficult because Elspeth had had so many men. Two of her sisters rode, so to speak, Elspeth's discarded mounts.

334   Nervous system from Pthodemy Club (Dean Clark's)

335   Switzerland is a country where very few things begin, but many things end.

336   A machine for blowing the movable snot from the nasal cavities of

337   No such word in the English language as Cannes.

338 An American—Ou allez-vous pour les huitre (meaning Easter.)

339 Irish chemist.

340 Cotton manufacturer who worries because African chiefs go in for rayon.

341 No grand idea was ever born in a conference but a lot of foolish ideas have died there. ★

342 Ye Old Hooke Shoppe

343 Movie man says about engaged current mistress of ★

344 Genius goes around the world in its youth incessantly apologizing for having large feet. What wonder that later in life it should be inclined to raise those feet too swiftly to fools and bores.

345 Death in most countries is considered practically fatal.

346 When anyone announces to you how little they drink you can be sure it's a regime they just started. ★

347 Thank gravity for working your bowels.

348 No such thing as a man willing to be honest—that would be like a blind man willing to see.

349 Hospitality is a wonderful thing. If people really want you they'll have you even if the cook has just died in the house of small-pox.

350 Suddenly he turned in bed and put both his arms around her arm. Her free hand touched his hair.

"You've been bad," she said.

"I can't help it."

She sat with him silently for half an hour; then she changed her position so that her arm was under his head. Stooping over him, she kissed him on the brow. (See Two Wrongs.)

351 Any walk through a park that runs between a double line of mangy trees and passes brazenly by the ladies' toilet is invariably known as "Lover's Lane."

352 Gynecologist to trace his pedigree.

353 Women are going to refuse to build with anything but crushed brick.

354 Not 1% of the dressed up biddies of the Junior League could possibly be regarded as ladies except by each other.

355 Brushes called Andy and Bill Gump

356 Few people die of sin, but a complications of sins

357 The Black Shirt
The Brown Shirt
The Stuffed Shirt

358 Wanted for
    6 C. grade for pipe laying
    1 A grade moron (experienced foreman)
    2 B grade imbeciles 3 o'clock ask for Mr. Jones ★

359 Magazine—the Parlor Pink

360 Proud words that eventually revenged themselves by meaning nothing at all

361 One of toughs: he's rich, he's got caviare between his teeth

362 Secret of the Balkans

363 Blackmail "Made sweet moan'

364 Shy beaten man named Victor
Clumsy girls named Grace
Great truck drivers named Earl and Cecil

365 She was one of those people who would just as soon starve in a garret with a man—if she didn't have to. ★

366   Beatrice Lillie broke up the British Empire with "March to the Roll of the Drums"

367   Mencken forgives much to the Catholic church perhaps because it has an index

368   All my characters killed each other off in the first act because I couldn't think of any more hard boiled things for them to say.

369   They thought a child would be nice too because they had a nursery and the Harold Lloyds had one.

370   They have more money (Earnest's wisecrack)

371   She's got to be a loyal, frank person if she's got to bitch everyone in the world to do it.

372   For a statesman—any school child knows that hot air rises to the top

373   Nothing to do but marry them (the Murphys)

374   Suicide and wife arrive in Cuba.

375   Let's all live together.

376   Debut—the first time a young girl is seen drunk in public.

377   He repeated to himself an old French proverb he had made up that morning.

378   A sleeping porch is a back room with no pictures on the walls. It should contain at least one window.

379   Kill the scrub sire is our slogan.

380   Why can't you be square? Well, when I was young I used to play with old automobile tires.

381   Forgotten is forgiven.

382   If all your clothes are worn to the same state it means you go out too much.

383   American actresses now use European convents as a sort of female Muldoon's.

384   You must stoop a little in order to jump.

385   For a car—Excuse my lust.

386   Andre Gide lifted himself by his own jockstrap so to speak—and one would like to see him hoisted on his own pedarasty.

387   Creditors' jokes

388   Like the man that crossed the ocean three times on the same woman.

389   Test of a good mind.

390   The guy that played Sergeant Quirt in Romeo & Juliet.   ★

391   A poet named Constantly Aching did all the plagiarism for me.

392   Three men better known as Christ's nails.

393   The spiritual stomach of the race was ruined those fifty years when mid-western women didn't go to the toilet.

394   Take us to the Cambridge Legs—I mean the Cambridge Arms. Or any place around there.

395   To bring on the revolution it may be necessary to work inside the communist party.

396   They try to be Jesus (Forsyth) while I only attempt to be God, which is easier.

397   He said: Our Rhododendrons (roads are demned 'uns)

398   He had Cheyne-Store breathing.

399   To most women art is a form of scandal.   ★

400   Impersonating 46 Presidents at once.

401   All things come to him who mates.   ★

402   Trained nurses on duty should not be allowed to talk in their sleep.

403   "What kind of man was he?"   ★
"Well, he was one of those men who come in a door and make any woman with them look guilty."

404   Grown up, and that is a terribly hard thing to do. It is much easier to skip it and go from one childhood to another.

405   We put an ashtray in the window (for a lamp).

406   I'm on such a rigid diet they won't even let me lick a   ★
stamp.

407   Dietitians: They have made great progress in the last few years. They know pretty definitely that bichloride of mercury or arsenic in the right dose will kill you and that food should probably be eaten rather than taken in gas form or over the radio.

408   Honi soit que Malibu

409   1870 made Clemenceau and Clemenceau made 1933

410   Trained nurses who eat as if they didn't own the food but it was just lent them.

411   parked his pessimism in her sun-parlour.

412   No such thing as graceful old age

413   Vitality shows in not only the ability to persist but the ability to start over.

414   Bookkeeping is a subject without sex appeal

415   What is the point at which loan becomes property of loanee and at the offer of a refund one says "But I don't like to take your money." What is the point when one accepts return of loan with most profuse thanks.

416   The inevitable shallowness that goes with people who have learned everything by experience.

417   Somebody's specimen hijacked on way to doctor's.

418   The biggest temptation we can offer people to let *us* talk is to cry "say" (or dites) to them

419   "EX-WHITE-SLAVER,"—the authorship being identified with touching modesty as "By a Man Who Still is One."

420   "This isn't the south. This is the center of the country. We're only polite half the time."

421   "What'll we do with the animals when you're away?" "You mean the roaches in the kitchen? We'll leave those with the veterinarian—he'll take care of them."

422   A girl with ankles like that has no privileges.

423   I'm going through the crises of my life like railroad ties.

424   I'm from Washington
        Fine—what's the news from Moronsville

425   Lincoln's "all the people."

426   For Esther M. in memory of an old friendship or a prolonged quarrel that has gone on so long and accumulated so much moss that it is much the same thing.

427   Mr. and Mrs. Jay O'Brien moving like the center of population.

428   There are no second acts in American lives.   ★

429   My Spitback, my Error, my Mistake (for divorsed husband)

430   Somewhat relieved to find he was fired—he had, so to   ★
        speak, stuck it out to the end.

431   "I can't pay you much," said the editor to the
        author, "but I can give you some good publicity."
            "I can't pay you much," said the advertiser to the
        editor, "but I can give you some beautiful ads."

432   God appears to man who discovers that he has unmistakable Japanese features.

433   When he buys his ties he has to ask if gin will make them run.

434   Pacifism like bringing boy up to have brown skin on his—

435   Very bad jokes should be known as "employer's jokes" or "creditor's jokes." The listener has to laugh heartily so it seems wasteful to use up a good story on him.

436   The kiss originated when the first male reptile licked the first female reptile, implying in a subtle, complimentary way that she was as succulent as the small reptile he had for dinner the night before.

437   You are contemplating a gigantic merger between J.P. Morgan and the Queensboro Bridge.

438   To Mathews: I certainly do wish I could grow up like you fellows and write about all the wonderful things that are happening in the newspapers. But here I sit like a big fat fairy thinking that maybe if I really knew why (club stuff here) I would really know almost as much about the social revolution as those deep thinkers Mike Gold ect.

439   Beware of him who would give his last sou to a beggar in the street. He would also give it to you and that is something you would not be able to endure.

440   Fashion Blessing. Think how many flappers would have been strangled like Porphyria except for bobbed hair.

441   Don't get thinking it's a real country because you can get a lot of high school kids into gym suits and have them spell out "bananas" for the news reels.

442   I used to hie you up to a nervous excitement that bore a ★ resemblance to intelligence.

443   The priesthood: a method eating the cake of Christian ascetism and having it too.

444   I may be just an old visionary—but I seem to see Scottie walking around without overshoes.

445   Turnbull idea—Neo-post-thoreau

446   The young architect referred to women's protuberances as "flying buttresses."

447   It grows harder to write because there is much less weather than when I was a boy and practically no men and women at all.

Feelings & Emotions (without girls)

448   Ah, it was a great feeling to relax—the best feeling, unlike any sinking down he had ever known before.

"I have half an hour, an hour, two hours, ten hours, a hundred hours. God Almighty, I have even time to take a drink of water from the cooler in the hall; I can sleep eight full hours tonight, with a piece of paper stuffed in the telephone buzzer; I can face everybody in the office knowing they'll be paid again this week, the week after, the week after next!"

But most of all—he had that first half an hour. Having no one to communicate with, Andrew Fulton made sounds. One was like Whee-ee-ooo, but though it was expressive for awhile it palled presently, and he tried a gentle yawning sigh, but that was not enough. Now he knew what he wanted to do—he wanted to cry. He wanted to drink but there was nothing to drink, or to take his office force for an aeroplane ride or wake up his parents out of their graves and say, "Look—I too can rest."

449   He might find the ecstasy and misery, the infatuation that he wanted.

450   The thrilling staccato joy of the meeting.   ★

451   "I feel as if I had a cannon ball in my stomach."

452   Wait for what? Wait while he swam off into a firmament of his own, so far off that she could only see

his feathers gleaming in the distance, only hear distantly the clamor of war or feel the vacuum that he created when sometimes he fell through space. He came back eventually with spoils, but for her there was always another larger waiting—for the end of youth, the blurring of her uniqueness—her two menacing deaths beside which mortal death was no more than sleep.

453   She looked lovely, but he thought of a terrible thing she had said once when they were first married—that if he were away she could sleep with another man and it wouldn't really affect her, or make her really unfaithful to him. This kept him awake for another hour, but he had a little fine deep restful sleep toward morning.

454   the blind luck that had attended the industry, and he ★ knew croupiers who raked in the earnings of that vast gambling house. And he knew that the Europeans were impressed with it as they were impressed with the sky-scrapers, as something without human rhythm or movement. They had left rhythm behind them and it was their rhythm he wanted. He was tired of his own rhythm and the rhythms of the people in Hollywood. He wanted to see people with more secrets than the necessity of concealing a proclivity for morphine.

455   *Two Dreams*   (1) A trip to Florida with Howard Garrish and many bathing beauties. Asleep standing on the prow the beach and girls dancing. The one one skates like skiis. Like Switzerland, far castles and palaces. The horseman in the sea, the motor truck on sand, the horsemen coming ashore, the Bishop rears, falls, the horse saves him. My room, suits and ties, the view, the soldiers drilling under arcs in khaki, the wonderful water man is now Tom Taylor, I buy and ties wake in strange room. Blunder into Mother who nags me. My mean remarks.

        (2) The colored burglar. Found clothes in hotel—underwear, suit; I discover pocket book, Echenard, my accusation.

456 By the next morning she realized that she was the only
one who cared, the only one who had the time and
youth for the luxury of caring. Her aunt, her old
cousins were mercifully anaesthetized against death—
her brother was already worrying about his wife and
children back in West Virginia. She and her father were
alone; since the funeral had been held over for her the
others somehow looked to her to summarize their grief.
They were thin-drawn, worn out Anglo-Saxon stock
and all that remained of their vitality seemed to have
flowed by a mysterious distillation into her. They were
chiefly interested in her. They wanted boldly to know
whether it was true about the Prince of—

457 Slaves may love their bondage but all those in slavery
are not slaves. What joy in the threat that the solid wall
surrounding us is falling to rack and ruin—the
whispers of measles running through the school on
Monday morning, the news that the supply officer has
run away with the mess fund, the rumor that the floor
manager has appendicitis and won't be downtown for
two weeks! "Break it up! Tear it down!" shout the *sans
cullottes*, and I can distinguish my voice among the
others. Striped and short rations tomorrow, but for
God's sake, give us our measure of hysteria today.

458 It was not an American bar any more—he felt polite in
it, and not as if he owned it. It had gone back into
France.

459 Fed up with it—he wanted to deal again in the vapid,
to deliver a drop of material solid out of the great
gaseous world of men, and never again waste his
priceless hours watching nothing and nothing with
nothing.

460 she was alone at last. There was not even a ghost left   ★
now to drift with through the years. She might stretch
out her arms as far as they could reach into the night
without fear that they would brush friendly cloth.

461   Liking man when he's tired.   ★

462   The voices fainter and fainter—How is Zelda, how is
       Zelda—tell us—how is Zelda

463   Felt utterly forlorn and defeated and outlasted by
       circumstances.

464   She wanted to crawl into his pocket and be safe forever.   ★

465   She fronted the appalling truth. She could never love
       him, never while he lived. It was as if he had charged
       her to react negatively and so long as the current flowed
       she had no choice. Passionately she tried to think back
       to a few minutes before when the world had been tragic
       and glorious, but the moment was gone. He was alive
       and as she heard his feet take up the chase again the
       wings of her mind were already preening themselves for
       flight.

466   Proxy in passion.

Descriptions of Girls

467   She turned her slender smile full upon Lew for a   ★
moment, and then aimed it a little aside, like a pocket
torch that might dazzle him.

468   She was the dark Gunther—dark and shining and driven.

469   He had not realized that flashing fairness could last so   ★
far into the twenties.

470   Nevertheless, the bright little apples of her cheeks, the
blue of the Zuyder Zee in her eyes, the braided strands
of golden corn on the wide forehead, testified to the
purity of her origin. She was the school beauty.

471   Her beauty was as poised and secure as a flower on a
strong stem; her voice was cool and sure, with no
wayward instruments in it that played on his emotions.

472   She was not more than eighteen—a dark little beauty
with the fine crystal gloss over her that, in brunettes,
takes the place of a blond's bright glow.

473   Becky was nineteen, a startling little beauty, with her   ★ ★
head set upon her figure as though it had been made
separately and then placed there with the utmost
precision. Her body was sturdy, athletic; her head was a
bright, happy composition of curves and shadows and
vivid color, with that final kinetic jolt, the element that
is eventually sexual in effect, which made strangers

stare at her. [Who has not had the excitement of seeing
an apparent beauty from afar; then, after a moment,
seeing that same face grow mobile and watching the
beauty disappear moment by moment, as if a lovely
statue had begun to walk with the meager joints of a
paper doll?] Becky's beauty was the opposite of that.
The facial muscles pulled her expressions into lovely
smiles and frowns, disdains, gratifications and
encouragements; her beauty was articulated, and
expressed vividly whatever it wanted to express.

474   Anyone looking at her then, at her mouth which was
simply a kiss seen very close up, at her head that was a
gorgeous detail escaped from the corner of a painting,
nor mere formal beauty but the beholder's unique
discovery, so that it evoked different dreams to every
man, of the mother, of the nurse, of the lost childish
sweetheart or whatever had formed his first conception
of beauty—anyone looking at her would have
conceded her a bisque on her last remark.

475   She was a stalk of ripe corn, but bound not as cereals   ★
are but as a rare first edition, with all the binder's art.
She was lovely and expensive, and about nineteen.

476   A lovely dress, soft and gentle in cut, but in color a   ★
hard, bright, metallic powder blue.

477   An exquisite, romanticized little ballerina.

478   He imagined Kay and Arthur Busch progressing
through the afternoon. Kay would cry a great deal and
the situation would seem harsh and unexpected to them
at first, but the tender closing of the day would draw
them together. They would turn inevitably toward each
other and he would slip more and more into the
position of the enemy outside.

479   Her face, flushed with cold and then warmed again   ★
with the dance, was a riot of lovely, delicate pinks, like
many carnations, rising in many shades from the white

of her nose to the high spot of her cheeks. Her
breathing was very young as she came close to him—
young and eager and exciting. (used)

480   The intimacy of the car, its four walls whisking them   ★
along toward a new adventure, had drawn them
together.

481   A beauty that had reached the point where it seemed to
contain in itself the secret of its own growth, as if it would
go on increasing forever.

482   Her body was so assertively adequate that someone   ★
remarked that she always looked as if she had nothing
on underneath her dress but it was probably wrong.

483   Her ash-blond hair seemed weather-proof save for   ★
a tiny curtain of a bang that was evidently permitted,
even expected to stir a little in a mild wind. She had an
unmistakable aura about her person of being carefully
planned. Under minute scallops that were scarcely
brows her eyes etc. Her teeth were so white against the
tan, her lips so red, that in combination with the blue
of her eyes the effect was momentarily startling—as
startling as if the lips had been green and the pupils
white.

484   A few little unattached sections of her sun-warm hair   ★
blew back and trickled against the lobe of the ear
closest to him, as if to indicate that she was listening.

485   A square chinned, decided girl with fleshy white arms
and a white dress that reminded Basil domestically of
the lacy pants that blew among the laundry in the yard.

486   He saw that she was lying, but it was a brave lie. They   ★
talked from their hearts—with the half truths and
evasions peculiar to that organ, which has been famed
as an instrument of precision.

487   I look like a femme fatale

488   After a certain degree of prettiness, one pretty girl is as pretty as another.

489   shimmering with unreality for the fancy-dress party

490   Popularly known as the "Death Ray." She was an odd   ★
little beauty with a skull-like face and hair that was a
natural green-gold—the hair of a bronze statue by
sunset.

491   He rested a moment on the verandah—resting his eyes
on a big honey suckle that cut across a low sickle
moon—then as he started down the steps his abstracted
glance fell upon a trailer from it sleeping in the
moonlight.

492   She was the girl from foreign places; she was so   used
asleep that you could see the dream of those places in
the faint lift of her forehead. He struck the inevitable
creaky strip and promptly the map of wonderland
written on the surface of women's eyebrows creased into
invisibility.

493   His brisk blond sidelocks scratched her cheek while a
longer tenuous end of gold silk touched him in the
corner of his eye

494   She wore the usual little dishpan cover.

495   She was small with a springy walk that would have been
aggressive if it had been less dainty.

496   Her mouth was made of two small intersecting cherries
pointing off into a bright smile.

497   What's a girl going to do with herself on a boat—fish?

498   The girl hung around under the pink sky waiting for
something to happen. There were strange little lines in
the trees, strange little insects, unfamiliar night cries of
strange small beasts beginning.
—Those are frogs, she thought, or no, those are *grillons*—
what is it in English?—those are crickets up by the pond.

—That is either a swallow or a bat, she thought; then again
the difference of trees—then back to love and such
practical things. And back again to the different trees
and shadows, skies and noises—such as the auto horns
and the barking dog up by the Philadelphia turnpike. . .

499   Her face, flowing out into the world under an amazing
Bersaglierri bonnet, was epicene; as they disembarked at
the hotel the sight of her provoked a curious sigh-like
sound from a dense mass of women and girls who
packed the side-walk for a glimpse of her, and Bill
realized that her position, her achievment however
transient and fortuitous was neither a little thing nor
an inheritance. She was beauty for hundred afternoons,
its incarnation in millions of aspiring or fading lives. It
was impressive, startling and almost magnificent.
Half an hour later sitting a few feet from the judgment dias
he saw a girl detach herself from a group who were
approaching it in threes—it was a girl in a white evening
dress with red gold hair and under it a face so brave and
tragic that it seemed that every eye in the packed hall must
be fixed and concentrated on its merest adventures, the
faintest impression upon her heart.

500   Women having only one role, their own charm—all the   ★
rest is mimicry.

501   If you keep people's blood in their heads it won't be   ★
where it should be for making love.

502   Men got to be a mixture of the charming mannerisms
of the women one has known.

503   Her air of saying "This is my opportunity of learning
something, beckoned their egotism imperatively near."

504   A frown, the shadow of a hair in breadth appeared
between her eyes.

505   The little 14 year old nymph in the Vagabonds.

506   Wearing a kimono bright with big blue moons, she sat
up among the pillows drawing her lips by a hand-glass.

507   He had thought of her once as a bubble and had told   ★★
her about it, an iridescent soap-blown bubble with a
thin delicate film over all the colors of the rainbow. He
had stopped abruptly at that point but [he was
conscious too of the sun panning gold from the clear
brooks of her hair, of her tawny skin]—hell! He had to
to stop thinking of such things.

to]

508   She was eighteen with such a skin as the Italian   ★
painters of the decadence used for corner angels,] and
all the wishing in the world glistening on her grey eyes.

509   [Wherever she was, became a beautiful and enchanted   ★★
place to Basil, but he did not think of it that way. He
thought the fascination was inherent in the locality, and
long afterward a commonplace street or the mere name of
a city would exude a peculiar glow, a sustained sound,
that struck his soul alert with delight. In her presence he
was too absorbed to notice his surroundings; so that her
absence never made them empty, but, rather, sent him
seeking for her through haunted rooms and gardens that
he had never really seen before.]

510   The glass doors hinged like French windows, shutting
them in on all sides. It was hot. Down through three
more compartments he could see another couple—a girl
and her brother, Minnie said—and from time to time
they moved and gestured soundlessly, as unreal in these
tiny human conservatories as the vase of paper flowers
on the table. Basil walked up and down nervously.

511   Life burned high in them both; the steamer and its
people were at a distance and in darkness.

512   What was it they said? Did you hear it? Can you
remember?

513   She was a thin, a thin burning flame, colorless yet fresh.
Her smile came first slowly, shy and bold, as if all the
life of that little body had gathered for a moment around
her mouth and the rest of her was a wisp that the least

wind would blow away. She was a changeling whose lips were the only point of contact with reality.

514   Came up to him taking his hand as though she was stepping into the circle of his arm.

515   The tilted shadow of her nose on her cheek, the point of dull fire in her eyes.

516   Mae's pale face and burning lips faded off, faded out, against the wild dark background of the war.

517   The copper green eyes, greener than the green-brown ★ foliage around them.

518   She gave him a side smile, half of her face, like a small ★ white cliff.

519   Flustered, Johanna fumbled for an apology. Nell jumped up and was suddenly at the window, a glitter of leaves in a quick wind, a blond glow of summer lightening. Even in her state of intimidation Johanna noticed that she seemed to bear with her, as she moved, a whole dream of women's future; bore it from the past into the present as if it were a precious mystery she held in the carriage of her neck and arms.

520   A girl who could send tear-stained telegrams.

521   The lady was annoyed, and so intense was her personality that it had taken only a fractional flexing of her eyes to indicate the fact. She was a dark, pretty girl with a figure that would be full-blown sooner than she wished. She was just eighteen.

522   Hallie Bushmill was young and vivid and light, with a boy's hair and a brow that bulged just slightly, like a baby's brow.

523   Sat a gold-and-ivory little beauty with dark eyes and a moving childish smile that was like all the lost youth in the world. (Used?)

524   He bent and kissed her braided forehead.

525   Helen Avery's voice and the drooping of her eyes when   ★
       she finished speaking, like a sort of exercise in control,
       fascinated him. He had felt that they both tolerated
       something, that each knew half of some secret about
       people and life, and that if they rushed toward each
       other there would be a romantic communion of almost
       unbelievable intensity. It was this element of promise
       and possibility that had haunted him for a fortnight and
       was now dying away.

526   Standing at the gate with that faint glow behind her,
       Dinah was herself the garden's last outpost, its most
       representative flower.

527   Lola Shisbe had never wrecked a railroad in her life. But
       she was just sixteen and you had only to look at her to
       know that her destructive period was going to begin any
       day now.

528   He saw now, framing her face in the crook of his arm,
       her resemblance to Kay Phillips, or rather the genus to
       which they both belonged. The hard little chin, the
       small nose, the taut, wan cheeks, it was the way actresses
       made up to play the woman wronged and tubucular, a
       matter of structure and shadows of course, for they had
       fresh cheeks. Again, in Dinah the created lines were
       firmness—in Kay they had an aesthetic value alone.

529   Your eyes always shine as if you had fever.

530   Passing within the radius of the girl's perfume.

531   Then for a moment they faded into the sweet darkness   used
       so deep that they were darker than the darkness, so that
       for awhile they were darker than the black trees—then so
       dark that when she tried to look up at him she could but
       look at the wild waves of the universe over his shoulder
       and say, "Yes, I guess I love you too."

532   Nymph of the harvest.

533   She was the tongue of flame that made the firelight vivid.

534   "Sometimes I'd see you in the distance, moving along like a golden chariot." After twenty minutes of such eloquence, Alida began to feel exceedingly attractive. She was tired and rather happy, and eventually she said: "All right, you can kiss me if you want to, but it won't mean anything. I'm just not in that mood."

535   Long white gloves dripping from her forearms.

536   Her eyes shone at Bill with friendly interest, and then, just before the car shot away, she did something else with them—narrowed them a little and then widened them, recognizing by this sign the uniqueness of their relationship. "I see you," it seemed to say. "You registered. Everything's possible."

537   Emily, who was twenty-five and carried space around with her into which he could step and be alone with their two selves.   ★

538   She was a bundle of fur next to Caros Moros, and he saw the latter drop his arm around her till they were one mass of fur together.

539   He took them each in one arm, like a man in a musical comedy, and kissed the rouge on their cheeks.

540   Her low voice wooed him casually from some impersonal necessity of its own.

541   It was fine hearing Nora say that she never looked behind.   ★

542   A woman's laughter when it's like a child—just one syllables, eager and approving, a crow and a cry of delight.   ★

543   She took it to the rocker and settled herself to a swift seasick motion which she found soothing.   ★

544   Her voice seemed to hesitate after consonants and then out came resonant and clear vowels—ahs and ohs and joyful ees lingering on the air.

545   Her hair was soft as silk and faintly curling. Her hair was stiff fluff, her hair was a damp, thick shiny bank. It was not this kind or that kind, it was all hair.

Her mouth was (different things about her mouth, contrary things, impossible to reconcile—and always with:) It was not this kind or that kind of mouth, it was all mouths.

Also nose, eyes, legs, etc., same ending.

546   Always a glisten of cold cream under her eyes, of wet rouge on her lips.

547   Griselda was now unnaturally calm; as a woman becomes when she feels that, in the main, she has fulfilled her intuitive role, and is passing along the problem to the man.   ★

548   Her lovely straggled hair.

549   She felt nice and cool after a dip in the lake, felt her pink dress where it touched her, frothy as pink soda water, all fresh in the new wind. When Roger appeared, she would make him sorry for his haughtiness of the last twenty-four hours.   ★

550   Tremendous resemblance between Bijou and Beatrice.

551   He had once loved a girl with a blight (describe) on her teeth who hid it by reaching down her upper lip when any emotion was in sight—laughter or tears—and laughing with a faint bowing of her head—and then, being absolutely sure she had not exposed her scar, laughing quite freely and exposing it. He had adopted the mannerism, and, to get on with what happened and why, he was still doing the same thing, etc.

552   Nora's gay, brave, stimulating, "tighten up your belt, baby, let's get going. To any Pole." I am astonished   ★

sometimes by the fearlessness of women, the recklessness—like Nora, Zelda, Beatrice—in each case it's partly because they are all three spoiled babies who never felt the economic struggle on their shoulders. But it's heartening when it stays this side of recklessness. In each case I've had to strike a balance and become the cautious *petit bourgeoise* after, in each case, throwing them off their initial balance. Yet consider M. . . T. . . who was a clergyman's daughter—and equally with the others had everything to lose and nothing to gain economically. She had the same recklessness. It's a question of age and the times to a great extent, because, except for the sexual recklessness, Zelda was cagey about throwing in her lot with me before I was a money-maker, and I think by temperament she was the most reckless of all. She was young and in a period where any exploiter or middle-man seemed a better risk than a worker in the arts. Question unsolved. Think further back.

553   Frances Strah looks like a trinket.   ★

554   Some impressions of the Carnival. What made everyone walk all through the train to get out; the boys smashing baggage at the station; the high snowdrifts; the girls faces in the car windows drifting ghost-like past the watchers; the yell of recognition as a last watcher found some last girl; the figures in the dark passing the frat houses on their way to the carnival. The comparative bareness of the scene where the queens were chosen. How did some of those girls get there—some must have been accidents or at least chosen by pull or the wrong girl tapped—they weren't the 20 prettiest girls there. Some pretty girls must have ducked it.

555   A young woman came out of the elevator and wavered uneasily across the lobby.

556   Myron Selznick's "Beautiful—she'll lose that pudgy baby fat."

557   Beggar's lips that would not beg in vain

558   My cousin Corrinne is still a flapper. Fashions, names, manners, customs and morals change but for Corrine it is still 1920. This concerns her for there is no doubt that she originally patterned herself upon certain immature and unfortunate writings of mine so I have a special indulgence for Corrine as for one who has lost an arm or leg in one's service.

559   She was a ripe grape, ready to fall for the mere shaking of a vine.

560   The sunlight dodged down to her hair thought bright red maple and bronze encorepus leaves that bent down low to say to the young men: See, we are nothing beside her cheeks, her russet hair.

561   One of those girls who straighten your necktie to show that in her lay the spirit of the eternal mother.

562   A girl who thought the whole thing was awfully overestimated.

563   She's all tied up in knots that girl.

564   Anything added to beauty has to be paid for, that is, the   ★
       qualities that pass as substitutes can be liabilities when added to beauty itself.

565   The car was gay with girls whose excited chatter filled   ★
       the damp rubbery air like smoke.

566   Women are fragile that way. You do something to them at certain times and literally nothing can ever change what you've done.

567   Your voice with the lovely pathetic little peep at the crescendo of the stutter.

568   "IT"

569   Scotty comes up to people when she meets them as if she   ★
       were going to kiss them on the mouth, or walk right thru them, looking them straight in the eye—then stops

a bare foot away and says her Hello, in a very disarming understatement of a voice. This approach is her nearest to Zelda's personality. Zelda's was always a vast surprise.

570   She kissed him several times then in the mouth, her face getting big as it came up to him, her hands holding him by the shoulders, and still he kept his arms by his side.

571   Among the very few domestics in sight that morning was ★ a handsome young maid sweeping the steps of the biggest house on the street. She was a large simple Mexican girl with the large, simple ambitions of the time and the locality, and she was already conscious of being a luxury—she received one hundred dollars a month in return for her personal liberty.

572   who with every instant was dancing further and further off with Caros Moros into a youthful Spanish dream.

573   at voice full of husky laugher his stomach froze

574   Josephine's lovely face with its expression of just having led the children from a burning orphan asylum did the rest.

575   She admired him; she was used to clasping her hands ★ together in his wake and heaving audible sighs.

576   She wore a blue crepe-de-chine dress sprinkled with soft ★ brown leaves that were the color of her eyes. (More than Just a House?)

577   Instead she let the familiar lift and float and flow of love ★ close around them, pulling him back from his far-away uniqueness.

578   It was a harvest night, bright enough to read by. Josephine sat on the veranda steps listening to the tossing of sleepless birds, the rattle of a last dish in the kitchen, the sad siren of the Chicago-Milwaukee train.

579   She saw through to his profound woundedness, and something quivered inside her, died out along the curve of her mouth and in her eyes.

580   Their hearts had in some way touched across two feet of Paris sunlight.

581   Of a despairing afternoon in a little speakeasy on Forty-eighth Street in the last sad months.

582   Crackly yellow hair.   (used)

583   A girl with a bright red dress and a friendly dog jumping at her under the arcs. (Are there arcs now?)

584   Her face was a contrast between herself looking over a frontier—and a silhouette, an outline seen from a point of view, something finished—white, polite, unpolished—it was a destiny, scarred a little with young wars, worried with old white faiths. . .
        . . . And out of it looked eyes so green that they were like phosphorescent marbles, so green that the scarcely dry clay of the face seemed dead beside it.

585   The white glints in her eyes cracked the heavens as a diamond would crack glass, and let stream down a whiter light than he had ever seen before; it shown over a wide beautiful mouth, set and frightened.

586   Looking for a last time into her eyes, full of cool secrets.

587   Pushing s strand of indefinite hair out of her eyes.

588   They swayed suddenly and childishly together. (used?)

589   Mae Purley, without the involuntary quiver of an eyelash, fitted the young man into her current dream.

590   For some years there had been the question as to whether or not Boops was going to have a nose. There was a sort of button between her big dark eyes, eyes that were round at the bottom, half moons hinting that half a person lay undivulged—but at eleven the button was still rudimentary and so unnoticeable that of a winter her elders were often driven frantic by its purls and mutterings, its gurgles, hisses and back firings, before it occured to them to say "Blow it."

591   He had passed the wire to her, to a white rose blooming
       without reason at the end of a cross-bar on the edge of
       space and time like a newly created tree.

592   Bright, unused beauty still plagued her in the mirror.   ★

593   She was desperately adaptable, desperately sweet-natured.

594   Her face was heart shaped, an impression added to by   ★ ?
       honey-colored pointed-back hair which accentuated the
       two lovely rounds of her temples.

595   She was a key-board all resonent and gleaming.

596   He smoothed down her plain brown hair, knowing for
       the thousandth time that she had none of the world's
       dark magic for him, and that he couldn't live without
       her for six consecutive hours.

597   Her childish beauty was wistful and sad about being so
       rich and sixteen.

598   Much as the railroad kings of the pioneer West sent their
       waitress sweethearts to convents in order to prepare them
       for their high destinies.

599   Basil's heart went bobbing off around the ballroom in a
       pink silk dress.

Descriptions of Humanity (Physical)

600   They rode through those five years in an open car with
the sun on their foreheads and their hair flying. They
waved to people they knew but seldom stopped to ask a
direction or check on the fuel, for every morning there
was a gorgeous new horizon and it was blissfully certain
that they would find each other there at twilight. They
missed collisions by inches, wavered on the edge of
precipices and skidded across tracks to the sound of the
warning bell. Their friends tired of waiting for the
smash and grew to accept them as sempiternal, forever
new as Michael's last idea or the gloss on Amanda's hair.
One could almost name the day when the car began to
splutter and slow up; the moment found them sitting in
a Sea Food place on the water-front in Washington;
Michael was opening his letters, his long legs thrust way
under the table to make a footstool for Amanda's little
slippers. It was only May but they were already bright
brown and glowing. Their clothes were few and sort of
pink in general effect like the winter cruise adver-
tisements.

601   The Uni-cellular child effect—short dress.

602   Cordell Hull—Donald Duck eyes?

603   The sinister faces of Elsa Maxwell, of Gloria Vanderbilt
with her frozen whine, of Foreskin Gwinne, of Mr. and

Mrs. J. O'Brien (Dolly Fleishman), the fatuous William Rhinelander Stuart and the stricken boredom in the eyes of his beautiful wife.

604   His hair was grey at 35 but people said the usual things—that it made him handsomer and all that, and he never thought much about it, even though early grey hair didn't run in his family.

605   When Jill died at last, resentful and bewildered to the end, Cass Erskine closed up his house, cancelled his contracts and took a boat around the world as far as Constantinople—no further because he and Jill had once been to Greece and the Mediterranean was heavy with memories of her. He turned back, loitered in the Pacific Isles and came home with a dread of the years before him.

606   Rosalind gave up thinking some time between the Civil war and the depression, and when I want to get anything over to her I tell it to her two dozen times till she begins to parrot it back to me as it were an idea of her own. A satisfactory arrangement but somewhat a nuisance if a decision has to be arrived at in a hurry. Scotty thinks of her as a sweet old bore—she had the impression at first that she was expected to sit in the room when Scotty's beaux called, as if the first guns were going off at Fort Sumter.

607   Attractive people are always getting into cars in a hurry   ★
or standing still and statuesque, or out of sight.

608   Stark's expression, as if he could hardly wait till you   ★
did something else funny—even I was ordering soup.

609   His mannerisms were all girls' mannerisms, rather   ★
gentle considerations got from. . . . . . girls, or
restrained and made masculine, a trait that far from
being effeminate gave him a sort of Olympic stature
that in its all kindness and consideration was masculine
and feminine alike.

610   Captain Saltonville—the left part of his hair flying.

611   For better or worse the awkward age has become shorter
and this youth seemed to have excaped it altogether.
His tone was neither flip nor bashful when he said:

612   Ernest—until we began trying to walk over each other
with cleats.

613   His features were well-formed against the flat canvas of
his face.

614   Dr. X's story about the Emperor of the world.

615   Big fingers catching lisps from unintended notes. Arms
crowded against his sides.

616   Max Eastman—Like all people with a swaying walk he
seemed to have some secret.

617   Romanticism is really a childish throwback horror of   ★
being alone at the top—which is the real horror: Vide:
Zelda's necessity of creating a straw man of me.

618   Photographed through gauze.

619   Pretty girl with dandruff in Rome.

620   A long humorous pimply chin.

621   A panama hat, under which burned fierce, undefeated
Southern eyes.

622   His heart made a dizzy tour of his chest.

623   Amusing of K. Littlefield to call up Zelda about Lydig
and Widener.

624   The gleam of patent Argentine hair.

625   A lady whose lips in continual process of masking buck
teeth, gave her a deceptively pleasant expression.

626   He was a tall, even a high young man.

627   His old clothes with their faint smell of old clothes.

628   The boy's defence of his mother's innocence in the
Lausanne Palace Bar. His mother sleeping with the son
of the Consul.

629   Single way of imitating, distend nostrils, wave his head
from side to side and talk through his nose.

630   Francis' excitability, nerves, eyes against calm
atmosphere.

631   They went to sleep easily on other people's pain.

632   The air seemed to have distributed the applejack to all
the rusty and unused corners of his body.

633   His long, lanky body, his little lost soul in the
universe, sat there on the bathroom window seat.

634   The young man with a sub-Cromagnon visage.

635   Notes on Accident Room.

Afternoon—Rolling table with splints, gauze bandages,
rotten
Tiled floor—wall halfway
Tubes nitrous oxide (gas)
Deaf man—humble. Man with broken arm. Whether I
took my coat off or not. Coat like intruding. Fireman's
child (make it wife) take wings, notices on door,
smoking. Red headed conceited interne who took
me other ward. Laughter of O' O'Donovan's nurse.

First Night—Thrice told story of the night before about
the transfusion from the assailant to the victim.
Why it was necessary. Crowding medical student.
Barber. Barrel of fish. Souture with flap, the
ordinary needle and black thin gut. The two lady
dactors. "Externes" Blonde nurse. Bad cut of
uniforms. Injections, pink disinfectant, needle and
tweezers to draw it through, the flap. Negresses
with gonorrhea probably. Zinder's wife. Barber's

pretentiousness—wonderful. Oyster barrel from biggest sea food dealer in X. Can I work? Wiggles fingers. Straps on chair. Orderly and board washed; his morality. Big legs of doctoresses, petit bourgeousie manners of Zinder. Negroes by first name even by northerners. Discussion about dyes. Difference and relation between lady doctors one already the prom girl, her coat.

Second Night—Jamaica negro. His name. Writing it. Two wounds, one found. Drunk named Katy or Casey (damn good name he says; hesitation saying it) Medical students in evidence. Princeton spies, Trimbles schedule (relatives, diet, time—other doctors' rounds) Blood transference—won't you have a chair? Not a wrinkle in the colored woman's face—nor a flicker—her disease. How it sounded bad faucet, looked—wine sloshed around looking for vein, lost pump, elevators, close both doors, upstairs in biology laboratory. Previous memories "never mind how much" and "it'll do you good" and joking while they do it and change of tone as if patient wouldn't understand "Awful trouble getting this blood." Little boy, fanning wet cast. Dirty feet. Miss Brady—her psychology. Miss Brady knowing everything. The stitches through the eyebrows, Niagara Falls, North Falls, Miss Brady kidding. The student who got fresh. The policeman. The sick negro kid with 103 degrees. The father with "six head of children" and the son with the dislocated arm that would have to be operated on.
He had other commission from outside. One of the nurses in the accident room, an abandoned movie fan, wanted to know if she was really going to marry a certain star. It was in all the magazines— all Bill had to ask her was yes or no.

636   She did not plan; she merely let herself go, and the overwhelming life in her did the rest. It is only when

youth is gone and experience has given us a sort of
cheap courage that most of us realize how simple
such things are.
(used in Tender?)

637   The oily drug store sweat that glistens on battle and   ★
       struggle in films.

638   He swelled out the muscles of his forehead but the
       perfect muscles of his legs and arms rested always
       quiescent, tranquil.

639   Her dress wrapped around her like a wrinkled towel
       unnecessarily exposing her bottom.

640   Always seems to be one deaf person in every room I'm
       in now.

641   Receiving line—girls pirouette, men shifting   ★
       from one foot to the other. Very gracious man shaking
       hands like crawl.

642   The continual "don't remember" of amateur singers is
       annoying.

643   Small black eyes buttoned to her face.

644   Herman Manowitz, bound as Gulliver, vomiting on
       treadmill, 1932 etc.

645   Gus first learned to laugh not because he had any sense
       of humor but because he had learned it was fun to
       laugh—think of other types in society—as a girl
       learns it's pretty.

646   Deep belly laughs of H. L. M.

647   He was not the frock-coated and impressive type of
       millionaire which has become so frequent since the
       war. He was rather the 1910 model—a sort of cross
       between Henry VIII and "our Mr. Jones will be in
       Minneapolis on Friday."

648   He was one of those unfortunate people who are always constrained to atone for their initial aggressiveness by presently yielding a more important point.

649   A white handsome face aghast . . imprisoned eyes that had been left out and stepped on and a mouth   at the outrage.

650   She held her teeth in the front of her mouth as if on the point of spitting them delicately out.

651   Harlot in glasses

652   South—aviation caps, southern journalism, men's faces ˙

653   glass fowl eyes

654   A hand-serrated blue vein climbing the ridges of the knuckles and continuing in small tributaries along the fingers.

655   Girls pushed by their arm in movies.   ★

656   Thornton Wilder glasses in the rosy light

657   He was dressed in a tight and dusty readymade suit which evidently expected to take flight at a moment's notice for it was secured to his body by a line of six preposterous buttons.
There were supernumerary buttons upon the coat-sleeves also and Amanthis could not resist a glance to determine whether or not more buttons ran up the side of his trouser leg.

658   rather like a beach comber who had wandered accidentally out of a movie of the South Seas.

659   The good looking, pimply young man with eyes of a bright marbly blue who was asleep on a dunnage bag a few feet away was her husband—

660   Fat women at vaudeville or the movies repeating the stale wisecracks aloud and roaring at them.

661 On a aime le haliene mauvais quand elle etait malude parcequ'il a ete a lui.

662 The steam heat brings out Aquilla's bouquet.

663 Jews lose clarity. They get to look like old melted candles, as if their bodies were preparing to waddle. Irish get slovenly and dirty. Anglo Saxons get frayed and worn. ★

664 There was no hint of dissipation in his long warm cheeks.

665 She carried a sceptre and wore a crown made by the local costumer, but due to the cold air the crown had undergone a peculiar chemical change and faded to an inconspicuous roan.

666 Those terrible sinister figures of Edison, of Ford and Firestone—in the rotogravures.

667 Round sweet smiling mouth like the edge of a great pie plate.

668 She took an alarming photograph in which she looked rather like a marmoset.

669 The bulbs, save for two, were dimmed to a pale glow; the faces of the passengers as they composed themselves for slumber were almost universally yellow tired.

670 He saw that they made a design, the faces profile upon profile, the heads blond and dark, turning toward Mr. Schofield, the erect yet vaguely lounging bodies, never tense but ever ready under the flannels and the soft angora wool sweaters, the hands placed on other shoulders, as if to bring each one into the solid freemasonry of the group. Then suddenly, as though a group of models posing for a sculptor were being dismissed, the composition broke and they all moved toward the door.

671   His restless body, which never spared itself in sport or danger, was destined to give him one last proud gallop at the end.

672   He had leaned upon its glacial bosom like a trusting child, feeling a queer sort of delight in the diamonds that cut hard into his cheek. He had carried his essential boyishness of attitude into a *milieu* somewhat less stable than gangdom and infinitely less conscientious about taking care of its own.

673   Aquilla's brother—a colored boy who had some time ago replaced a far-wandering houseman, but had never quite acquired a name of his own in the household.

674   A tall, round-shouldered young man with a beaked nose and soft brown eyes in a sensitive face.

675   Her buck teeth always made her look mildly, shyly pleasant.

676   Then, much as a postwar young man might consult the George Washington Condensed Business Course, he sat at his desk and slowly began to turn the pages of Bound to Rise.

677   So poor they could never even name their children after themselves but always after some rich current patron.

678   The chin wabbling like a made-over chin, in which the paraffin had run—it was a face that both expressed and inspired disgust.

679   Men mouthed cigars grotesquely.   ★

680   A handsome girl with a dirty neck and furtive eyes.

681   As an incorrigible masterbater he was usually in a state of disgust with life. It came through however, etc.

682   For the first time a dim appreciation of the problems which Dr. Hines was called upon to face brought a dim, sympathetic sweat to his temples.

683   She reminds me of a record with a blank on the other side.

684   The ones who could probably drive looked as if they couldn't type; the ones who looked as if they could type looked also as if they couldn't drive with any safety—and the overwhelming majority of both these classes looked as though that even if they liked children, the child might not respond.

685   "The German Prince is the horse-faced man with white eyes. This one—" He took a passenger list from his pocket, "—is either Mr. George Ives, Mr. Jubal Early Robbins and valet, or Mr. Joseph Widdle with Mrs. Widdle and six children."

686   A young man with one of those fresh red complexions ribbed with white streaks, as though he had been slapped on a cold day, did not appear to be

687   Family like the last candies left in dish

688   She was so thin that she was no longer a girl, scarcely a human being—so she had to be treated like a grand dame

689   His face over his collar was like a Columbia salmon that had flopped halfway out of a can.

690   A thin young man walking in a blue coat that was like a pipe

691   Run like an old athlete

692   She reminds me of a turned dress by Molyneux

693   They look like brother and sister, don't they, except that her hair is yellow with a little red in it and his is yellow with a little green in it

694   He sat so low in the car that his bullet head was like a machine gun between the propellers of a plane.

Ideas

695

People Born in -		Childhood	Youth	Y.M.
1840	Cleveland	40s	50s	60s
1850	Father	50s	60s	70s
1860	Wilson & Roosevelt	60s	70s	80s
1870	Coolidge & Harding	70s	80s	90s
1880	(Mencken)	80s	90s	00s
1890	Max P.	90s	00s	teens

65	10 in 75	20 in 85	30 in 95
70	" " 80	" " 90	" " 00
75	" " 85	" " 95	" " 05
80	" " 90	" " 00	" " 10
85	" " 95	" " 05	" " 15

696   Play in which revolutionist in big scene "Kill me," etc.
displays all bourgeoise talents hiterto emphasized,
paralyzes them with his superiority and then shoots
them.

697   Lois and the bear hiding in the Yellowstone.   ★

698   A person perfectly happy succumbing to the current
excitement and looking for trouble. Each time he or

she is rescued except the last. Begin with her attempt to achieve real point with her husband—end with her losing it because of this superimposed excitement hunting. One scene where she's pathetic Zelda-Gimma natural—another where you want to wring her neck for ignorant selfishness.

699   *For Play*
    Personal charm.
    Elsa Maxwell.
    Bert.
    Hotels.
    Pasts—great maturity of characters.
    Children—their sex and incomprehension of others.
    Serious work and worker involved. No more patience with idlers unless *about* them.

700   *Helpmate*—Man running for congress gets hurt in line of other duty and while he's unconscious his wife, on bad advice, plans to run in his stead. She makes a fool of herself. He saves her face.

701   Family breaks up. It leaves mark on three children, two of whom ruin themselves keeping a family together and a third who doesn't.

702   A young woman bill collector undertakes to collect a ruined man's debts. They prove to be moral as well as financial.

703   Sam Ordway running away from it all and finding that new menage is just the same.

704   Man wants to see Bermuda. Goes there and is sick the   ★ whole time and sees it only as he leaves.

705   Widely separated family inherit a house and have to live there together.

706   Fairy who fell for wax dummy

707   Three people caught in triangle by desperation. Can't resolve it geographically, so it is chrystallized and they have to go on indefinitely living that way.

708   Evelyn's tragedy: Vagabonds and Debut

709   Plot—if I were rich. He became such Dream (not told) starts with who he wouldn't help, unsympathetic. Goes through schemes Princeton, etc. People that he wouldn't help become more and more sympathetic in bad place. Other schemes fail. Wakes up disillusioned. Would now help—those people

710   *Early Contacts* —When I was young I had the opportunity of meeting a very few great men anonymously. They were all in varying degrees unconscious of the fact that they were meeting one of the—but no, let that pass it has no place in a perfectly serious piece which is to describe the influence of big people on a once pure and sensitive— plasm.

711   Caruso
        A. D. Hurt (Alger boy)
        W. J. Bryan
        Hobey Baker
        Stuart Hienzeman
        Taft (?)
        Duc de Richlieu and Lord Aberdeen
        Freddy McLaughlin

712   Andrew Fulton, a facile character who can do anything is married to girl who can't express herself. She has a growing jealousy of his talents. The night of her musical show for the Junior League comes and is a great failure. He takes hold and saves the pieces and can't understand why she hates him for it. She has interested a dealer secretly in her pictures (or designs or sculptures) and plans to make independent living. But

the dealer has only been sold on one specimen. When he sees the rest he shakes his head. Andrew in a few minutes turned out something in putty and the dealer perks up and says "That's what we want." She is furious.

713   A Funeral—His own ashes kept blowing in his eyes. Everything was over by six and nothing remained but a small man to mark the spot. There were no flowers requested or proferred. The corpse stirred faintly during the evening but otherwise the scene was one of utter quietude

714   Story about man trying to live down his crazy past and encountering it everywhere.

715   Ballet Story —Baseball-Lifar

716   Movie talk-back idea   ★

717   A tree finding water pierces roof and solves a mystery

718   Father teaches son to gamble on fixed machine; later the son unconsciously loses his girl on it.

719   A criminal confesses his crime methods to a reformer, who uses them that same night.

720   Girl and giraffe

721   Marionettes during dinner party meeting and kissing

722   Play opens with man run over

723   Play of gangster—balloons

724   Play about a whole lot of old people—terrible things happen to them and they don't really care.

725   Dolly Wilde

726   Flower shop, Bishop, Malmaison, Constantine, clinics, black men, nurses

727   Caulkins *or* Eduardo story

728   Snubs—Gen. Mannsul, Telulah phone, Hotel O'Con-   ★
nor, Ada Farewell, Toulman party, Barrymore, Talmadge, and M. Davies. Emily Davies, Tommy H. meeting
and bottle, Frank Ritz and Derby, Univ. Chicago,
Vallambrosa and yacht, Condon, Gerald in Paris,
Ernest apartment.

729   The Tyrant Who Had To Let His Family Have Their
Way For One Day.

730   Idea of accidental death of wife husband is tired of.
Makes a hero of her after.

731   For Sketch—Memories of the war
How I took the brass band to etc.

732   *Story*: A man who wanted an elephant, or some such
one of the wisest of beasts who could not talk. Then
began to try to teach him to talk.

733   The Dancer Who Found She Could Fly

734   Words

735   Boobs Bones Mistaken for John The Baptist

736   There was once a moving picture magnate who was   ★
ship-wrecked on a desert island with nothing but two
dozen cans of film. (Herbert Howe)

737   Angered by a hundred rejection slips he wrote an
extroadinarily good story and sold it privately to
twenty different magazines. Within a single fortnight it
was thrust twenty times upon the public. The
headstone was contributed by the Author's League.

738   Idea—like in *The Gallows Wait* (unsuccessful in   ★
Fortitude) of a man taking girl for granted and coming
back upon girl changed. Unable to understand at first.
Examine the situation. In light of previous pop-into-
bed spirit.

739   Short Story—man's admission to himself that he's no
longer in love.

740   Somebody buying an old State car. (suggested by the car having belonged to a president)

741   The man who killed the idea tanks in England—his after life.

742   Play—The Office—an orgy after hours during the boom.

743   Gerald's story of Clews.

744   Two things. Two parties at Ellerslie Smith and Lois.

745   Unusual death—man pierced by his own belt buckle.

746   Two middle-aged well dressed men meet on bridge where each intends suicide. They exchange stories. One has succeeded too late after terrible struggles, loss of girls etc. The other begins with great dreams, hint frustration, etc. But suprise end is, "No, I got it."

747   A bat chase. Some desperate young people apply for jobs at Camp, knowing nothing about wood lore but pretending, each one.

748   Man who gives up just before his chance comes—but happy end and girl.

749   Bijou as a girl in Athens meeting German legacy people in secret. Representing her mother.

750   Seven instead of ten (crank's idea)

751   Idea of husband who had on convention badge and lover on tram who pretends he doesn't know husband and convinces indirectly of innocence. When he's gone husband remembers badge.

752   Mrs. William Mitchell robbed.

753   Jesse or Shep, the bootlegger was deaf. W.C.T.U. preaching in St. Petersburg. $67,000 in three months during boom rum running. Girls on the street.

754   Phillip Marshall Brown on train about Buchmanism.

755   Marberry's story about catcher who threw sweet potatoes.

756   Negro accused of chicken stealing makes up tragic and sympathetic defense—then pockets chickens and goes home.

757   Day with a busy man. Combine the day of Ernest's ★ pictures, the man of genius episode,

758   To make a study of Japanese humility—with myself as Japanese. Idea of height etc. Sharp differentiation from Jewish humility.

759   Story: Photographer looking for a picture surprised on a man's face Crook Gambler looking for truth. Man being the one who gained the Sweepstakes. Both have to know the truth and suspect each other.

760   Driving over the rooftops on a bet.

761   Revenge plan: Man hates to vacate apartment. Gets notice must pull down blind while undressing. Plan made, he writes back snootily and at last moment fixes shade so it won't lower so new tenant will be catch it.

762   Shoes used as man talking to woman. Or in musical comedy cartoon.

763   Story idea: Great man dies in sleep under unusual circumstances. Unusual tribute paid to him—this as main background. (men, women, children, niggers, old men, old women. Pick some vignettes) Story told thru eyes of daughter and beau retelling their affair. She is about 25 and has been her father's secretary. Perhaps is sick and couldn't be told. Look out for Browning story or Hardy.

764   Play founded on Highlands: ★
           IT WAS JUST TOO BAD
      Scene: A drug store. A woman crying.

Scene: A country club. Lover in the distance.
Scene: A hotel—3 in the afternoon. Rain.

Curtain

Scene: A drug store.
Scene: A hotel room. Parting.
Scene: A hotel room showing all involved.
Scene: A drug store.
Scene: The wreck afterwards.
Scene: The drug store.

765   The going to the Riviera. The 35,000 a year. The table at Villa Marie. The attempt at adjusting swimming time. The aviation field. The garden in the morning. The Seldes. Night in St. Maxime. Feeling of proxy in passion strange encouragement. Costume—shaved legs. Invitation from the (Humersteins). Pictures of the picnic. The trip to Avignon. Down the street. The Rumanian army. He was sorry, knowing how she would pay. Bunny Burgess episode.

766   About being high up to insure direction.

767   A famous writer fakes his own death but things *make* him come back.
        Or else *he can't*.

768   G. men as Samurai class.

769   Life and death of love affairs.

770   Magician: 97 out of 100 things being the same. Says characteristic, really characteristic only of unusualness during honeynoon.

771   Josephine in War
        Piggy Back Voyage
        Candy Town
        The Littlefields
        Ball Player Possessed
        The Casting Room   ★

        Revenge by making a person a dope fiend.

Siren System

The Carmagnole

Hog call
Zelda's "not Judas."
Jess old nigger prototype of master
Handshaking, and Pauline's comment and mine.
Pigs and acorns
His good manners
Davenport moon-making
Tenant who sent his son through Sarycuse
The "Settlement."
Calling cattle from one range to another

772   Old Ida finds bills and thinks they're assets, presents and is sued and makes great reputation in her neighborhood.

773   Girl whose ear is so sensitive she can hear radio. Man ★ gets her out of insane asylum to use her.

774   Boredom is not an end product, is comparatively rather an early stage in life and art. You've got to go by or past or through boredom as through a filter before the clear product emerges.

775   A man hates to be a prince, goes to Hollywood and has ★ to play nothing but Princes. Or a general—the same.

776   He's got 'em on his arms (Gerald's Indian.)

777   Jackie Merkle, the mind-reader.

778   Book: It might have been me. My old idea of half truth half lie, including all notes and everything. Shoot the works.

779   I went on one of those Armistice Day bats and the girl I was with drove my car into a hotel lobby and knocked down a major. He really wasn't hurt but he was shocked and they put me in Leavenworth to see whether he'd die or not. Only a couple of months—the girl's father was a big man in Kansas and they acted very well about it.

780   A boy who always says about himself "I ain't got no ker-r-ricketer, I ain't got no self respect." He has no confidence. Finally gets it.

781   Famous Drunks of History

782   The $\begin{bmatrix} \text{ther}\textit{mom}\text{eter} \\ \text{ther}\textit{pape}\text{ter} \end{bmatrix}$ and the man with his head under his arm.

783   Break up of family and mark on children

784   Scribner & Transon.

785   Vagabonds.

786   Machine gun scandal in Balkans.

787   Shooting at the Moon (play idea).

788   Virginia Graham.

789   Boat to Norfolk.

790   Begin with Connie Bennett being nice to Converse who is down and out, nicer and nicer, then jilting him. Exact reverse of what happened to her.

791   Esquire idea about Othello's speech.

792   Hand car in story. (Something about Carter Brown)

793   The gypsies at Hopkins.

794   "At Pauline's"
Pure Gold,
Holy rollers, childrens' faces, voice of preacher
Gypsies
Toilet
Getting Sherry, Burnsville.
Fitzgeralds vs. Brownells.
Rivierra House
Your property

Zelda's eyes
Grandfather apostles beard
(con't)

795   Astonishing story of Kelly; American College in Rome
to Harry's bar and whore-house.

796   Ghost of Vercingetorix crazy man.

797   *Comparisons—Europe* and *America—* for New
Yorker article. Englishman who can't get
passport.

Cities

Stockholm	St. Paul and Minneapolis (Twin Cities)
London & Paris	New York and Washington
(their suburbs)	(Long Island)
Moscow	Chicago
Geneva, Munich	Boston
Manchester	Pittsburgh
Lyons	Detroit, Los Angeles
Berlin	Philadelphia
Marseilles	New Orleans, San Francisco
Milan	Baltimore, Cleveland
Bordeaux	St. Louis

Towns and Resorts

Gstaad	Asheville, N.C. Tryon. Lake Placid
Oxford	Princeton
Hiedelburg	Univ. Virginia, Leland Stanford
French Riviera	Palm Beach, Miama (Florida)
Italian "	Coronado, Santa Barbara (Calif.)
Monte Carlo	Aga Caliente
Hyeres, France	St. Petersburg, Fla.
St. Moritz	Western Place
Aix Les Bains and Vichey	Hot Springs, Va. and White Sulphur
Interlaken	Lake Champlain
Deauville and Trouville	The Main Coast (Kennebunkport &
	the 1000 Islands
Biarritz	Newport R. I.
Avignon, Aix-en-Provence	Charleston and Mobile
Valence (Provence)	Montgomery
Brighton	Atlantic City

798   Story—What becomes of old whores

799   Man has perfectly good case of hate and revenge against other—his liver (fact prepared for) falls out and it's all changed yet he's committed to idea—*Reverse* of suicide story. Or—he has to stop drinking to beat him up and no longer wants to beat him up.

800   The morning young Jackson came over about Ring on telephone

801   Play about boys from Newman

802   Play about wife and Prince Droit de Seigneur   ★

803   Father and Polonius
       Something that began from Greenland's etc.
       Whittier's Barbara Fritchie with the words traitor and shame inked out and replaced by substitutes in the margin, and sections of Hamlet. Principly
           Lend not etc.
           Well, this brings up—"your father" (loan to that man)
           Morgan affair. Smith parallel
           My principles of loan
           English cadging
           Loaning in the morning
           Finish
       Father telling me about man who went to prison for telling lie (Shuttleworth)

804   The celebrity

805   John Jackson tries to get son to stop drinking

806   Man and crime. Through *his* eyes the guilty
       Begin in mediores. Perhaps golf

Two ex-poor girls married to rich men try to return
to former lives

807   Contemplating suicide a man does all he wants to do.
Circumstances prevent and he lives in terror. But it was
all good for him.

808   Basil of Bar Twenty or another

809   Josephine's marriage or rather in Camp

810   Foley Family

811   Woman envies another for meeting Prince of Wales

812   Masseur blinded in war—Goucher wife, Baby seen
through her eyes.

813   Could you have believed in 1929

>   That Kreuger —and Insull
>   That Colonel Lindbergh
>   That Princeton
>   That Hoover
>   That a Mob
>   That the Japanese
>   That U. S. Steel
>   That Spain
>   That the Hohenzollerns

814   Psychological movie with Rex Inghram.

815   For Esquire: Jealous husband meets wife's lover on
train. The bluff that convinces all, including the reader
that the wife has "boasted."

816   Scottie's houseparty

817   The old "Smile for Sylvo" "Canary for two" "Dinner at
Eight" theme, this time with a person ignorant of
imminent and tragic parting of two lovers following
them through what seems a perfect day in New York.

818   On Becoming a Bore

819   Bad parties we've given

820   Unattractive things girls do.

821   The Barnyard boys

822   Play—Two men alternately bored with city and country share country house.

823   For New Yorker "Getting Out." Quiet couple go to Scarface.

824   Save the Indo-Chinese soldiers. Remember they don't laugh.

825   Eye in back of head

826   The piano-movers. Man in one act analogistic play instructs four waiting piano movers in the higher conception. When the piano arrives they are unable to use it.

827   The Fellows yacht scandal

828   Easy Fables for Business Men

829   Fairy play laid in 1940. The pioneer.

830   The walking seven times around the deck after the most terrible stuff. Different line for each seven times. In novel with a new woman in Section II.
Why   Explanation of each of their lives like in advertising article

831   Title for Communist Article. "The Burning of the Book" from Chinese History.

832   Story of Fred Murphy

833   "Time Lapse"
    (1)   Man, girl, friend. Former thinks may happen but won't—it is happening.
    (2)   Later—thinks it is now. Has happened and is over.

834   *The Grotesque Stories*
        The Horror (St. Sulpice)
        The Devil (A day of my Life)
        Tiggy's Dress Suit
        Dr. Fay and the three colleges

835   AN AUTHOR TELLS ALL

Escape and so we have the Escape Autobiography

Youth, Rich Ancestry
Football
War (Escape from Germany capture Kaiser) and
    Revolution
Hollywood
Money making. Bull market
Flying Pacific
Marriages. Giving up Mary, Gretta, etc.
Civil murder and Dot King Case
Breaking up gangs
Writing success. Nom de Plumes
To the South Seas and back
Charming retreat at etc.
Rescues at sea, fire.
All the things I'd like to have done. And you better hurry
up with the check for this or I won't be able to pay my
week's hotel bill.

836   The great Morons of the world (their Ages)

837   New Masses. Father Baron and the nun (for an actor)

838   The Pardners

839   That September 1924, I knew something had happened
      that could never be repaired.

840   Clarence Brown's stories

841   Girl married a dissipated man and keeps him in
      healthy seclusion. She meanwhile grows restless and
      raises hell on the side.

842   The Party Dress (Hergy)

843   My idea about depth in three dimension pictures about submarines.

844   Hollywood Doctor

845   This is the first of six original stories written for the Screen. They will not be offered to magazines. This is not because, in any sense, they are inferior products but because the magazines expect from this author descriptive and "mental" values rather than dramatic values. Also the lengths.

846   Trinidad: The Redlegs are the rear guard of Monmouth's army.

847   Story about 1st flight—man can't marry dumb girl in last flight because of eugenics. Fixes test to prove value of beauty.

848   "—I hadn't been within miles of the lines and I was very bored and had nothing to write home. I wrote my mother that I'd just saved the lives of Pershing and Foch—that a bomb had fallen on them and I'd picked it up and thrown it away. And what did mother do but telephone the news about her brave boy to every paper in Philadelphia."

Jingles and Songs

849   *ONE SOUTHERN GIRL*

Lolling down on the edge of time
    Where the flower months fade as the days move over,
Days that are long like lazy rhyme,
    Nights that are pale with the moon and the clover,
Summer there is a dream of summer
    Rich with dusks for a lover's food—
Who is the harlequin, who is the mummer,
    You or time or the multitude?

Still does your hair's gold light the ground
    And dazzle the blind 'till their old ghosts rise;
Then, all you cared to find being found,
    Are you yet kind to their hungry eyes?
Part of a song, a remembered glory—
    Say there's one rose that lives and might
Whisper the fragments of our story:
    Kisses, a lazy street—and night.

850   FOR A LONG ILLNESS
                    by
            F. Scott Fitzgerald

I.   Where did we store the summer of our love
        Come here and help me find it
    Search as I may there is no trove
        Only a dusty last year's calendar.

Without your breath in my ear
   Your light in my eye to blind it
  I cannot see in the dark.
      Oh tender
Was your touch in Spring, your barefoot voice—
In August we should find graver music and rejoice.

II. A long Provence of time we saw
    For the end—to march together
  Through the white dust.
      The wines are raw
  Still that we will drink
   In the groves by the old walls in the old weather.
  Two who were hurt in the first dawn
    Of battle; first to be whole again (let's think)
     If the wars grow faint, sweep over. . .
  Come, we will rest in the shade of the *Invalides*, the
                        lawn
   Where there is luck only in three leaf clover.

851   I don't need a bit assistance
      That's just—just music in the distance

852   Little by little
      Little by little
      That's the way to do things every day
      Little by little
      That's the way to whittle your troubles away

853   If Hoover came out for the N. R. A.
      And babies were born with an extra thumb
    My daughter would eyebrow me and say
      It was cute, pathetic, juicy or dumb.

If they found a dinosaur in the park
    If Einstein failed on an easy sum
I'd hear from my daughter the bored remark
    It was cute, pathetic, juicy or dumb.

854   *ANSWER TO A POEM*

Yours is received—and I discreetly burn it.
I could hardly do less with such advice than to return it.
Your words are bold enough, may I be bolder?
Try out the plan for me—go lay your shoulder
On the mellow breast of Mr. Holt (don't knock the feller)
Or Mr. Rickey—or even Mr. Rockefeller.
They're kind, they're wise (or think they are) they're
                                   through with fighting.

Infinitely fitter for love—if less exciting!
They'll feel romance for both, and in addition
There'll be less worry—there's less competition
So cease such vaporings. The girls you mention
Have in their time been not without attention
But if their very mattresses were wet
With tears, they could not now play Juliet.

855   Listen to the hoop la
       That's for Betty Boop—ah

856   A god intoxicated fly
           Got in a room with men
       He heard them talk with flashing eye
           Of deeds of fist and pen
       He heard them laugh, he heard them lie
           He watched them leave and then
       He flew to where each sticky hand
           Had left upon a chair
       The sort of drink.

857   THOUSAND-AND-FIRST SHIP

In the fall of sixteen
    In the cool of the afternoon
I saw Helena
    Under a white moon
I heard Helena
    In a haunted doze
Say: "I know a gay place
    Nobody knows."

Her voice promised
  She'd live with me there
She'd bring everything
  I needn't care
Patches to mend my clothes
  When they were torn.
Sunshine from Maryland
  Where I was born.

My kind of weather
  As wild as wild
And a funny book
  I wanted as a child
Sugar and you know,
  Reason and Rhyme
And water like water
  I had one time.

There'd be an orchestra
  Bingo! Bango!
Playing for us
  To dance the tango
And people would clap
  When we arose
At her sweet face
  And my new clothes.

But more than all this
  Was the promise she made
That nothing, nothing,
  Ever would fade
Nothing would fade
  Winter or fall
Nothing would fade,
  Practically nothing at all.

Helena went off
  And married another,
She may be dead
  Or some man's mother
I have no grief left

But I'd like to know
If she took him
   Where she promised we'd go.

            ——F. Scott Fitzgerald

858   *FIRST LOVE*

All my ways she wove of light,
  Wove them all alive,
Made them warm and beauty bright—
    So the trembling, ambient air
    Clothes the golden waters where
  The pearl fishers dive.

When she wept and begged a kiss
  Very close I'd hold her,
And I know so well in this
    Fine fierce joy of memory
    She was very young like me
  Though half an aeon older.

Once she kissed me very long,
  Tiptoed out the door,
Left me, took her light along,
    Faded as a music fades—
    Then I saw the changing shades,
  Color blind no more.

859   *CLAY FEET*

Clear in the morning I can see them sometimes:
  —Men, gods and ghosts, slim girls and graces—
Then the light grows, noon burns, and soon there come
                         times
  When I see but the pale and ravaged places
Their glory long ago adorned—And seeing
  My whole soul falters as an invalid
Too often cheered. Did something in their being
  Of worth go from them when my ideal did?

Men, gods and ghosts, cast down by that young damning,
  You have no answer; I but heard you say
"Why, we were weak. We failed a bit in shamming."

—So I am free! Will freedom always weigh
   So much hung around my heart? For your defection
      Break! You who had me in your keeping, break! Fall!
From that great height to this great imperfection!,
      Yet I must weep—Yet, can I hate you all?

860   *HORTENSE—TO A CAST OFF LOVER*

He loved me too much; I could not love him!
   Opened my eyes so wide I did not see;
For all I left unsaid I could not move him;
   He did not love himself enough for me.

He dropped the helm, he let his ship, unruddered,
   Ride the calm waters of my youth and sin—
His was the blameless past, and still I shuddered
   Seeing the dark spot where his lips had been.

"How you must loathe me, child of youth and brightness!
   All my—well, sentiment. Ah—I'm a bore—"
. . . I smile and lie, and pray for more politeness,
   And shiver when his curled hair nears once more.

Trembling before the fire I gasp and rise,
   Yawn twice and hint of sleep, profess to nod,
—An image flashes, flares to life and dies;
   A devil screaming in the arms of God.

He'd gone too far, lost all his pride somewhere
   On my small heart—And all that I could see
Was his stark soul that labored, grovelled there:
   I loathed him for that soul—that love of me.

861   *THE POPE AT CONFESSION*

The gorgeous Vatican was steeped in night,
   The organs trembled on my heart no more,
But with a blend of colors on my sight
   I loitered through a somber corridor;
When suddenly I heard behind a screen
   The faintest whisper as from one in prayer;
I glanced about, then passed, for I had seen
   A hushed, dim-lighted room—and two were there.
A ragged friar, half in a dream's embrace,

Leaned sideways, soul intent, as if to sieze
The last grey ice of sin that ached to melt
And faltered from the lips of him who knelt
A little bent old man upon his knees
With pain and sorrow in his holy face.

862   **MARCHING STREETS**

Death shrouds the moon and the long dark deepens,
   Hastens to the city, to the great stone heaps,
Blinds all eyes and lingers on the corners,
   Whispers on the corners that the last soul sleeps.

Gay grow the streets now, torched by yellow lamp-light,
   March all directions with a staid, slow tread;
East West they wander, through the sodden city
   Rattle on the windows like the wan-faced dead.

Ears full of throbbing a babe awakens startles,
   Lends a tiny whimper to the still, dark doom;
Arms of the mother tighten round it gently
   Deaf to the marching in the far flung gloom.

Old streets hoary with dead men's footsteps,
   Scarred with the coach-wheels of a gold old age;
Young streets, sand-white, fresh cemented, soulless
   Virgin with the pallor of the fresh-cut page.

Black mews and alleys, stealthy eyed and tearless,
   Shoes patched and coats torn, torn and dirty old;
Mire-stained and winding, poor streets and weary,
   Trudge along with curses, harsh as icy cold.

White lanes and pink lanes, strung with purple roses,
   Dancing from a meadow, weaving down a hill,
Beckoning the boy streets with stray smiles wanton,
   Strung with purple roses that the dawn must chill.

Soon will they meet, tiptoe on the corners
   Kiss behind the foliage of the leaf-filled dark.
Avenues and highroads, bridlepaths and parkways,
   All must trace the pattern that the street-lamps mark.

Steps stop sharp! A clamor and a running!
   Light upon the corner spills the milk of dawn.
Now the lamps are fading and a bluewinged silence
   Settles like a swallow on a dew-drenched lawn.

863 .   PILGRIMAGE

There was a country horse, they say
   Who one day came to town.
Chalked on his side (he was a bay)
   Was "Send me to Carter Brown."

So chaperoned by villagers
   From friendly bin to bin
The nag arrived by easy staggers
   Up at the *Pine Crest Inn.*

And with surprise in every pore
   Twas noted by the country masses
This singular old gee-gee, wore,
   Instead of blinders, *Horn-rimmed glasses!*

Now Carter seldom off his base is—
   But this exceptionable horse
Drew him out briskly from his office
   To ask (in Polish, Welsh, and Norse):

"O horse!" he cried, "What occulist
   Concocted this, to thus surprise us?
Is there a watch upon your wrist?
   Or other quaint and queer devices?"

"O Carter!" said the steed (and balked
   At grooms, quite dumb and ineffectual
Who tried to snub him while he talked):

   "Carter," he said, "I'm intellectual."

"I've had my little shot at knowledge.
   My name's not Jones or Smith or Johnson,
"But—" (and to prove he'd been to college,
   He neighed a bar from "On, Wisconsin!")

"My name is Fido," he confessed,
   "It's true, yes, by it I'll be bound
With that sad moniker I am blessed
   Because they thought I'd be a hound.

"That is my tragedy, my cross,
   That's what still keeps my heart a'burning,

Am I a dog or just a hoss?—
  (I've sublimated it in Learning.")

* * * * * *

His host had fainted. When he came
  To life, he shouted with a frown:
"Why did you bring, in Heaven's Name
  Your problem here to Carter Brown?"

"Because—" the Beast replied—"they tell
  You've heard so many horsey lies, you
'll ne'er be told in heaven or hell
  One fact on horse-flesh to surprise you."

864 She lay supine among her pekinese
  Her dress was pink; she had a lot of guests
All had been given long intelligence tests
  (Square carrots ought to fit octagonal peas)
She used to dandle God upon her knees
  And tell him how—and still kepp nicely humble
Take us to ride with Jesus in the rumble
  Drunk as a fool on wine that had no leas

Poor Sarah—brown back hanging from her pearls
  Poor us who wanted her to be the same
Never to change for she had made us stable
  She was as good and bad as she was able
Change and live on, sweet metal, ours the blame
  Ours is the wig forever yours the curls

865   BEG YOU TO LISTEN.

It is hot tonight—my hand sticks to this paper
  Listen—in the unrequited years
Wasn't it me you looked for sometimes at the races
  beaches, tables? Didn't your odd delicacies and fears
melt away one time when we made funny faces?

  at each other on a canal boat,
galley, floating palace—fifty months ago?
  Didn't we tell the whole story, sit and dote,
stare pop-eyed at each other? Didn't we though?

Cast us as Mona Liza and Jack Horner
Will you! With neither of us supposed to care a damn?
   —My version is the last sight of your head around a
                                          corner—
And the awful unsaid blankness of a telegram.

It is hot tonight but the humidity will not show in the
                      typewriting.

866   *SAD CATASTROPHE*

We don't want visitors, we said
   They come and sit for hours and hours
They come when we have gone to bed
   They are imprisoned here by showers
They come when they are low and bored
   Drink from the bottle of your heart
Once it is emptied the gay horde
   Shouting the Rubyiat, depart

I balked—I was at work, I cried
   Appeared unshaven or not at all
Was out of gin—the cook had died
   Of small pox, and more tales as fall
On boor or friend I turned the same
   Dull eye, the same impatient tone—
—The ones with beauty, sense and fame
   Perceived we wished to be alone

But dull folk, dreary ones and rude
   Long talker, lonely soul and quack
Who hereto hadn't dared intrude
   Found us alone, swarmed to attack
Thought silence was attention; rage
   An echo of their own home's war
Glad we had ceased to "be upstage"—
—But the nice people came no more.

867   Pretty Boy Floyd
And School Boy Rowe
      Went walking up the street.

If you want a flapper—shake her

If you want a maiden—make her
If you want a woman—take her

In a jitney heaven on a cheap gilt street etc.
    (finish) It's me
        (Good Lord)
           It's me.

868   Counter Song to the "Undertaker"
        Bingo Bingo
        Boola-a-boola-boola-boola
        Bingo—Bingo
           Princeton only boasts
           When it roasts
              Old El-i-Yale.

869   Touchdown song based on
        Whoo-oo won
        Prince-ince-ton

870   "Patty's Pulling Parties."

871   Song—
    Near-ya
    There's a kind of magic near ya.

872   Colors has she in her soul
    Dusky gold and green and white

    So if eyes peer out to see
        Rain a-slanting down the street
           Washing through the colonade
    Let us smile and say that she
        Paints in green.

    Rain a-slanting down the street
        By the first lamps of the night
           Overhead the willows meet
    Bells from hidden places toll
        (Colors has she in her soul
           Dusky gold and green and white)

    Hurried dots upon the day
        Little figures scurry by

873   "Sticking along." The voice so faint sometimes I could
                    scarcely hear it.
        Sticking along? For what, we had forgotten years ago.
        Sometimes there was only the cold frim comfort of not
                    being near it,

874   First a hug and tease and a something on my knees
        And then everything
        And that's everything

875   Hooray
        Hooray
        For the boys that say Hurray

876   I hate their guts
        The lowsy mutts

877   If you have a little Jew
            Beat him (when he sneezes)

878   *You'll never know*
            the
                la—
                    —zy
        Spring in my heart

879   Bath tub torch song

880   Oh where are the boys of the boom-boom-boom
        Where are the boys of the boom

881   For Song—Idea—He's just a friend he said. But
        knowing what I (know
                        (do
        I'd be contented If I could be just a friend.

882   "I got a suit of silk pajamas—I'm savin' for you."

883   Refrain for a Poem. How to Get to So and So.
            You go to X and turning there
                Continue on to Berkely Square
                    etc. etc.

You go to X and something X
    And four miles on

884   In a dear little vine covered cottage
        On Forty-second Street
A butcher once did live who dealt
        In steak and other meat

His son was very nervous
        And his mother him did vex
And she failed to make allowance
        For his matracide complex
        And now in old Sing Sing
        You can hear that poor lad sing.

Just a boy that killed his mother
        I was always up to tricks
When she taunted me I shot her
        Through her chronic appendix
I was always very nervous
        And it really isn't fair
I bumped off my mother but never no other
        Will you let me die in the chair?

II

He was only sixteen and a fraction
        A had ne'er been ail in his life
He had scarcely been fired from his high school
        For raping the principal's wife
Now he sits in the laws foulest dungeons
        Instead of his families embrace
Oh how would you like it your ownself
        If you stared the hot seat in the face
        So write Franklin D. if you can
        To send him to old Mattewan
Just a boy that killed his mother
        Now he's in a sorry fix
Since he up one day and plugged her
        Through her perfect thirty-six
It was no concern of no one's
        And his trial wasn't fair

The fact that he shot her was a family matter
    Will you let him die in the chair?

III

Do you think that our civilization
    Should punish an innocent lad
Why he said to the judge in the court room
    He was aiming the gun at his dad

But the judges denied his petition
    And at dawn on the 9th of July
Unless Governor Roosevelt shows kindness
    Gus Schnlitski must certainly die
And the death house once again
Does ring to this refrain
Just a boy that killed his mother
    With a brace of stolen colts
On July 9 they'll fill me
    With a hundred thousand volts
It was dope that made me do it
    Otherwise I wouldn't dare
'Twas ten grains of morphine that made me an orphinc
    Will you let me die in the chair?

885   *OUR APRIL LETTER*

    This is April again. Roller skates rain slowly down
the street

        Your voice far away on the phone
Once I would have jumped like a clown through a hoop—
                but

    "Then the area of infection has increased? . . . oh . . . What
can I expect after all—I've had worse shocks.
Anyhow, I *know* and that's something." (Like hell it is,
but it's what you say to an X-ray doctor.)
        Then the past whispering faint now on another
                phone:
    "Is there any change?"
    "Little or no change"
    "I see"

The roller skates rain down the streets,
The black cars shine between the leaves,
  Your voice far away:
  "I am going with my daughter to the country. My
husband left today. . . No he knows nothing."
   "Good".

  I have asked a lot of my emotions—one hundred
and twenty stories, The price was high, right up with
Kipling, because there was one little drop of something
not blood, not a tear, not my seed, but me more
intimately than these, in every story, it was the extra I
had. Now it has gone and I am just like you now.
  Once the phial was full—here is the bottle it came
in.
  Hold on there's a drop left there. . . No, it was just
the way the light fell
  But your voice on the telephone. If I hadn't
abused words so what you said might have meant
something. But one hundred and twenty stories

  April evening spreads over everything, the purple
blur left by a child who has used the whole paint-box.

886 Don't you worry I surrender
 Days are long and life's a bender
  Still it's true that
   Tender is the Night

887   SONG
 You have got to take a bath
  Just a wee one—a beginner
  Cause my mother's here to dinner
 So you're going to take a bath
  Don't you put me off with maybe
  Get your scrubbing brush for baby
   We must ride through life
   In the very same boat
 But I never counted on a billy goat
  I am used to your aroma

But to others it means—coma
You have got to take a bath

Oh I will not take a bath
    You can lead me to the slaughter
    But I'll just let out the water
Oh I will not take a bath
    For the soap it makes me itchy
    And the whole idea is bitchy
        For you-see-my-dear
        When you married your lad
You married his habits so you might as well be glad
    Baths are only for the dirty
    Haven't needed one since thirty
And I will not take a bath

There's no room to swim around dear
You will end up in the pound dear
    But you've given me your oath, love
    You can take baths for us both, love
And I'm quite content to be a Billy goat
But I never counted on a Billy goat
Do you like to be so high, dear
I am aiming at the sky, dear

888   Mr. Berlin wrote a song about forgetting to remember
        A song that I would never dare to borrow
    For they sang it East and West from January to December
        And we felt for Mr. Berlin in his sorrow
    But here the situation is entirely different

        If I can remember to forget your way (smile)
        To forget a fingers fussing with your hair
            (If I can remember to forget)

889   Mother taught me to—love things
    Now you tell me to—hate things

    Mother taught me to   things
    Now you tell me to doubt things.   etc.

890   Truth and—consequences
        Bobby loved who—it's a big do

Bill loved Ruth—but you mustn't play truly
Truth and consequences

891   Everytime I blow my nose I think of you
          And the mellow noise it makes
              Says I'll be true
      With beers and wines
      With Gertrude Steins
          With all of that
                  I'm through
      Cause every time I blow my no-o-ose
          I—think—of—you.

892   For the time that our man spent in pressing your suit
      For the books and the towels that you took off as loot
      For your general idea you were out on a toot

          For my debutante daughter you threw for a loss
          For the way you insulted my husband's big boss
          For the crap game you won with that *singular* toss
      Thank you so much Mr. Porter for coming here. For the
          servants to whom you did not come across

      For the way that you smashed up our sweet little car
      For your hoggish attacks on our nicely stocked bar
      For the bed you set fire with your God damn cigar
          Never ask you to a week end again

893   Keep the watch!
          When-the-tread-of the many feet is still
          Hold our place on the heights until
          We—come—back—many thousand strong
              Keep the watch
              —At Princeton

894   She's pimply, etc.
      But when she gets together with the giggely girls, she's
      pimply a succoream

895   *Half-and-Half Girl*

      Half-hearted Half-a-Miss
          Half-hearted measures

Are causing you to miss
  Half of life's pleasures

Half rude and half polite
  Half time endeavor
Half wrong but always right
  Justified ever

Half truths that make a lie
  Half kept intentions
(And need one mention, Pie
  Half learned declensions)

Half of a bathing suit
  Half of a mitten
Half the time (when it's cute!)
  Love for a kitten

Half finished stories
  Sewing—got mired in it
Literature's glories
  Gave up—got tired in it

Half of a language done
  Half of a lesson
Half study-time for fun
  Half work to guess on

Half of an exercise
  Heavens who *can* know
How one can memorize
  Half the piano!

Half liking half a friend
  Grow warm or colder
When cross don't half unbend
  Turn the cold shoulder

Half with your duty—Aye!
  Fluid like water
Seeking half beauty—my
  half-and-half daughter

896   *OH, SISTER, CAN YOU SPARE YOUR HEART*
VERSE: I may be a What-ho, a No-can-do
             Even a banker, but I can love you

As well as a better man
a letter-man of fame
As well as any Mr. Whosis you can name

_____

The little break in my voice
—or Rolls-Royce
take your choice
I may lose
You must choose
So choose

_____

A hundred thousand in gold
and you're sold
to the old
and I'm broke
when our days a
are gold
I'm begging
begging
Oh, Sister, can you spare your heart?

****

Those wealthy goats
In racoon coats
can wolfe you away from me
But draw your latch
For an honest patch
the skin of necessity
(we'll make it a tent, dear)

****

The funny patch in my pants
take a chance
ask your aunts
What's a loss
You must toss
So toss!
A gap inside that's for good.
You'll be good
As you should

Touch *wood!*
I'm begging
begging
Oh, Sister, can you spare your heart?

897   *You've driven me crazy*
       What'll Jung do   what'll Jung do
       My yen for you makes everything hazy
       What Jung do to you

       How true—were the doctors who
           psychked me
           who liked me
       Believe me they knew
           but you—were
               the kind of neurotic
               schitzotic when
               I needed you
       You've driven me crazy
       I'll do the same to you

898   A SONG NUMBER IDEA:

       DOWN—LONG—ILE—LAND
       Where the Choo-Choo trains go
           All the yellow cabs are rushing
           To the seven-ten for Flushing (etc.)
       (with three trains—Winchester, Long Island, New
               Jersey—
       events *en route*, false legs over seats, etc.)

899   *A BLUES*
           Sway-yed and driven
               by forces I don't understand
       (high) Sway-ed and driven
               Got to eat out a somebody's hand
               Gotta eat
               Gotta eat out a somebody's han'
                   But gotta eat
           Sway-ed etc.

900   *THE EARTH CALLS*

The ground cried out to him
It clasped his middle
He knew finally
The end of the riddle.

Some things we know
About death and birth
He knew he was due to go
Down back into the earth

901   Life's to short to
Wait for a boy like you to make up his mind.
Life's too short to
Meddle with anyone else but you.

Karacters

902   A Portrait

　　She will never be able to build a house. She hops
herself up on crazy arrogance at intervals and wanders
around in the woods chopping down everything that
looks like a tree (vide: sixteen or twenty short stories in
the last year *all of them* about as interesting as the
average high-school product and yet all of them
"talented.") When she comes near to making a clearing
it looks too much to her like all the other clearings
she's ever seen so she fills it up with rubbish and debris
and is ashamed even to speak of it afterwards. Driven,
ordered, organized from without, she is a very useful
individual—but her dominant idea and goal is freedom
without responsibility which is like gold without metal,
spring without winter, youth without age, one of those
maddening, coo-coo mirages of wild riches which make
her a typical product of our generation. She is by no
means lazy yet when she chops down a tree she calls it
work—whether it is in the clearing or not. She makes
no distinction between *work* and mere sweat—less in
the last few years since she has had arbitrarily to be led
or driven.

903   Someone who was as if heart and brain had been
       removed and were kept in canopic vase.

904   Lonsdale: You don't want to drink so much because you'll make a lot of mistakes and develop sensibility and that's a bad trait for business men.

905   He had once been a pederast and he had perfected a trick of writing about all his affairs as if his boy friends had been girls, thus achieving feminine types of a certain spurious originality. (See Proust, Cocteau and Noel Coward.)

906   A dignity that would have been heavy save that behind it and carefully overlaid with gentleness, something bitter and bored showed through.

907   There was, for instance, Mr. Percy Wrackham, the branch manager, who spent his time making lists of the Princeton football team, and of the second team and the third team; one busy morning he made a list of all the quarterbacks at Princeton for thirty years. He was utterly unable to concentrate. His drawer was always full of such lists.

908   He abandoned the younger generation which had treated him so shabbily, and, using the connections he had made, blossomed out as a man of the world. His apprenticeship had been hard, but he had served it faithfully, and now he walked sure-footed through the dangerous labyrinths of snobbery. People abruptly forgot everything about him except that they liked him and that he was usually around; so, as it frequently happens, he attained his position less through his positive virtues than through his ability to take it on the chin.

909   He was a warrior; for him, peace was only the interval between wars, and peace was destroying him.

910   "Sure, more strong here. More peasants come, with strength and odor of ground." (About U. of M. in eyes of Japanese.)

911   Frank Crowninschild and coffee house.

912   "Against my better judgment," he would say, having no judgment and "obviously" and "precisely."

913   About that. From the moment when, as a boy of twenty, his handsome eyes had gazed off into imaginary distance of a Griffith Western, his audience had been really watching the progress of s straightforward, slow-thinking, romantic man through an accidentally glamorous life.

914   Young Fox "America missed a great opportunity by not forgiving debts."

915   A young lady "in pictures" who once, in the boom days of 1919, had been almost a star. It had been announced in the movie magazines that she was to "have her own company" but the company had never materialized. The second girl did interviews with "cinema personalities" interviews which began "When one thinks of Lottie Jarvis, one pictures a voluptuous tigress of a woman."

916   The man who entertained Scottie in Brittany.

917   Minnie the Moocher stabbed me.

918   He has a dark future. He hates everything.

919   But if they haven't it all comes out the same. Only if they control themselves they forget their emotion and so they think they haven't missed anything.

920   "Don't get the idea that Seth doesn't ask anything. He's lived all his life off better minds than his own."

921   "Stick-around" spirit from Duffy

922   Uncle Phil idea about this kind uncle or aunt—how far is he indulging himself—(not that it matters except how far is his—self-indulgence to be trusted.)

923   Nicole's attitude toward sickness was either a sympathy toward a tired or convalescent relation who didn't need it, and which therefore was mere sentimentality, or else a fear when they were absolutely threatened with death, toward real sickness—dirty, boring, unsympathetic she could control no attitude—she had brought up selfish in that regard. Often this was a source of anger and contempt in her to Dick.

924   Idea about Nicole can do everything, extroverts toward everything save people so earth, flowers, pictures, voices, comparisons seem to writhe—no rest wherever she turns, like a tom-tom beat. Escapes over the line where in fantasy alone she finds rest.

925   No first old man in an amateur production of a Victorian comedy was ever more pricked and prodded by the daily phonomens of life than was

926   Mrs. Rogers' voice drifted off on an indefinite note. She had never in her life compassed a generality until it had fallen familiarly on her ear from constant repetition.

927   Instinct of Peggy Joyce collecting jewelry instead of bonds

928   NORA LANGHORNE FLYNN (Now 1935—age 42 or 43)
Born 1892—11th child—Greenwood, Virginia
Stuff from little niggers for Corbett-Fitzsimmons movie
Visited oldest sister Lady Astor
Married 1910—Age 18—Two children
Met Lefty Flinn summer 1914. Lefty at piano. Like children. Picture of Madonna. One month—bigamy—West Nora to England. Letters intercepted

Lefty married (1) Palmer—children 2		Nora celebate from husband
		War nurse (Capt.)
	(2) Viola Dana	Officer tying tie.
		Scotsman who wishes

she had been born a
housemaid

15 years pass. Chil-
dren grown

Letter in 1931. Lefty arrives Carleton drunk. Flight to Paris,
Riviera,
    Africa—followed by lover with mustache. Lady Astor
    hell, Hoyty,
    etc.
    Marriage. America 1931-1935
    His disappearances.

929   *List of troubles*
    Heart burn
    Eczema
    Piles
    Flu
    Night sweats
    Alcoholism
    Infected Nose
    Insomnia
    Ruined Nerves
    Chronic Cough
    Aching teeth
    Shortness of Breath
    Falling Hair
    Cramps in Feet
    Tingling Feet
    Constipation
    Cirocis of the liver
    Stomach ulcers
    Depression and Melancholia

930   He was wearing old white duck trousers with a
    Spanish flair and a few strange coins nodding at their
    seams and a striped Riviera sweater and straw shoes
    from the Bahamas, and an ancient Mexican hat. It was,
    for him, a typical costume Diana thought. Always at
    Christmas she arranged to get him some odd foreign
    importation from parts as far away as possible from
    Loudoun County.

931   Boyd's lordly manner not quite carried off. Contrast
        with Hitchcock's.

932   Erskine Gwynn

933   Eleanor Hill

934   Tuolmans

935   For the first week he was called Aquilla's brother ("That
        Frenchman," he reported at home, "kep' a-callin me
        Aquilla's brother. 'Aquilla's brother!' he'd call, till I
        hardly knew who I was.") because Aquilla's return was
        expected daily, and as time passed the question was
        never investigated as to whether he had a name of his
        own. So that during the hours he spent in Rene's house
        he had, to himself at least, hardly any identity at all.

936   Called him Aquilla with a sort of noise after it like
        Aquilla boom as a sort of recognition that it was not
        quite his name.

937   A small tongue-tied colored boy. He had come one day
        to replace Aquilla who had an aching tooth.

938   When I like men I want to be like them—I want to lose
        the outer qualities that give me my individuality and be
        like them. I don't want the man I want to absorb into
        myself all the qualities that make him attractive and
        leave him out. I cling to my own inards. When I like
        women I want to own them, to dominate them, to have
        them admire me.

939   Like so many "men's women" she hid behind girls
        when available, as if challenging a man to break
        through and rescue her. Any group she was with
        became automatically a little club, protected by her
        frail, almost ethereal strength, tensile strength of thin
        fine wires.

940   The old woman afraid of aeroplanes

941   Alec had a terrible temper and had once chased him for ten blocks with a sharp butcher knife intending to cut him smaller. Claire once chased him half that far with a dead rat. But he was actually braver than either of them—he caught behind the bat without a mask and when he was thirteen he broke three ribs in football tackling a boy who weighed a hundred and seventy.

942   When he was despised it was rather more than usually annoying, the last stages of throwing him over I mean. For he knew it as soon if not sooner than you, and seemed to hang about analyzing your actual method of accomplishing the business.

943   *Fatality of Beauty*

944   Man who instinctively with people he liked turned the left side of face the ugly half people, had corresponding reacton on brain, spinal chord etc. and had charm.
       Contrariwise right side of face exact opposite. Perfect, made him self conscious paralyzed mental and nervous etc.
       To be worked out.

945   Mr. Chambers of Montgomery as character

946   The nervous quarrel between husband and wife, which had already caused sensitive passengers to have their tables changed in the dining salon

947   Jitters clinic, given by Ruby Robert Kelly who had died of jitters there.

948   Seemed to extend in its own right out of the ordinary world of courtesy.

949   He had a knowledge of the interior of Skull and Bones

950   You were so brave about people, George. Whoever it was, you walked right up to them and tore something aside as if it was in your way and began to know them. I tried to make love to you, just like the rest, but it was difficult. You drew people right up close to you and held them there, not able to move either way.

951   Addresses in his pocket—mostly bootleggers and psychiatrists.

952   Inescapable racial childishness. In the act of enjoying anything wanted to tell. Sandy Annabel etc. trying to get everything out of first meeting.

953   He seldom exuded liquor because now he had tuberculosis and couldn't breathe very freely.

954   Just when somebody's taken him up and is making a big fuss over him he pours the soup down his hostess' back, kisses the serving maid and passes out in the dog kennel. But he's done it too often. He's run through about everybody, until there's no one left.

955   "You mustn't do that, Abe," protested Mary. "Abe spends half his time living up to engagements he make when he's tight. This spring in Paris he used to take dozens of cards and scraps of paper out of his pockets every morning, all scrawled with dates and obligations. He'd sit and brood over them for an hour before he dared tell me who was coming to lunch."

956   I've given parties that have made Indian rajahs green with envy. I've had prima donnas break $10,000 engagements to come to my smallest dinners. When you were still playing button back in Ohio I entertained on a cruising trip that was so much fun that I had to sink my yacht to make the guests go home.

957   Mother had explained his faults to Seth and found him extremely understanding.

958   She wanted to be ringmaster—for awhile. In somebody else's circus—a father's circus. "Look here my father owns this circus. Give me the whip. I don't know how or why I snap it but my father owns this circus. Give me your mask, clown, acrobat your trapeze, etc.

959   Elsa was a social impressario of considerable ability but her ambition had driven her to please so many

worthless people that she had become, so to speak, a
sort of lowest common denominator of all her clients.

960   Zelda on Gerald's Irishness, face moving first.

961   Hates old things, the past, Provence. A courtier.

962   Constance Talmage on my middle-class snobbishness.
        Also Fanny Bryce

963   Throw blood from one side of the head to another
        (Cuban)

964   There is undoubtedly something funny about not being
        a lady, or rather about being a gold digger. You've got
        to laugh a lot like Constance Talmage and Ruth.

965   Rosalind always hiding in closets till the battle is over
        and then coming back to say, "I told you so."

966   Don, unlike Elsa Maxwell, yearned after higher
        things. This yearning he indulged in a series of modest
        parodies which he declared were "better than Candide."
        However the attempt to convince himself brought on a
        short paranoia during which he made efforts to pull
        down the pillars on all our heads and hide in the ruins.
        We were through, he said,—then, satisfied he returned
        to suck. The Whitneys bought him up cheap and
        turned him out to grass on the private golf links—for
        all I know he is still there.

967   Once tried to get up a ship's party on a ferry boat.

968   You had to have head lettuce and mayonaise and she
        realized vaguely that the latter was seldom found in a
        wild state. Brought up in apartment hotels and married
        at the beginning of the delicatessen age, Vivian had not
        learned to cook anything save a strange liquid that in
        emergencies she evolved from the coffee bean; she was
        most familiar with the product of the soil in forms in
        such highly evolved forms as "triple combination
        sandwiches." A farm to her was a place where weary

butterflies retired with their lovers after the last fade out in the movies.

969   Vivian Barnaby was just what her husband had made her, no masterpiece. She was pretty in a plaintive key, so was the child, and momentarily when you first met them you liked them for a certain innocence, a blowy immaturity—momentarily, that was all.

970   Perhaps a drunk with great bursts of sentimentality or resentment or maudlin grief.

971   He saw men acutely and he saw them small, and he was not invariably amused—it was obvious that his occasional dry humor was washed over the brim of an over full vessel. Francis' first instinct was to defer to him as to an older man, a method of not bothering him, but he saw that Herkimer turned away from delicacy even more than from the commonness to which he was adjusted.

972   Roscoe's gestures increasingly large and increasingly fall short. Again he "hates old things."

973   Greatest vitality goes into displeasure and discontent

974   Irving—on the bust at 50

975   Paul Nelson from School Play Onward

976   He said that no matter what happened he always carried about his own can of olive oil. He had a large collection of lead soldiers and considered Ludendorf's memoirs one of the greatest books ever written. When McKisco said that history was already ruined by too much about war Monsieur Brugerol's mouth twisted fiercely under his hooked nose and as he answered that history is a figured curtain, hiding that terrible door into the part through which we all must go.

977   Capable of imaginative rudeness

978   Mother always waiting in waiting-rooms an hour early, etc. pulled forward by an irresistible urge of boredom and vitality.

979   Egloff as being the typical uncertain tentative attitude

980   Weaver

981   Rosalind talks in several more syllables than she thinks in.

982   He was one of those men who had a charger; she always knew it was tethered outside, chafing at its bit. But now, for once, she didn't hear it, though she listened for the distant snort and fidgeting of hoofs.

983   Like most men who do not smoke he was seldom still and his moments of immobility were more taut and noticeable.

984   Someone with a low voice who feels humble about it.

985   About a man looking as if he was made up for a role he couldn't play.

986   Fat people—good humor vs. Romance—sweat

987   Mrs. Smith had been born on the edge of an imaginary precipice and had lived there ever since, looking over the precipice every half hour in horror and yet unable to get herself away.

988   surprised that a creature so emotionally tender and torn as himself should have been able to set up such strong defenses around his will.

989   My father is very much alive at something over a hundred and always resents the fact that the fathers of most of the principal characters in my books are dead before the book begins. To please him I once had a father stagger in and out at the end of the book but he was far from flattered—however, this is a short word on money lending. Father passed on to me certain

inerradicable tastes in peotry. The Raven and the
Belles, The Prisoner of Chillon (it's the fact that at the
moment I'm looking down at the original that makes
me write this)

990 One button always showed at front of his trousers.

991 Please? screamed English girl.

992 Family explained or damned by its dog

993 English girl: "For over 250 years there hasn't been
a battle there—match that."

994 Girl's tenderness against man's bogus humanity.

995 The drunk on Majestic and his 100 yard dash.

996 Mrs. Widdle in my book either—she was bound to sleep
with someone or to humiliate them—she didn't care
which.

997 Some of those who have known him would be content
to have him spared my bitterness which roams in and
out of sacred gardens. And some day I may meet him
again it might be his whim to honor me once more
with a moment or so of—, hand me my self respect, my
justification on a platter as he had a way of doing.

998 How if I said I was impressed by "can" motif in E. M.

999 Roscoe made up Dinah

1000 Roscoe as a reader. A reader's mind. One's own
experience, the necessity for using which educated
many fiction writers never existed for him. Indeed he is
one of those for whom the visual world does not exist.
He reads and his mind is stimulated; before it is
assimilated (i.e. associate it with?) he has an elation, as
if he had thought of it himself, almost a creative
ecstacy. He can hardly wait to get at a chance to work it
in

1001   Bogus girl who reads Ulysses, Wharton gives her a pain in the eye.

1002   As to Ernest as a boy—reckless, adventurous, etc. Yet it is undeniable that the dark was peopled for him. His bravery and acquired characteristics.

1003   Donald Stewart ecstacy about Lew Cody in the act.

1004   All girls know some way to kill time but Scottie knows all the ways.

1005   I never know what Scottie is—I only know what she's like. This year she seems to have a certain community of purpose with the Scarlet Pimpernel.

1006   Hank the cop and the clapper.

1007   For Don communism is a spiritual exercise. He's making it his own.

1008   Don: An intellectual simpleton. He pleases you not by direct design but because his desire to please is so intense that it is disarming. He pleases you most perhaps when his very words are irritants.

1009   Zeld is frou-frou, her frou-frou characteristics.

1010   Boy from the Tropics
          That wonderful book, *Soldiers of Fortune* was a "gross representation". He was least objectionable when he talked about what they did to Igarottes and how there were natives in the backhills of Luzon who had tails of real fur.

Literary

1011   ***Charles Brackett's Book***
It was wonderful. I couldn't lay it down, was impelled on the contrary to hurry through it. In fact I finished it six and a half minutes while getting shaved in the Continental Hotel. It is what we call a book written at a fine pace as for the high spots there are so many that it is difficult to pick them but I could select.

1012   Nothing is any more permitted in fiction like stage convention of keeping people on stage by coincidences.

1013   Edgar Wallace—G. A. Henty

1014   Long rhythm based on Essie's full excuse and thank you to Aquilla's I mean.

1015   Barnaby Rudge ran in Sat Eve Post

1016   Must listen for conversation style a la Joyce

1017   Livid
Demean   all misused
Jejune

1018   In a transition from say:
        fight or action interest
            to
        love and woman interest
The transition *cannot* be abrupt. The man must be *before*

or *after* an event to be interested in women; that is, if he *is* a man and not a weakwad.

Fault in transition in Musa Dag book. After battle right to Julia. Sometimes clumsy. Better an interval. You cannot tie two so different masculine emotions by the same thread.

1019   Nevertheless value of Ernest's feeling about the pure heart when writing—in other words the comparatively pure heart, the "house in order."

1020   Zelda's style formed on her letters to her mother—an attempt to make visual etc.

1021   T. S. P. A Romance and a Reading List
Sun also Rises. A Romance and a Guide Book

1022   The only reason the artist's judgment is better is because his reason, if it is really for his work, is his opinion on the various top swayings of men and ideas is less disinterested than any other people's reason for unlike the philosophers he can at any point discountenance the whole method of his reasoning unlike the scientist he can claim being closer to nature. He reverts again and again to martyr and clown. Not apropos consider Shaw and The Bohemian Mrs. Swann and Co.

1023   Cisebeo for gigolo.

1024   Resent the attempt of the boys and girls who tried to bury me before I was dead.

1025   Books are like brothers. I am an only child. Gatsby my imaginary eldest brother, Amory my younger, Anthony my worry. Dick my comparatively good brother but all of them far from home. When I have the courage to put the old white light on the home of my heart, then—

1026   Stuf about Grande Guignol (serious).

1027   Shakespeare—whetting, frustrating, surprising and gratifying.

1028   Forebearance, good word.

1029   I can never remember the times when I wrote
anything—This Side of Paradise time or Beautiful and
Damned and Gatsby time for instance. Lived in story.

1030   Idea for an essay on the "Lilies that fester," sonnet.

1031   That Willa Cather's poem shall stand at beginning of
Mediaval and that it shall be the story of Ernest.

1032   What are successful backgrounds now-a-days—think—
Coquette?

1033   Shows in which you forget background, remember no
help from description. Gas stations is the type.

1034   Just as Stendahl's portrait of a Byronic man made *Le
Rouge et Noir* so couldn't *my* portrait of Ernest as
Phillipe make the real modern man.

1035   But there was one consolation:
They could never use any of Mr. Hemingway's four
letter words, because that was for fourth class and fourth
class has been abolished—
(The first class was allowed to cheat a little on the
matter.)
But on the other hand they could never use any two
letter words like NO. They *had* to use three letter words
like YES!

1036   A character who spends all his time trying to break
down a stray and careless aphorisms of great men. Give
him a name and list him under characters and note
aphorisms as they pop up in reading.

1037   There never was a good biography of a good novelist.
There couldn't be. He is too many people if he's any
good.

1038   Robert ("Gastric") Forsite   (Kyle Creighton)

1039   The great hitch hike to glory that's going to make them
         good artisans—able to repair the car much in the
         manner of the cars in this jacket freize.

1040   And such condescension toward the creative life—
         Tolstoi caught the sense of the Napoleonic wars out in
         the street from the man in the street; his comments on
         fiction which would make any old 1864 copy of Leslie's
         more humanly valuable than *The Red Badge of
         Courage*—the idealization of all that passes through his
         empty mind; his hatred of all people who formed the
         world in which he lives—a political Oscar Wilde
         peddling in the provinces the plums he took from our
         pudding; his role of Jesus cursing. You can see him
         going from prize fight to first night to baseball game—
         maybe even to women—trying to put back into
         movement the very things Lenin regretted that he
         might have destroyed—gracelessness and ugliness for its
         own sake. Gentlemen, proletarians—for a prize skunk I
         give you Mr. Forsite.

1041   D. H. Lawrence great attempt to synthesize animal and
         emotional—things he left out. Essential pre-Marxian.
         Just as I am essentially Marxian.

1042   She had written a book about optimism called Wake up
         and Dream which had the beautiful rusty glow of a
         convenient half-truth—a book that left out illness and
         death, war, insanity, and all measure of achievement,
         with titillating comfortability. She had also written a
         wretched novel and a subsequent volume telling her
         friends how to write fiction, so she was on her way to
         being a prophet in the great American Tradition.

1043   When Whitman said "Oh Pioneers" he said all.

1044   Byron's mountains warm.

1045   Didn't Hemmingway say this in effect:
             If Tom Wolfe ever learns to separate what he gets
         from books from what he gets from life he will be an

original. All you can get from books is rhythm and technique. He's half-grown artistically—this is truer than what Ernest said about him. But when I've criticized him (several times in talk) I've felt bad afterwards. Putting sharp weapons in the hands of his inferiors.

1046   Reporting the extreme things as if they were the average things will start you on the art of fiction.

1047   "Inviscera" instead of "Invictus."

1048   Work out my hard luck season—my most productive seasons, etc

1049   Conrad's secret theory examined.
He knew that things do transpire about people. Therefore he wrote the truth and transposed it to parallel to give that quality, adding confusion however to his structure. Nevertheless there is in his scheme a desire to imitate life which is in all the big shots. Have I such an idea in the composition of this book?

1050   Conrad influenced by Man Without a Country

1051   Gene Stratton-Porter. What a cheap old harpy she was. If Frank Norris had written one more chapter to the Octopus she'd have had one more novel.

1052   No English painting because of their putting everything into words.

1053	Bracket Book (See Notes)	Merde Siphilis Couchez avec Miscarriage Ass (for arse) Fag

1054   List of Zelda's faults and virtues as a writer.

1055   Chapter in slow motion.

1056   Right to Pretty heroines

1057   Exact equivalent of escape mechanism in Little Colonel books is in escape mechanism of Greta Garbo films.

1058   Tie up with Faulkner—Lord Fauntleroy.

1059   Art invariably grows out of a period when in general the artist admires his own nation and wants to win its approval. This fact is not altered by the circumstances that his work may take the form of satire for satire is the subtle flattery of a certain minority in a nation. The greatest artists grow out of these periods as the tall head of the crop. They may seem not to be affected but they are.

1060   Great art is the contempt of a great man for small art.

1061   Tarkington: I have a horror of going into a personal debauch and coming out of it devitalized with no interest except an acute observation of the behavior of colored people, children and dogs.

1062   The queer slanting effect of the substantive, the future imperfect, a matter of intuition or ear to O'Hara, is unknown to careful writers like Bunny and John.

1063   My feelings on re-reading "Imagination and a Few Mothers" and realizing that it had probably influenced Mrs. Swann's whole life.

1064   I thought Waldo Frank was just the pen name that a whole lot of other writers used for symposiums.

1065   When the first rate author wants an exquisite heroine or a lovely morning, he finds that all the superlatives have been worn shoddy by his inferiors. It should be a rule that bad writers must start with plain heroines and ordinary mornings, and, if they are able, work up to something better.

1066   Man reads good reviews of his book so many times that he begins finally to remodel his style on them and use their rhythms.

1067   Realistic details like Dostoiefski glasses

1068   *Re* Cole Porter: *vide* the ending of Mrs. Lowseboro
          Something which does not bother even to be a
          paraphrase of Tchaikowski's *Chanson Triste*

1069   The scandal of "English Teaching".

1070   The Thackeray at Edward Everett Horton's.

1071   The two basic stories of all times are Cinderella and
Jack the Giant Killer—the charm of women and the
courage of men. The 19th century glorified the
merchant's cowardly son. Now a reaction.

1072   Taking things hard—from Genevra to Joe Mank—:
That's stamp that goes into my books so that people
can read it blind like brail.

1073   The Steinbeck scene. Out of touch with that life. The
exact observation there.

1074   Bunny Wilson writing his Renan before Christ is
deified.

1075   Analysis of Tender:

I	Case History	151-212	(1 pps.(change moon) p.212
II	Rosemary's Angle	3-104 101 pps.	P.3
III	Casualties	104-148, 213-224	55 pps.(-2)(120 & 121)
IV	Escape	225-306	82 pps.
V	The Way Home	306-408	103 pps.(-8)(332-341)

1076   To write a series of children's books illustrated by
someone like Job or Orgeille.

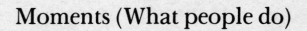

Moments (What people do)

1077   *DOGS*

We went through a routine, with a lot of false starts, charges, leg and throat holds, rolling overs, and escapes.

I only barked a little in the base to stretch my throat—I'm not one of the kind always shooting off their muzzle

We followed a tall lady for awhile—no particular reason except she had a parcel with meat in it—we knew we wouldn't get any but you never can tell. Sometimes I just feel like shutting my nose and just following somebody pretending they're yours or that they're taking you somewhere.

The Brain wasn't there yet but the Beard was. He got out that damn pole and tried to kid me again, holding it out and jabbering—a long time ago I figured out that his object is to see if I'm fool enough to jump over it. But I don't bite, just walk around it. Then he tried the trick they all do—held my paws and tried to balance me on the end of my spine. I never could figure out the point of that one.

I wanted to lick him, but when I came really close he snarled, "Scram!" and got half up on his haunches. He thought I was going to eat him just because he was down.

The little boy said, "Get away you!" and it made me feel bad because I've never eaten a dog in my life and would not unless I was very hungry.

I must have a hundred bones around here and I don't know why I save them. I never find them again unless accidentally, but I just can't stand leaving them around.

1078   Thinking the world was going to start over with the things they could make of cellophane. Because for a moment everyone was making things of cellophane.

1079   Moving on to hot seat in theatre.

1080   In processions I always look at the coach man and see what he looks like.

1081   The idea of the grand dame slighly tight (a la Margaret Harriman) is one of the least impressive in the world. You know: "The foreign office will hear about this, hic!"

1082   I once financed the great grandson of the great Morgan.

1083   Who did I kiss who said, "Don't tell Zelda"? Sandy?

1084   It was an old pistol for as he took it away from her a slice of pearl came off the handle and fell on the floor.

1085   Some kind of small animal that looked all wrong "as if it were turned inside out," had emerged from the forest, regarded them curiously for a moment and hurried mysteriously away.

1086   They were all hungry now, and sitting jaded beside the stream they developed individual tendencies to look around for a sign "Restaurant" or strain their ears for the tinkle of a dinner bell.

1087   In Manilla Mr. Barnaby had struck her with a whist broom because she had ruined his life.

1088   Nurses clucking. As if that confirmed some idea of life that they had held for long

1089   Dorothy Parker going Victorian, making up fortune in the past by weeping—a sort of deliberate retrogression

1090   He put out a mosquito on the paper and erased its body with the rubber

1091   Her mouth fell open comically, she balanced a moment

1092   Almost release but scene broken by local music

1093   She was asleep—he stood for a moment beside her bed sorry for her, because she was asleep, and because she had set her slippers beside her bed.

1094   Waiting for the lady to take out the bag on bus

1095   Everyone suddenly stiffened—after a terrible moment Mrs. Littleton, by making herself figuratively into oil managed to ooze a few words through.

1096   Only a fat Victorian pincushion filled with an assorted variety of many-colored-headed pins seemed to assure her that a well-brought-up girl would do the right thing.

1097   They ran for it through a blinding white hot crash.

1098   He cocked one miserable eye at the bright tropical stars.

1099   Belina the young Corsican yelled with glory as he bounced his aeroplane across the sky.

1100   The inebriated American who had invited him to lunch thought at first that Val was a son of the czar.

1101   "Dramatic club! Oh, gosh!" cried the girl. "Did you hear that? She thinks it's a dramatic club, like Miss Pinkerton's school." In a moment her uninfectious laughter died away.

1102   Back in the sitting room he resumed his walking; unconsciously he was walking like his father, the judge, dead thirty years ago; he was parading his dead father up and down the room.

1103   The cuff button dropped to the floor; he stooped to pick it up and then said "Helen!" urgently into the mouth-piece to cover the fact that he had momentarily been away.

1104   The water went into his nose and started a raw stinging; it blinded him; it lingered afterward in his ears, rattling back and forth like pebbles for hours.

1105   The silence was coming from some deep place in Mrs. Ives' heart.

1106   The almost regular pat-smack, smack- pat- pat of the balls, the thud of a jump and the overtone of the umpire's "Fault;" "Out;" "Game and st,6 —2, Mr. Oberwalter."

1107   Our fathers died. Suddenly in the night they died and in the morning we knew.

1108   They laughed, ending with yawning gurgles that were not laughed out but sucked in.

1109   She yet spoke somewhat sharply, as people will with a better refusal to convey.

1110   To ride off into the sunset in such a chariot, into the very hush and mystery of night, beside him the mystery of that baby-faced girl.

1111   Couple treading water dancing.

1112   Wiping his chin with a long rag which he took from some obscure section of his upholstery.

1113   When he left the house their engagement was over, but her love for him was not over and her hope was not gone, and her actions had only begun.

1114   If Teddy had played the current sentimental song from Ermine, and had played it with feeling, she would have understood and been moved, but he was plunging her suddenly into a world of mature emotions, whither her nature neither could nor wished to follow.

1115   A chorus of pleasant envy followed in the wake of their effortless glamour.

1116   He threw his hands up so high it seemed as if they left his wrists and were caught again on their descent.

1117   Hesitation before name doesn't displease.

1118   Behind them a long haired Nebraska pederast (not Van Vechten) told the plot in mournful numbers.

1119   He went back into the bathroom and swallowed a draught of rubbing alcohol guaranteed to produce violent gastric disturbances.

1120   He put his mind in order with a short resume of the history of music, beginning with some chords from The Messiah and ending with Debussy's La Plus Que Lent, which had an evocative quality for him, because he had first heard it the day his cat died.

1121   Clubbing him with his taller fist his head side-swiped a fence with blood tasting on his mouth and going cold on his ear lobes.

1122   Trying to dismiss him as a sort of inspired fairy.

1123   Opens magazine several times at the fact that poetry is at crossroads.

1124   A beam, soft and pleasant fell across his spirit. Those two beings, tender and cloud-like, unreal, with the little sins of little people. They were no more than sick room flowers where he lay.

1125   But at the look of childish craftiness in her eyes he took it back quickly.

1126   She leaned back confortably against the water pipe, as one enjoying the moment at leisure. He lit her a cigarette impatiently and waited.

1127   She walked toward the dressing table as though her own reflection was the only decent company with which to foregather.

1128   De Sano tearing the chair

1129   The funeral carriages—a man smoking in the last

1130   Two brown port bottles appeared ahead, developed white labels, turned into starched nuns who seared us with holy eyes as we went by.

1131   We left him there dancing with a fluttering waiter.

1132   Dog arrives. I call him. Doesn't like me. Expressionless he passes on.

1133   *In the big halt of night, an arrow fell in camp*—it was neither poisoned nor pigeon-burdened—only pointed, and during big halt the enemy was a friendly thing.

1134   Her voice trying to blow life into the dead number 2-0-1-1

1135   Mother majestically dripping her sleeves in the coffee.

1136   His ecstacy made him use the cane. He pointed it at little patches of snow that still remained on the ground and then raised it overhead dragging it through the lower limbs of the trees.

1137   There was a flick of the lip somewhere, a bending of the smile toward some indirection, a momentary lifting and dropping of the curtain over a hidden passage.

1138   he sat back robbed and glowering.

1139   Hats coming off, thought it was his head

1140   Went into the bathroom and sat on the seat crying because it was more private than anywhere she knew.

1141   When he urinated it sounded like night prayer.

1142   The feeling that she was (his) began between his shoulders and spread over him like a coat going on.

1143   A thing called the Grand Canyon Symphony which seemed to me to lean heavily on Horses Horses Horses.

1144   breaking into an "Off to Buffalo" against a sudden
        breath of wet wind.

1145   Shocked at five razor blades instead of twelve.

1146   Shuddering with pleasure at the difficult idiom.

1147   The young people got back into the boat—they all felt
        fine and quietly passionate.

1148   When she heard his footsteps again she turned frankly
        and held his eyes for a moment until his turned away,
        as a woman can when she has the protection of other
        men's company.

1149   An idea ran back and forth in his head like a blind
        man, knocking over the solid furniture.

1150   He had written a complimentary letter to Mr. X, the
        humorist, for an autograph and had received Mr. X's
        form letter which was a joke. About bunions 'Dear Sir,'
        the letter said, 'My advice to you is to

1151   Her mother had handed the passenger list across the
        table—her fingers so meticulously indicating the name
        that Rosemary had to pry it up to read.

1152   Person driving away after seeing friend off (Sheilah)
        "I'm glad you've gone John", and does a takem
        glancing back.

1153   Going home at night—lights out—newsboy remind me.

1154   "Bring me a box of Elizabeth Arden" you'd wired me
        and how our love shone through any old trite phrase in
        a telegram.

1155   After a while a skittish lady with an air of being
        pursued slipped in and not without a few wary glances
        around achieved sanctuary in the front row.

1156   The moment of closeness between savagry and
        civilization never closer than in the self-consciousness
        of truces and surrenders of men in love with the same

girl, or in common life when we handle money. Scene to show this—paying Flora setting down money on bureau—no you keep it, etc.

1157   Moss Hart's compliment and me calling him author of Babes in Arms.

1158   The pins and the napkin ring I swallowed.

1159   ———for a moment the sparkler went in four directions, exploded. The end of four stars. They exploded in four directions, detonated. The corner of the room—stars—just for a moment. He did not what he had done.

1160   "And Nanny's Trunk."

1161   I have known and analyzed too much charm to be impressed by ladies who recompose their features after an interdict.

Nonsense and Stray Phrases

1162   Kings Own Leopards.

1163   He would be part of that great army driven by the dark
        storm.

1164   "I've arranged that if anything should happen to you
        the remains will be kept in cold storage until I return."

1165   They were startled—that was inevitable; one couldn't
        crash right in on people without tearing a little bit of
        diaphanous material.

1166   The car waited tenderly for a minute.

1167   All around her he could feel the vast Mortmain fortune
        melting down, seeping back into the matrix whence it
        had come.

1168   Scott Fitzgerald climax runner for the Cal.
        "Courtesans" today passed his zenith. It was rushed
        after him to Peoria, Indiana, but by that time the soap
        on the nursery floor had become a shambles.

1169   You're not talking to a scared picker full of hookworm.

1170   With your practically brilliant faculty for supposing
        that whatever isn't in the foreground of your conscience
        has ceased to exist.

1171   There's nothing like a good dog—unless it's a good cow or a good slice of underdone tripe.

1172   At the pound they would call off the names of the dogs. Some had to be carried out barking, others walked nobly. They were taken in little carts to place of execution and then one by one they disappeared down the sausage machine.

1173   Have you ever known a man who could bark? I have not. Or who liked to be led out on the end of a chain? I have not.

1174   He had long forgotten whether Darrow called Scopes a monkey or Bryan called Darrow a scope or why Leopold-Loeb was ever tried in the first place.

1175   BURLESQUE ON MOTHER PITCHER IN DOS-
         PASSOS MANNER:
         Continentals starving for want of coal finally get some but can't digest it because it's hard coal. After the war—hollow victory—they lost Montreal and it's wet. Profiteers in daguerreotypes. Everybody tired of Yankee Doodle. Men seasick crossing the Delaware. Rammed her petticoat down cannon, she was restrained. British walked away with hands over their eyes.

1176   In an instant the combination of atoms that was Eva Coo was dissolved.

1177   Ernest Hemingway, while careful to avoid cliches in his work, fairly revels in them in his private life, his favorite being Parbleu ("So what?") French, and "Yes, We Have No Bananas." Contrary to popular opinion he is not as tall as Thomas Wolfe, standing only six feet five in his health belt. He is naturally clumsy with his body, but shooting from a blind or from adequate cover, makes a fine figure of a man. We are happy to announce that his work will appear in future exclusively on United States postage stamps.

1178   Thomas Wolfe or "Loup" (Anthony Adverse, Time and the River, N.Y. Telephone Directory 1935) is a newcomer to American Skulldugery. Born during a premium contest.

1179   The Barnyard boys
          or Fund on the Soil
                George Barnyard
                Thomas   ″
                Glenway   ″
                Lladeslas   ″ , their uncle
                Knute   ″ , their father
                Burton Smalltown, the hired man
                Chambers, a city dude
                Ruth Kitchen
                Martha Kitchen
                Willa Kitchen, their mother
                Little Edna, an orphan
                Margaret Kitchen

          It was winter, summer, spring, anything you like, and the Barnyard Boys were merrily at work getting together epics of the American soil in time for the next publishing season. All day long they dug around in the great Hardy fields taking what would come in handy in the next winter (or spring, summer the seasons follow one another tearing up growths of by the roots)

                How Hanson you are looking cried the fan
                Chambers dressed 1903
                There is no such thing as willing to be honest—like blind man willing to see

1180   To dine at a "serious" restaurant.

1181   He's a roll call, that fellow

1182   Proximity of her tan legs

1183   The Blue Ribbon Boys

1184   *ECONOMY STATEMENTS:*
                They're much less expensive to run
                It's all right to run around in

It'll do to wear around the house
It'll keep us from being extravagant and inviting too
many people to dinner
It'll do when we have another
We're saving that up so we'll have something to look
forward to
That's good for the moths
It (a carpet) just gets worn out in this house
We want to wait until we get a really nice one

1185   A weak heart, a sick heart, a broken heart or a chicken heart?

1186   Shot through bald forehead—like where a picture and its nail has been removed from wall

1187   The Thyroid Islands

1188   This is to say the least Miss Rosemary Prince

1189   rules that fight through all the weather like six wheeled cars crossing the Sahara.

1190   Listen little Elia, draw your chair up close to the edge of the precipice and I'll tell you a story.

1191   Drifting towards some ignoble destiny they could not evade.

1192   Then I was drunk for many years, and then I died.

1193   it would have been a bigger picture if he could have had everyone gilded.

1194   since his wife ran off one windy night and gave him back the custody of his leisure hours.

1195   A whole bunch of men kidnapped to take blackheads out of their neck

1196   He had hit her before and she him

1197   Far gone, far called, far crowned

1198   We gave the corpse twenty-four hours to leave town.

1199   *Esprit Frondeur*

1200   As twice as a double bumble bee

1201   The aristocratic nose and the vulgar heart

1202   Superfluous as a Gideon Bible in the Ritz

1203   Given at his birth a spoonful of noxema just brought
        from Palestine.

1204   One can do little more than deny the persistent rumors
        that hover about him; for instance that he was born in
        a mole cave near Schenectady, in a state of life-long
        coma—conversely that his father was a certain well-
        known international munitions manufacturer of pop-
        guns, a notorious blatherskite who earned a precarious
        living in the dives of Zion City or as others say a line
        coach at a famous correspondence school.

1205   Simile about paper they paste on glass during building

1206   The awful reverberating thunder of his absence

1207   Father bought her a Christian

1208   I have never wished there was a God to call on—I have
        often wished there was a God to thank.

1209   "Sure—you did a sequence for Collins with a watch
        face and some little card-board silhouettes. It was very
        interesting."

1210   I have had more trouble getting people out from under
        stamps. I just love people under stamps. I remember
        when I first got under a stamp with a girl—

1211   Better Hollywood's bizaare variations on the normal,
        with George Collins on the phone ordering twelve girls
        for dinner, none over eighteen.

1212   We'll find you a pooch that'll say *Arp.*"

1213   That I was as ill behaved on one stick of furniture as you were on another.

1214   Dive back Aphrodite, dive back and try for the fish undersea.

1215   The three rich neurotics.

1216   Ordered twisted fish and a cat's handle bar.

1217   The blue-green unalterable dream.

1218   A day full of imaginary telegrams.

1219   The Blue-eenum. . . carried 12 professors and a five ton truck sealed in a vaccuum bubble all over Western Europe in an hour.

1220   Joke about am I supposed to eat it—or have I and left it in the incinerator.

1221   Oh wild weekend, thou breath of autumn's being.

1222   Wit born in darkness of college movie houses.

1223   The "Wyn" in Metro Goldwyn Mayer. Explain its presence.

1224   I think I'd better go out and stay too long—don't you?

1225   At two-thirty this afternoon the Countess of Frejus will be fired out of this cannon.

1226   Section ending. And that brings us to that Goddamn word "compare".

1227   Antibes before the merchants came.

1228   Dr.'s take Oath of Hypocracy.

1229   Kid's Magazine: The Prospective Detective.

1230   Seething Sam from Seething Springs.   ★

1231   I may as well spend this money now. Hell, I may never get it.

1232   Drunk scooter-ing.

1233   When the thing began to begin.

1234   TURKEY REMAINS AND HOW TO INTER THEM
           WITH NUMEROUS SCARCE RECIPES
by
F. Scott Fitzgerald

At this post holiday season the refrigerators of the nation are overstuffed with large masses of turkey, the sight of which is calculated to give an adult an attack of dizziness. It seems, therefore, an appropriate time to give the owners the benefit of my experience as an old gourmet, in using this surplus material. Some of the recipes have been in my family for generations. (This usually occurs when rigor mortis sets in.) They were collected over years, from old cook books, yellowed diaries of the Pilgrim Fathers, mail order catalogues, golfbags and trash cans. Not one but has been tried and proven—there are headstones all over America to testify to the fact.

Very well then: Here goes:

1. *Turkey Cocktail*
     To one large turkey add one gallon of vermouth and a demijohn of angostura bitters. Shake.

2. *Turkey at la Francais.*
     Take a large ripe turkey, prepare as for basting and stuff with old watches and chains and monkey meat. Proceed as with cottage-pudding.

3. *Turkey and Water*
     Take one turkey and one pan of water. Heat the latter to the boiling point and then put in the refrigerator When it has jelled drown the turkey in it. Eat. In preparing this recipe it is best to have a few ham sandwiches around in case things go wrong.

4. *Turkey Mongole*
     Take three butts of salami and a large turkey skeleton from which the feathers and natural

stuffing have been removed. Lay them out on the table and call up some Mongole in the neighborhood to tell you how to proceed from there.

5. *Turkey Mousee*

Seed a large prone turkey, being careful to remove the bones, flesh, fins, gravy, etc. Blow up with a bicycle pump. Mount in becoming style and hang in the front hall.

6. *Stolen Turkey*

Walk quickly from the market and if accosted remark with a laugh that it had just flown into your arms and you hadn't noticed it. Then drop the turkey with the white of one egg-well, anyhow, beat it.

7. *Turkey a la Creme.*

Prepare the creme a day in advance, or even a year in advance. Deluge the turkey with it and cook for six days over a blast furnace. Wrap in fly paper and serve.

8. *Turkey Hash*

This is the delight of all connoisseurs of the holiday beast, but few understand how really to prepare it. Like a lobster it must be plunged alive into boiling water, until it becomes bright red or purple or something, and then before the color fades, placed quickly in a washing machine and allowed to stew in its own gore as it is whirled around.

Only then is it ready for hash. To hash, take a large sharp tool like a nail-file or if none is handy, a bayonet will serve the purpose—and then get at it! Hash it well! Bind the remains with dental floss and serve.

And now we come to the true aristocrat of turkey dishes:

9. *Feathered Turkey.*

To prepare this a turkey is necessary and a one pounder cannon to compel anyone to eat it. Broil the feathers and stuff with sage brush, old clothes, almost anything you can dig up. Then sit down and simmer. The feathers are to be eaten like artichokes (and this is not to be confused with the old Roman custom of tickling the throat).

10. *Turkey at la Maryland*
Take a plump turkey to a barber's and have him shaved, or if a female bird, given a facial and a water wave. Then before killing him stuff with with old newspapers and put him to roost. He can then be served hot or raw, usually with a thick gravy of mineral oil and rubbing alcohol. (Note: This recipe was given me by an old black mammy.)

11. *Turkey Remnant*
This is one of the most useful recipes for, though not, "chic", it tells what to do with the turkey after the holiday, and extract the most value from it.

Take the remants, or if they have been consumed, take the various plates on which the turkey or its parts have rested and stew them for two hours in milk of magnesia. Stuff with moth-balls.

12. *Turkey with Whiskey Sauce.*
This recipe is for a party of four. Obtain a gallon of whiskey, and allow it to age for several hours. Then serve, allowing one quart for each guest.

The next day the turkey should be added, little by little, constantly stirring and basting.

13. For Weddings or Funerals. Obtain a gross of small white boxes such as are used for bride's cake. Cut the turkey into small squares, roast, stuff, kill, boil, bake and allow to skewer. Now we are ready to begin. Fill each box with a quantity of soup stock and pile in a handy place. As the liquid elapses, the prepared turkey is added until the guests arrive. The boxes delicately tied with white ribbons are then placed in the handbags of the ladies, or in the men's side pockets.

There I guess that's enough turkey to talk. I hope I'll never see or hear of another until—well, until next year.

Left Out—Stand live turkey in ice box until quite stiff ect.

Observations

1235   Strater trying to carry with him the good of every age—
one must discard no matter from how unworthy a
motive. Trying to see good in everyone he saw only his
own good.

1236   Thinking is a development of talking and not talking—
thereby furnishing a contrast between if I had and I
didn't.

1237   Parallel of Ernest's and French conversation as opposed
to Gerald and me and U.S.A. emotional bankruptcy.

1238   Drunk at 20, wrecked at 30, dead at 40
Drunk at 21, human at 31, mellow at 41, dead at 51.

1239   Like all men who are fundamentally of the group, of
the herd, he was incapable of taking a strong stand
with the inevitable loneliness that it implied.

1240   Voices—American doubtful. "Well, I don't know,"
English saying "Extraordinary" refusing to think,
French saying "Well there you are."

1241   Apropos of Cocteau—perverts love of perverted children
M. or F. is compensation for missing women who are,
in their social aspect, children with guile and
sometimes wisdom, but still children.

1242   Like all self-controlled people the French talk to
themselves.

1243   She knew that she herself was superior in something to the girls who criticised her—though she often confused her superiority with the homage it inspired.

1244   Too soon they were responding to Josephine with a fatal sameness, a lack of temperament that blurred their personalities.

1245   Cocktails before meals like Americans, wines and brandies like Frenchmen, beer like Germans, whiskey-and-soda like the English, and as they were no longer in the twenties, this preposterous *melange*, that was like some gigantic cocktail in a nightmare.

1246   Do you know what your affair was founded on? On sorrow. You got sorry for each other.(Did Ernest borrow this one?)

1247   Young people do not perceive at once that the giver of wounds is the enemy and the quoted tattle merely the arrow.

1248   Arbitrary groups formed by the hazards of money or geography may be sufficiently quarrelsome and dull, but for sheer unpleasantness the condition of young people who have been thrust together by a common unpopularity can be compared only with that of prisoners herded in a cell. In Basil's eyes the guests at the little dinner the following night were a collection of cripples.

1249   I can even live with a lie (even someone else's lie— can always spot them because imaginative creation is my business and I am probably one of the most expert liars in the world and expect everybody to discount nine-tenths of what I say) but I have made two rules in attempting to be both an intellectual and a man of honor simultaneously—that *I do not tell myself lies that will be of value to myself,* and secondly, *I do not lie to myself.*

1250   They went on to the party. It was a housewarming,
        with Hawaiian musicians in attendance, and the guests
        were largely of the old crowd. People who had been in
        the early Griffith pictures, even though they were
        scarcely thirty, were considered to be of the old crowd;
        they were different from those coming along now, and
        they were conscious of it.

1251   The combination of a desire for glory and an inability
        to endure the monotony it entails puts many people in
        the asylum. Glory comes from the unchanging din-din-
        din- of one supreme gift.

1252   France was a land, England was a people, but America,
        having about it still that quality of the idea, was harder
        to utter—it was the graves at Shiloh and the tired,
        drawn, nervous faces of its great men, and the country
        boys dying in the Argonne for a phrase that was empty
        before their bodies withered. It was a willingness of the
        heart.

1253   The real plot of all Little Theatre plays the one that
        transpires through whatever play they're officially
        acting is how the young gosling actor of fourteen ever
        managed to be in love with the leading woman of forty
        and what's going to come of the situation. The reality
        of this gives that blurred air that the performances
        always have.

1254   It is difficult for young people to live things down. We
        will tolerate vice, grand larceny and the quieter forms
        of murder in our contemporaries, because we think of
        ourselves as so strong and incorruptible, but our
        children's friends must show a blank service record.

1255   What would you rather be loved for, your beauty,
        your intrinsic worth, your money?
            First two vanish and are replaced by their equivalents,
        beauty and charm and tact spirituality and energy, by
        experience and intelligence. Third never knows any
        change.

1256   Why do whores have husky voices?

1257   After all, any given moment has its value; it can be questioned in the light of after-events, but the moment remains. The young princes in velvet gathered in lovely domesticity around the queen amid the hush of rich draperies may presently grow up to be Pedro the Cruel or Charles the Mad, but the moment of beauty was there.

1258   Perhaps that life is constantly renewed, and glamour and beauty make way for it.

1259   "A pair of thoroughbreds, those two," said the other woman complacently, meaning that she admitted them to be her equals.

1260   Parallel of Zelda to me, and the hunter who got back the third time with lions.

1261   Family quarrels are bitter things. They don't go according to any rules. They're not like aches or wounds; they're more like splits in the skin that won't heal because there's not enough material.

1262   One advantage of politeness is to be able to deal with women on their own grounds, to please or to torture the enemy, as it may prove necessary. And not to fire random shots and flowers from the pure male camp many miles away.

1263   It is in the thirties that we want friends. In the forties we know they won't save us any more than love did.

1264   But the world is always curious, and people become valuable merely for their inaccessibility.

1265   You can usually scare a certain amount of brains into a woman but usually you can't make them stick.

1266   Force of a proverb in another language.

1267   He felt then that if the pilgrimage eastward of the rare poisonous flower of his race was the end of the adventure which had started westward three hundred years ago, if the long serpent of the curiosity had turned too sharp upon itself, cramping its bowels, bursting its shining skin that at least there had been a journey; like to the satisfaction of a man coming to die—one of those human things that one can never understand unless one has made such a journey and heard the man give thanks with the husbanded breath. The frontiers were gone—there were no more barbarians. The short gallop of the last great race, the polyglot, the hated and the despised, the crass and scorned, had gone, at least it was not a meaningless extinction up an alley.

1268   Dispairingly and miserably, to what purpose neither knew, as people in fire save things they don't want and have long disliked.

1269   Advantage of politeness. Extending out of ordinary world, etc.

1270   Actors the clue to much

1271   He had one of those minds so imconprehensible to the literary man which are illiterate not through insensibility but through the fact that the past and future are with them contemporary with the present, having no special value or pathos of their own.

1272   No learning without effort—educational movies.

1273   Each of us knows much more about us than you'd think to read the novels. Give you a few strong lines here says photographer, etc. Loss in dignity but—

1274   When we do something mean to a friend we think of it as an exception in our relations with them but as a matter of fact it has immediately become the type thing. We have just one time.

1275   My sometimes reading my own books for advice. How much I know sometimes—how little at others.

1276   This being in love is great—you get a lot of compliments and begin to think you're a great guy.

1277   Very strong personalities must confine themselves in mutual conversation to very gentle subjects. Everything eventually transpired—but if they start at a high pitch as at the last meeting of Ernest, Bunny and me their meeting is spoiled. It does not matter who sets the theme or what it is.

1278   If you're strong enough there *are* no precedents.

1279   Gertrude Harris about pleasure of giving. The excess.

1280   Didn't finish idea today that lack of success of physical sheer power in my life made trouble. Fighting through intellectual power—parallel in life of modern woman—courage in Zelda, etc.

1281   They had a dignity and straightforwardness about them from the fact that they had worked in pictures before pictures were bathed in a golden haze of success. They were still rather humble before their amazing triumph, and thus, unlike the new generation, who took it all for granted, they were constantly in touch with reality. Half a dozen or so of the women were especially aware of being unique. No one had come along to fill their places; here and there a pretty face had caught the public imagination for a year, but those of the old crowd were already legends, ageless and disembodied. With all this they were still young enough to believe that they would go on forever.

1282   Large or small house. Foul or clean mouth.

1283   Like a bad play where there is nothing to do but pick out the actors that look most like real people and watch them until, like amateurs, their true existance has become speculatively interesting

1284   Something in his nature never got over things, never accepted his sudden rise to fame because all the steps weren't there.

1285   Francis says he's tired of a life like a full glass of water, relations with people a series of charades, you never do the whole world.

1286   Is snubbed when he dramatized himself as victim of American failure.

1287   De Sano—If you use both logic and imagination you can destroy everything in the world between them.

1288   Men hate to stay in hotel run by woman
        Women vice versa

1289   The American capitol not being in New York was of enormous importance in our history. It had saved the Union from the mobs in sixty-three—but, on the other hand, the intellectual drifted to the Metropolis and our politics were childish from lack of his criticism.

1290   Each of us thinks his own life has been etc.

1291   Fairy can only stand young girls on stage, where they're speaking other people's lines.

1292   The laugh generated by Fred Stone's I'm so nervous in the Wizard of Oz justified a whole generation into cultivating nerves.

1293   I've seen that everytime Zelda sees Egerova and me in contact, Egerova becomes gross to her. Apart the opposite happens.

1294   Subject of control—
        British pitch—from strength easy, from nervous effort hard therefore a moral question?
        Dohan
            me etc.

1295   It seemed to her that the dance was woman's interpretation of music; instead of strong fingers, one had limbs with which to render Tschaikowsky and Stravinski; and feet could be as eloquent in Chopiniana as voices in The Ring. At the bottom it was something

sandwiched in between the acrobats and the trained
seals; at the top it was Pavlova and art.

1296   To record one must be unwary.

1297   They would like to have been her, but not to have paid
the price in self-control.

1298   Your first most typical figure in any new place turns
out to be bluff or local nuisance.

1299   . . . retrospect to have a more enduring value of their
own. Nights are their own fulfilment—we possess them
and not their memory, save for certain nights that open
out into a novel and startling dawn. But perhaps it is
only that it is easier to remember afternoon.

1300   "They come over so the children can learn French,"
said Abe gloomily. "Then they all just slip down
through Europe like nails in a sack, until they stick out
of it a little into the Mediterranean Sea."

1301   I heard a child called Venice in movie theatre at night.
First Michael Arlen generation. The sort of picture
you'd expect, and it was night.

1302   I've notice that the children of other nations always
seem precocious. That's because the strange manners of
their elders have caught our attention most and the
children echo those manners enough to seem like their
parents.

1303   Once a change of direction has begun, even though it's
the wrong one, it still tends to clothe itself as
thoroughly in the appurtenances of rightness as if it
had been a natural all along.

1304   A large personality is built on such a structure that we
scarcely realize its dimensions while it is being built; it
keeps up its monstrous development, flinging out as
many unaccountable commitments as the limbs on an
octopus, growing until we scarcely recognize its
shadow—so large has it become beyond that of ordinary

people. Except we can recognize the dimensions of the shadow in the horizontal twilight of the coffin.

It becomes such a valuable thing that it is a pity when it is killed, and those nature lovers among us should watch its growth; it is difficult to reproduce scientifically; and if allowed to die may not re-occur for many years.

1305   You and Seth can be radicals and show your children how you look in the bathtub, because you're both so good, but people who really experiment with themselves find out that all the old things are true.

1306   My theory of partial arbitrary covering of skin as protection from cold—furred Dolmans, Roman shin guards, etc.

1307   "You can be nice to someone without falling into their arms" almost always means "You can be awful to somebody without their knowing it."

1308   She never realized that whenever she mustered all the cold cruelty with which she could dominate, over the wide open sensitivity that she lived on but could never know—she never knew that later in a form of revenge, when his wounds were well, his sores closed, he would inevitably crush down on her with a pressure she could no more comprehend than his sensitivity; it contained the same elements—only his suffering was now made over into suffering for her—even more fatal for not being deliberate.

1309   She was plagued by the devastating small one—ring selfishness of some women for instance to her statement that a man had been on sentry duty all night she would oppose the fragment of truth that he had somewhere snatched two legitimate hours of sleep, and thus discredit his ability to take the punishment of a twenty-one hour day. This seems to be one of the last achievements women are likely to wrest from men, but having made the confusion of mere patience with work they are not inclined to surrender the point graciously.

1310   The word "manly" ruined by commercial use.

1311   *On Operations*—Being a soldier takes the life out of you, as was the experience of Philip Sidney; being a good poet removes or invalidates the nervous system, being a politician or statesman operates only on the conscience, and is as simple as the removal of the heart which too often goes with doctoring. The removal of the soul consonant on being a successful merchant is accomplished practically without pain.

1312   Idea that in the higher levels of human achievement writing Thalberg etc. difference is so slight etc.

1313   Awful disillusion of arriving at center of supposed authority and finding need of flattery so as to be reinforced in that authority.

1314   The grand triumph of the people who don't care over the people who do—the well in the sick room, nurse over patient, doctor's jokes, their exquisite attention (Forel) to my egotism, the advantage of the beloved over the lover, and the lender over the borrower but also the sponge over the softee.

1315   Personality precludes inspection by vis-a-vis.

1316   Wanting to mother a man—wanting to keep him from spending his money on some other woman.

1317   The words gentleman and lady only have a concise meaning to a person just learning to be one, or just having ceased to be one.

1318   A woman's sense of men conspiring together and vice versa

1319   You can take your choice between God and Sex. If you choose both you're a smug hypocrite, if the choose neither you get nothing.

1320   Fairies' natures attempt to get rid of soft boys by sterilizing them.

1321   Some discussion of the facts that in general *Haut bourgeousie* training is so much more enlightened that more stuffed shirts survive. *Esprit de Corps.*
petite bourgeousie training is rougher and selects the fittest but *proletarian* training is the roughest of all, and has poorest education and least *esprit de corps* is hampered by race prejudices etc.

1322   Artistic temperament is like a king with vigour and unlimited opportunity. You shake the structure to pieces by playing with it.

1323   any given individual life or situation things progress from good toward less good. But life itself never does.

1324   Mankind has lived through three ideas (1) That the capacity for leadership is hereditary, (2) that the soul is immortal, (3) that he can govern as a mass and is fit and able to choose his leaders—and into a fourth i.e. that ethics are attractive in themselves.

1325   Zelda's idea: the bad things are the same in everyone; only the good are different

1326   It is necessary to emphasize the individual differences between men. If you are high enough in the air you can't even see the leader of the parade, sometimes you can't even see the way it's going—and it's necessary to know. Al Capone

1327   Women took over political-religious thought, with their lack of education, their almost universal lack of knowledge of things as they are, and turned this delegated prerogative inward, cultivating all tendencies in children as individualism. This can best be looked at in the case of a conscious mother and a conscious son such as your mother and you, where the dead or senile grandfather was still the head of the family.

1328   Does anyone think an angel of God appeared to George Washington and suddenly informed him that if he gave up all the allegiances that he had in Virginia, and the entire caste to which he had been born, that he would become a model hero of all the school children of 1933?

1329   The very elements of disintegration seemed to him romantic—the vague unrest that went on back of the big tranquil lawn, the incessant small bickering that seemed to prove that in their magnificence they had no need of solidarity. Actually it meant that the old Millers having nothing to teach had taught their children no common good, having traded their Bavarian field-wisdom for a sort of wisdom that was current in the middle west twenty to forty years ago which was of no value at all. Evolved under one set of conditions, the settlement and development of the west, it seemed as academic to children growing up in a static city as the morals of the amurai.

1330   He was in the safety zone. In a man this is the period between twenty-four and twenty-eight, and however precarious for a man to rely upon and belied by marriage statistics, such a safety zone is a reality. At that age a good man will not mistake the wide-eyed attention of eighteen for the wisdom of thirty, nor forgive thirty for lacking the freshness of eighteen. Let it even be insisted upon—a bachelor of twenty-six in his right mind is not a serious prospect.

1331   Women's continual reacting reacting reacting, almost to a point of self immolation, to forces that they haven't caused and can't do anything about.

1332   On such occasions as this, thought Scott as his eyes still sought casually for Yanci, occured the matings of the leftovers, the plainer, the culler, the poorer of the social world; matings actuated by the same urge toward perhaps a more glamorous destiny, yet for all that, less beautiful and less young. Scott himself was feeling very old.

1333   Learning of a word or place, etc. and then seeming to run across that word or place in your reading

constantly in the next few weeks.
Use as metaphor: "as when one" etc.

1334   You can stroke people with words

1335   Symington's white gloves initiated by school

1336   Advantages of children whose mother is dead

1337   Weaknesses of medium point of view
        (1) not attractive (2) always borne along in practise in
        the trial of extreme points of view, etc.

1338   A man being only the sum of his initials

1339   There are certain ribald stories that I heard at ten years
old and never again, for I heard a new and more
sophisticated set at eleven. Many years later I heard a
ten year boy telling another one of those old stories
and it occured to me that it had been handed on from
one ten-year old generation to the next for an
incalculable number of centuries. So with the set I
learned at eleven. Each set of stories, like a secret ritual
stays always within its age-class, never growing older
because there is always a new throng of ten-year olds to
learn them, and never growing stale because these same
boys will forget them at eleven. One can almost believe
that there is a conscious theory behind this unofficial
education.

1340   The easiest way to get a reputation is to go outside the
fold, shout around for a few years as a violent atheist or
a dangerous radical, and then crawl back to shelter.
The fatted calf is killed for Spargo, Papini, Chesterton,
and Henry Arthur Jones. There is a bigger temporary
premium put on losing your nerve in this regard than
in any other.

1341   When men agree on a subject of controversy, they love
to tell or listen to personal stories that seem to
strengthen their side of the question. They laugh
delightedly and enjoy a warm feeling that the case is
won.

1342   His mind full of the odd ends of all he had read, dim tracings of thoughts whose genesis was already far away when (their dim carbons) reached his ears.

1343   The reason morons can stand good entertainment is that they don't like to understand all the time. Like a nurse or child at a sophisticated lunch table. Something they could follow all through is a stirring nervous experience for them. Through a good picture they can drowse—as morons always drowse mentally through great events.

1344   Fifty years ago we Americans substituted melodrama for tragedy, violence for dignity under suffering. That became a quality that only women were supposed to exhibit in life or fiction—so much so that there are few novels or biographies in which the American male tangled in an irreconcilable series of contradictions is considered as anything but an unresourceful and cowardly weakwad.

1345   Nora's wit. Pleasure—Elsa. Happiness—Nora.

1346   All the sucks on the Astor and Whitney fortunes.

1347   Time marches on—ruthlessly—until the Russians tried to replace their artists and scientists—then time stood still and only the pendulum functioned.

1348   Rockefeller Center:
    That it all came out of the chicaneries of a dead racketeer.

1349   I can watch a cigarette burn, like Esquire's streamlines. Charley Petty's lines are all from a cigarette, even the hair where the smoke breaks.

1350   Never noticed Mother's eyes after living with her 20 years. Mrs. O. says they are like mine. Example of observation when I don't like to look at her.

1351   Like all "final"people—judges, doctors, great artists, etc.

1352   You began by pretending to be kind (politeness). It pays so well that it becomes second nature. Some people like Jews can't get past the artificiality of the first step.

1353   That Zelda's illness has wrecked our lives is no more important than the fact that it has cast a dark shadow over Mrs. Sayre's mature years.

1354   When people get mixed up, they try to throw out a sort of obscuring mist, and then the sharp shock of a fact—a collision! seems to be the only thing to make them sober-minded again.

1355   The luxuriance of your emotions under the strict discipline, which you habitually impose on them, makes that tensity in you that is the secret of all charm—when you let that balance become disturbed, don't you become just another victim of self-indulgence?—breaking down the solid things around you and, moreover making yourself terribly vulnerable.

1356   But scratch a Yale man with both hands and you'll be lucky to find a coast-guard. Usually you find nothing at all. Or else eleven bought iron men and 3000 ninnies. God preserve you from *that* vaccuum foundry!

1357   There is this to be said for the Happy Ending: that the healthy man goes from love to love.

1358   Reversion to childhood typical of the only child.

1359   Nine girls out of ten can stand good looks without going to pieces though only one boy out of ten ever comes out from under them.

1360   American farmer as a fighter comes of desperate stock as well as adventurous.

1361   Remember that women are ostriches about themselves; and that all men—and by this I mean *every* man, will tell everything, and usually more, within three months from date. Remember the daughter of Col. who owned the Charles St. Apt. I heard her story long before she'd left Baltimore.

1362   I left my capacity for hoping on the little roads that led to Zelda's sanitarium.

1363   There's quite a case for self-pity—save for that, I'd long ago have died of pitying you.

1364   But I am always guilty of an irreverent snort when I think of Cardinal Parker's "Hymn to Old Money Bags". What the rest of the Service must have been like in his nimble ecclesiastical hands would require a more hilarious pen than mine.

1365   You could tell a St. Mark's boy by his table manners. You see they ate with the servants while their parents divorced and remarried.

1366   Some men have a necessity to be mean as if they were exercising a faculty which they had to partially neglect since early childhood.

1367   In the beginning we are the split and splintered pieces of the basket in which we are all contained. At the end the basket, turned upside down has become a haystack in which we search for our own smooth identity—as if it had ever existed.

1368   Remember this—if you shut your mouth you have your choice.

1369   The flapper never really disappeared in the twenties— she merely dropped her name, put on rubber heels and worked in the dark.

1370   The tackles good or bad are a necessary fact in life. The Tiger Inn Type little nervous system, Dickinson, McGraw, etc. Their recognition of each other.

1371   I understand Duke has a beautiful shell—the tobacco workers who were sweated for it at sixty cents a day can see it in the rotogravures—I notice that the Atlantic

Monthly voted it 127th among American colleges in Faculty and Courses. They play professional football with hired truck-drivers and win great victories.

1372   About finding I am not a rational type, finding it in Hollywood, I mean, in script writing. How every director *must* be, for instance.

1373   Justification of happy ending. My father and Oscar Wilde born in the same year. One ruined at 40—one "happy" at 70. So Becky and Amelia are in fact *true*.

1374   A precociously tough boy makes jokes like old man. Like say (referring to 20 years ago) "So you laughed at me, eh?" Utterly safe kidding of people who don't want to hurt or be hurt.

1375   I believe what Zelda believed about her family until the wheels of her bicycle began to run backward.

1376   Beginnings of a bad education—when from Myers Ancient History and concentrated attention on Roman Columns I assumed that was standard and solid and indicative of mind and taste—and therefore was puzzled years later when Western bank architecture was deserted for more modern forms.

1377   I looked back at old pictures and thought of what you told me at Palm Beach and how it opened a window. There was an elaborate self-consciousness about our seduction which told of deep intuition that you were playing a role, though any one track mind didn't choose to notice it, and I should have guessed that it wasn't Paul Lagrand or anyone casual from your first story THE MAGNOLIA TREE—guessed there had been old emotional experience for you had learned to feel before I did.

1378   I didn't have the two top things—great animal magnetism or money. I had the two second things, tho', good looks and intelligence. So I always got the top girl.

1379   I wonder if it has been remarked by historians that the "final" victor for the Germany hegemony was a Hapsburg and not a Hohenzollern leader, Hitler the Austrian not Hindenburg the Prussian.

1380   In 1908 our Pacific and Carribbean adventures were as romantic as the G-Men exploits of today.

Proper Names

1381   A grand duke—"Jimber-jawed Serge."
       Name: Umphadel Piluski
       Gangster Salve Spitale—Saliva Spit.
       Gooshoofenstein Von Beasinghausen
       Meglomania McCarthy
       English clubman named Cumbersom   ★
       Names Lee Spurgeon, Stoner, Mortimer, Flieshhacker,   ★
       Henry P. Jacques. Borre.
       Bryon Appledeck
       Name for movie house "What's at the Dementia?"
       Mr. Schlchgd from *Notre Dame* in novel.   ★
       Beauty boy Johnston
       Name Howya Bartlett
       Joe Crusoe
       Hummer for name
       The Marquise de la Close d'Hirondelle
       Tookey Ledoux
       Harry Fantum
       George Gratteciel   ★
       Marylyn Miller Swann, Sherlock Holmes Swann
       Futility Trust Company
       Name of "La Paix" changed to "Thropaca"
       Grandfather called Mo'papa

1382   Names: Queer Justice. Pennsylvania Colman. . .
       Helen's name—Novida Veronica Helen Conway
       Prince Khnumba-ef
       Nuts Vandernut
       Darky Dolittle

1383   . . . .was named for the once celebrated star of the Pink
Lady, perpetuated her in dark mountainous flesh.

1384   Jim Bob

1385   Psychiatric sequence of nicknames;

>   Annabelle
>   Belly-Anne
>   Sap—Lawrenceville names. Owen J.
>   Goopher
>   Dudo
>   Doo
>   Babo
>   Pie
>   Nanny
>   Liza   Andrew's Dusa
>   Missy Owens.

1386   Name Luna Gineva.

1387   *BACKWOOD NAMES.*
Olsie, Hassie, Coba, Bleba, Onza, (Ozma—my own),
Retha, Otella, Tatrina, Delphia, Wedda, Zannis,
Avaline, Burtryce, Chalme, Glenola, Turla, Verlie,
Legitta, Navilla, Oha, Verla, Blooma, Inabeth, Versia,
Gomeria, Valaria, Berdine, Olabeth, Adelloyd.

1388   *NIGGERS*
Glee, Earvial, Aeiral, Roayna, Margerilla, Parolee,
Ferdiliga, Abolena, Iodine, Tooa, Negolna.

1389   *NAME:* Tycoonskins

Rough Stuff

1390   My mind is the loose cunt of a whore, to fit all genitals.

1391   His bowels, heavy with the night's catch groaned out
       new scenes.

1392   A man giving up the idea of himself as a hero. Perhaps
       picking his nose in a can.

1393   You can't take the son of a plough manufacturer, clip
       off his testicles and make an artist of him.

1394   "Did you ever see squirrels yincing?" he asked her
       suddenly.

1395   Scenario hacks having removed all life from a story   ★
       substituting the stink of life—a fart, a loose joke, a
       dirty jeer. How they do it.

1396   *Apology to Ogden Nash:*
            Every California girl has lost at least one ovary
            And none of them has read Madame Bovary.

Scenes and Situations

1397   "Did you ever read the books of Phillips Oppenheim?"

"I think I've read one."

"He's one of my favorite American writers," Tommy said simply. "He writes about the Riviera, you know. I don't know whether the things he writes about are true but this place is like that."

Standing before the gate they were suddenly bathed in a small floodlight, quick as a flashlight, that left them blinded for a moment. Then a voice from behind the gate.

"Who's this, please?"

"Tell Monsieur Irv that it's Monsieur Tommy. Tell him we can't come in the house, but can he come out in the garden a minute."

A section of the gate rumbled open like a safe and they were in a park, following a young Italo-American dandy toward a lighted house. They waited just out of range of the porch light, and presently the door opened and a dark thin man of forty came out and gazed blindly.

"Where you, Tommy?"

"Down here. Don't come. I have a lady with me who wants to remain anonymous."

"How?"

"I've got a lady with me who doesn't want to be seen—like you."

"Oh, I unestand, I unestand."

"We want to swim. Anybody on the beach?"

"Nobody, nobody. Go ahead, Tommy. You want suits, towels?"

"All right, some towels. Nodoby's going to come down, are they?"

"No, no, nobody. Say, did you see Du Pont de Nemours went up—"

"No stock market in the presence of ladies."

"All right, excuse me, lady. You wait now—Salve will take you down—don't want you to get in trouble."

As irv re-entered the house Tommy said, "Probably he's phoning the machine gunner to pass us. He was a fellow townsman of yours in Chicago—now he has the best beach on the Riviera."

Curiously Nicole followed down an intricate path, then through a sliding steel door that operated like a guillotine, out into a roofless cavern of white moonlight, formed by pale boulders about a cup of phosphorescent waters. It faced Monaco and the blur of Mentone beyond. She likes his taste in bringing her here—from the high-handed storming of Mr. Irv's fortress,

Then, starting back the lane by which they had come Tommy tripped over a wire and a faint buzzer sounded far away.

"My God!" he excalimed, "that a man should have to live like this!"

"Is he afraid of burglars?"

"He's afraid of your lovely city and came here with a bodyguard of a dozen monkeys—is that the right slang? Maybe Al Capone is after him. Anyhow he has one period between being drunk and being sober when he is very nice."

He broke off as again they were momentarily bathed in the ubiquitous spotlight. Then amber lamps glowed on the porch of the castellated villa and Mr. Irv, this time supported by the very neat young man, came out unsteadily.

"I kept them off the beach, Tommy," he announced.

"Thank you, very much."

"Won't you both change your minds and come in? In *greatest* confidence. I have some other ladies here." He raised his voice as if to address Nicole. "As you are a lady of background you will like 'em."

"It's four o'clock," said Tommy. "We have to get to our background. Good night."

Irv's voice followed them.

"You never make a mistake having to do with a lady."

1398   The soft swaying gowns that for a moment seemed to be the gowns of people that had waited for Jeb Stuart and the gallant Pelham to ride in out of the night; all the people there seemed to have for a moment that real quality which women have when they know that men are going toward death, and maybe will get there, and maybe not.

1399   Sir Francis Elliot, King George, the barley water and champagne.

1400   The big toy banks with candles inside that were really the great fashionable hotels, the lighted clock in the old town, the blurred glow of the Cafe de Paris, the pricked-out points of villa windows rising on slow hills toward the dark sky.

"What is everyone doing there?" she whispered. "It looks as though something gorgeous was going on, but what it is I can't quite tell."

"Everyone there is making love," said Val quietly.

1401   Blind man's buff and fiancee with no chin.

1402   Then he took a long breath and held it in him for an unnaturally long time. Then, quick and graceful, he died.

1403   Colored woman and dead Jewish baby.

1404   "Nothing to hang on to. No bridle—nothing. I'd like   ★
to be able to carry a swagger stick; fans break when you
get too nervous."

1405   The orchestra was playing a Wiener Waltzer, and
suddenly she had the sensation that the chords were
extending themselves that each bar of three-four time
was bending in the middle, dropping a little and thus
drawing itself out, until the waltz itself, like a
phonograph running down, became a torture.

1406   She feared the black cone hanging from the metal arm,   ★
shrilling and shrilling across the sunny room. It
stopped for a minute, replaced by her heartbeats; then
began again.

1407   She stood there in the middle of an enormous quiet.   ★
The pursuing feet that had thundered in her dream had
stopped. There was a steady, singing silence.

1408   Scottie presenting the garbage can and her proprietary
interest.

1409   The day in Annecy village the first time when Zelda
went shopping by herself and I watched from the hotel
johnny.

1410   Diabolic death scene: "Give 'em the cigar." (a high
explosive greased time bomb shoved up the rectum that
couldn't be extracted).

1411   Bunny Burgess episode of glass and wife.

1412   The realization came to her that the tracks of life would   ★
never lead anywhere and were like tracks of the

airplane; that of their plan no one knew it; if they were tracked with no particular Daniel Boone to hack trees; that the world had to go on and that it wasn't going to be inside her, there still had to be these tracks. It was an awful lonesome journey.

1413   Perhaps that slate we looked at once that was all the grey blue we'd ever know in life—where the dark brown tide receded, the slate came. It was indescribable as the dress beside him (the color of hours of a long human day)—blue like misery, blue for the shy-away from happiness, "If I could that shade everything would be all right forever. . ." Touch it? Touch.

1414   The opera singer and the pekinese in the taxi, "I did that."

1415   *For me an unhappy day on the Riviera. 1926*
The bouillabaisse.
The Baby gar.
(Marice—the 1st Peter Arno cartoons about Hic and Whoops.)
Who would save the weakest swimmer.
(The quarrel.)
Isolation of two in end of boat.
Gerald and Walker at Ville Franche
Archie and the oar on my eyebrow.
The swim au natural, but not.

1416   Lefty's psychiatry story: the bars, the barbers, the home, the pool balls, the hair combing, the slugs of vanilla and grain, etc. The printer and Lefty's being willing to sharpen the axe. The fake escape and coaxing.

1417   The man addressed took the jug slung from the leader's belt. But the concussion that Philippe had suffered was clearing. To his horse he whispered in one of those half-heard sentences that can be said only to very young children and to animals—"Don't fail me now. I'm going to lean against your neck and if you move a foot I fall. I'll do as much for you sometime."

The horse stabilized himself and, propped against him Philippe, who drew a breath, could even see; and with a second deep breath he could see as far as the horse's haunch. Then he could see as far as the nose of the Duke's horse; then the ribs of the Duke's horse were interrupted by something that presently became the Duke's stirrup. His eyes, clinging to it, found their way upward as if they were climbing a rope—found their way to other eyes, as hard and brown as his own.

1418   Didn't evenings sometimes end on a high note and not fade out vaguely in bars? After ten o'clock every night she felt she was the only real being in a colony of ghosts, that she was surrounded by utterly intangivle figures who retreated whenever she stretched out her hand.

1419   When he gets sober for six months and can't stand any   ★
of the people he's liked when drunk.

1420   The two young men could only groan and play   ★
sentimental music on the phonograph, but presently they departed; the fire leaped up, day went out behind the windows, and Forrest had rum in his tea.

1421   Josephine Baker's chocolate arabesques. Chorus from her show.

1422   In front of the shops in the Rue de Castiglione, proprietors and patrons were on the sidewalk gazing upward, for the Graf Zeppelin, shining and glorious, symbol of escape and destruction—of escape, if necessary, through destruction—glided in the Paris sky. He heard a woman say in French that it would not her

astonish if that commenced to let fall the bombs.
(Not funny now—1939)

1423   Why didn't they back away? Why didn't they back right
up, walking backward down the Rue de Castiglione,
across the Rue de Rivole, through the Tuileries
Gardens, still walking backward as fast as they could
till they grew vague and faded out across the river?

1424   Almost at once Josephine realized that everybody there
except herself was crazy. She knew it incontrovertibly,
although the only person of outward eccentricity was a
robust woman in a frock coat and gray morning
trousers. Their frightened eyes lifted to the young girl's
elegent clothes, her confident, beautiful face, and they
turned from her rudely in self-protection.

1425   "Well, what do you want do do?"
        "Kiss you."
        A spasm of timidity quickly controlled went over her
face.
        "I'm all dirty."
        "Don't you kiss people when you're all dirty?"
        "I don't kiss people. I'm just before that generation.
We'll find you a nice young girl you can kiss."
        "There aren't any nice young girls—you're the only
one I like."
        "I'm not nice. I'm a hard woman."

1426   The woman who snatched her children away on the
boat just to be exclusive—exclusive from what.

1427   "Tell that Spic to go count his piasters and I'll talk
turkey with you."
        She bestowed upon the puzzled darkling a healing
smile.
        "You won't mind, honey, if I sit this out? See you
later."
        When he had departed Tommy protested, " 'Honey!'
Do you call him 'Honey?' Why don't you call him
'greasy?' "

She laughed sweetly.

"Where you been?"

"Skiing. But every time I go away, that doesn't mean you can go dance with a whole lot of gigolo numbers from Cairo. Why does he hold his hand parallel to the floor when he dances? Does he think he's stilling the waves? Does he think the floor's going to swing up and crack him?"

"He's a Greek, honey."

1428   A small car, red in color and slung at that proximity to the ground which indicated both speed of motion and speed of life. It was a Blatz Wildcat. Occupying it, in the posture of aloof exhaustion exacted by the sloping seat, was a blond, gay, baby-faced girl.

1429   They floated off, immediately entering upon a long echoing darkness. Somewhere far ahead a group in another boat were singing, their voices now remote and romantic, now nearer and yet more mysterious, as the canal doubled back and the boats passed close to each other with an invisible veil between. The continual bump-bump of the boat against the wooden sides. They slid into a red glow—a stage set of hell, with grinning demons and lurid paper fires—then again into the darkness, with the gently lapping water and the passing of the singing boat now near, now far away.

1430   He paused speculatively to vault the high hydrant in front of the Van Schellinger house, wondering if one did such things in long trousers and if he would ever do it again.

1431   "Do away with yourself," he demanded, startled, "You? Why on earth—"

"Oh, I've almost done it twice. I get the horrors—usually when something goes wrong with my art. Once they said I fell in the bathtub when I only jumped in, and another time somebody closed a window before I could get to it."

"You ought to be careful."

"I am careful. I keep a lady with me always—but she couldn't come East because she was going to be married."

1432   Laughed with a sudden memory of Hopkins where going to a party he had once tried taking gin by rectum, and the great success it had been until the agony of passing great masses of burned intestine.

1433   Sending orchestra second rate champagne—never, *never* do it again.   ★

1434   Gerald walking Paris.

1435   Once in his room and reassured by the British stability of them, the ingenuity of the poor asserted itself. He began literally to wind himself up in his clothes. He undressed, put on two suits of underwear and over that four shirts and two suits of clothes, together with two white pique vests. Every pocket he stuffed with ties, socks, studs, gold-backed brushes and a few toilet articles. Panting audibly, he struggled into an overcoat. His derby looked empty, so he filled it with collars and held them in place with some handkerchiefs. Then, rocking a little on his feet, he regarded himself in the mirror

He might possibly manage it—if only a steady stream of perspiration had not started to flow from somewhere up high in the edifice and kept pouring streams of various temperatures down his body, until they were absorbed by the heavy blotting paper of three pairs of socks that crowded his shoes.

Moving cautiously, like Tweedle-dum before the battle, he traversed the hall and rang for the elevator. The boy looked at him curiously, but made no comment, though another passenger made a dry reference to Admiral Byrd. Through the lobby he moved, a gigantic figure of a man. Perhaps the clerks at the desk had a subconscious sense of something being wrong, but he was gone too quickly for them to do anything about it.

"Taxi, sir?" the doorman inquired, solicitous at Val's pale face.

Unable to answer, Val tried to shake his head, but this also proving impossible, he emitted a low negative groan. The sun was attracted to his bulk as lightning is attracted to metal, as he staggered out toward a bus. Up on top, he thought; it would be cooler up on top.

His training as a hall-room boy stood him in good stead now; he fought his way up the winding stair as if it had been the social ladder. Then, drenched and suffocating, he sank down upon a bench, the bourgeois blood of many Mr. Joneses pumping strong in his heart. Not for Val to sit upon a trunk and kick his heels and wait for the end; there was fight in him yet.

1436   Hannan married into a family of boarding house ★ aristocrats in Charleston and they didn't like him. But outside of Charleston their prestige depended on him so that they took it out in mild abuse. There was a coast guard officer in the family that was always going to jump down his throat with a loaded revolver. When his wife broke down the father used to go to the hospital and after getting his prestige with the doctors from poor Hannan's shows he'd tear into him. Hannan ducking around Europe at the time sleeping with chambermaids and raising hell on the quiet generally. Jesus Christ, he used to say, they climb up on your shoulders and then pull your nose.

1437   Ernest taking me to that bum restaurant. Change of station implied.

1438   Doll from window.

1439   A lot of young girls together is a romantic secret thing like the first sight of wild ducks at dawn (enlarge— Hotel Don Cesare at pink dawn—the gulf.)

1440   Kiddies' Children Hour—Kiddies, I'd be the last one to ask you to begin smoking before say, six, but remember we are in the depths of a depression—depth of a gepression from four to six through the courtesy of Amer. Cig. Co.—and you represent a potential market of forty million smokers.

1441   Moving picture scene where he infuriates people on beach trying to take picture after they've persuaded him to do it.

1442   The city had been merely an unfamiliar rhythm persisting outside the windows of an American Express Hotel, with days composed of such casual punctuation marks as going for the mail or taking auto rides that did not go back and forth but always in a circle.

1443   The rejection slips

1444   Soviet meeting
Looking at apartment—wife drops in from next room

1445   Mr. Slade and my father

1446   Dogs appraising buildings

1447   runs into again and again without ever being able to   ★
remember his name.

1448   A taxi tipping over on a nervous night.   ★

1449   Throwing away jewelry, burning clothes.

1450   Hypochronia—man thinks of thing at last moment—ostensibly an extra thing—yet that settles an affair that otherwise would have wrecked the whole thing.

1451   Jack Straw carried off screaming "I didn't want to sing the damn thing anyhow." (amateur theatricals)

1452   Dog ate up Buttercup's sausages (amateur theatricals)

1453   Beanpole as Buttercup (amateur theatricals)

1454   The pathos of "Now I am Complete."

1455   Unable to raise hands to fight.

1456   The stout man registered from Warsaw bent over a copy of the "Zuricher Nachrichten;" the big young American with the long pompadour and the flashing eyes spied him from the elevator and after a moment of thought, during which his eyes became almost imperceptible, came boldly over to the periodical table. He pawed through the magazines as if looking for something and meanwhile kept muttering aloud but as if to himself.

"Mr. Goldgarten from Warsaw. Huh! Maybe." He spoke the name reproachfully and insultingly but the stout man, though he was scarcely five feet away and couldn't have helped hearing, bent over his magazine as phlegmatically as a house detective. For a moment Frank Forrester was stumped and then driven on by the resourceful character which had probably accrued to his name "Frank Forrester in a Velicopter," "Frank Forrester in a Chinese Junk" during the eighteen years of his life, took a more determined step. Staring at a copy of the *Tatler* he said in a loud clear voice:

"We're getting a little tired of spies and we think we've seen that face before."

Still not a word from Mr. Goldgarten, commercial traveller from Warsaw. For a moment Frank Forrester— "Frank Forrester on the Matterhorn," Frank Forrester with Byrd at the South Pole,"—contemplated a further and even bolder step but at this point his cousin Emily, accompanied by that fellow McLane, came in the hotel door. Frank went over to them.

1457   She told him a wonderful plot she had for a "scenario," ★ and then repeated to him the outline of *The Miracle Man*. He gave her the address of Joe Gibney in Hollywood as someone who might be interested. Joe was the studio bootlegger. Perhaps she suspected his evasion for now she cast him an angry glance and whispered to her companions. She would go to his next six pictures to see if he had stolen her idea.

1458   Reformation of Hutchins

1459   The Jew in the Meadowbrook Club

1460   Grande Poisson scene.

1461 In the corner a huge American negro with his arms around a lovely French tart, roared a song to her in a rich beautiful voive and suddenly Melarky's Tennessee instincts were remembered and aroused.

1462 Phone ringing at Emily's.

1463 Memory of taking a a pee commencement night

1464 The heart Burst

1465 They had passed the time in making a collection of sticks and stones that "would do for things." They had found a stick somewhat like a comb and another one somewhat like a toothbrush. They had two stones that would make a nice book rack if they had only had books, and a stone that would dplendidly as an ash tray, when they had some ashes. They had also created a china closet by laying out fifty odd sections of cocoanuts in even rows.

 Donald regarded the exhibit impatiently and took out his notebook.

 "We've got to get some system. We'll make a list of things in the order of their importance. Now the first thing is—"

 "A good inexpensive brush and comb," suggested Vivian.

 "If I could have a doll," said Kitty, hopefully.

1466 The missing raft hurried desolately before a light wind with its sail tied, until the rotten canvas suddenly split and shred away. When night came it went off on its own again, speeding along the dark tide as if driven by a ghostly propeller.

1467 Scene equivalent to my last afternoon with Gerald, for benefit of two women. Portentousness.

1468 Man fascinated by girl finds she's showing off for   ★
someone else.

1469 Chauffer trying vainly to photo and preserve that group, his triumph

1470   Then Frances Daniels—Anna Biggs lack of taste on my part in referring to dead child.

1471   How I scared away a customer from the Hotel de la Paix

1472   Use about playing old tunes only at dance

1473   *Bootlegger and pas de bure*   ★

1474   Scene at dinner when Frenchman, pretending to criticize American life in general is really critisizing Francis, who repeats experiences of race.

1475   The problem as to whether it was a duty or a favor when she helped the English nurse down the steps with the perambulator. The English nurse always said "Please," and "Thanks very much," but Dolores hated her and would have liked without any special excitement to beat her insensible. Like most Latins under the stiumlus of American life, she had irresistible impulses toward violence.

1476   suddenly contemplated having a love affair with him. She looked at herself several times in the pantry mirror and stood close to him as she poured his coffee, but he read the paper and she saw that that was all for the morning.

1477   Jules had dark circles under his eyes. Yesterday he had closed out the greatest problem of his life by settling with his ex-wife for two hundred thousand dollars. He had married too young and the former slavey from the Quebec slums had taken to drugs upon her failure to rise with him. Yesterday, in the presence of lawyers, her final gesture had been to smash his finger with the base of a telephone.

1478   It was a cold winter for Tarleton, Georgia—the coldest in four hundred years. Old Black Great-Uncle Salambo said so and, as he was the only man left alive who had resided in Tarleton in 1524, no one around Tilly's garage ventured to dispute him.

"Reckon I'll take my body-servant and run down to Palm Beach for the season. You got any golf sticks?" he remarked after a minute, "an' couple old golf balls?"

Mrs. Tilly laughed.

"Dan Webster," he called to his helper, "Jim Powell here wants to practice up on golf. Get him a monkey-wrench and a couple of ball bearings."

"Got to buy me a parasol," continued Jim; "You know where I can get me a nice big red and white parasol—so's I can stick it up in the sand?"

1479   There was a Malay junk with a crew of four men praying for death, that had been blown off the Caroline Islands a week before; it revenged their wretched fate by drifting across the Aeolia's bow on the night of the first of June. The junk went down in half a minute, the Aeolia, listing slowly to starboard, took well over two hours.

1480   Before her eyes would pass in turn a prodigious,   ★ prodigal Latin American, or a lady whose title blazed with history or that almost mythological figure, an international banker, or *even a great Hollywood star with her hat pulled down over her face lest it be apparent that no one recognized her*—all these being great figures to her—and Dick would say something kind, really kind, about them and they would recede out of the far vista as a stark naked Argentine, a stuffed chemise of the society column, Dinah's uncle, or an actress pleased to see Seth—when we really possessed him, when he preferred us.

1481   That scene from Bridal Party where Powell accuses man of being unhappy with girl.

1482   *English Scene* (Bijou)
         Brazilian's departure
         Prado
         Phonograph
         Dog
         Money

1483   "I'm pretty tired," he said—unfortunately, because this gave her an advantage: she wasn't tired; while his mind and body moved in a tedious half time like a slow moving picture, her nerves were crowded with feverish traffic. She tried to think of some mischief.

1484   Percy Pyne in the limousine at Meadowbrook, getting as small as the man he was arguing with

1485   Scene toward end of *demenagement* distressing amount of good, five phonographs, eight pairs of dark glasses, wasteful reduplication, etc.

1486   During the ride the young man held his attention cooly away from his mother, unwilling to follow her eyes in any direction or even to notice his surroundings except when at a revealing turn the sky and sea dropped before them, he said, "It's hot as hell," in a decided voice.

1487   She sat down on the water closet with a coquettish smile. Her eyes, glazed a few minutes since, were full of impish malice.

1488   "I did say that, but I explained to you that waiting is just part of the picture business. Everybody's so much overpaid that when something finally happens you realize that you were making money all the time. The reason it's slow is because one man's keeping it all in his head, and fighting the weather and the actors and accidents—"   ★

    Francis looked at her, without anger now, but also without pity. She had long lost all power of moving him, yet he responded automatically to old stimuli and now he put his arm around her shoulders.

1489   "I would like to enjoy," said the man, "but I can only hope and remember. What the hell—leave me my reactions even though they're faint beside yours. Let me see things my own way."

    "You mean you don't want me to talk?"

    "I mean we come up here and before I can register, before I can realise that this *is* the Atlantic Ocean, you've analyzed it like a chemist, like a chemist who painted, or a painter who studied chemistry, and it's all diminished and I say 'Yes it does remind me of a delicatessen shop—' "

"Let you alone—"

1490   He lived his life then, as an honored man. But from time to time he would indulge his habit of eating mountain grass in preference to valley grass, a habit formed during those early days outside the herd.

"Oke!" said the herd.

Some of them would watch his curious munching and shake their heads. Some of them, though, grouped together and said: "If we eat that grass that will make us honored like him."

They tried it and it had the negative result of such follies.

1491   "Why, she's your wife—I can't imagine touching your ★ wife." Having heard this said to a husband ten minutes before the most passionate attempts to maneuver the wife into bed.

1492   He ran a low fever that evening and the mosquito netting bound him down into a little stifling space. But the morning was fresh and fair and he remembered that with a little vigilance there is seldom the necessity of being alone with oneself.

1493   He got up suddenly, stumbling through the shrubbery, and followed an almost obliterated path to the house, starting at the whirring sound of a blackbird which rose out of the grass close by. The front porch sagged dangerously at his step as he pushed open the door. There was no sound inside, except the steady slow throb of silence;

1494   *Trip to Virginia*

Tuesday—Off for Buffalo. The plan. Aquilla. Harper's Ferry. The Haynie family. The tourist place any my room. Curtains and drapes. John Haynie.

                    Night at Harrisonburg Hotel (?)

Wednesday—Calling home from Staunton. Rest in
                    Charlottesville. Locating Lee. The
                    garden that night. The campus in
                    afternoon. The President. Impressions
                    of University. Getting liquor. Cashing
                    check. Over the gap in Blue Ridge this
                    this day. The blow-out. The view. The
                    nickel machine.

Thursday— The reporter. Lunch with Lawrence
                    Lee. Phoning him. Another check. The
                    gallant Pelham. My remarks on dif-
                    ference between real and fake writing. J.
                    E. Thomason and old men.

                    Dinner in Warrenton.
                    Calling Mrs. R. Night in Alexandria.
                    The tough people. ?ame

Friday—   The Communist. Arrival home.

1495   The Court reporter scene in garden.

1496   "Let's not talk about such things now. I'll tell you
          something funny instead." Her look was not one of
          eager anticipation but he continued, "By merely
          looking around you can review the largest battalion of
          the Boys I've seen collected in one place. This hotel
          seems to be a clearing house for them—" He returned
          the nod of a pale and shaky Georgian who sat down at
          a table across the room, "That young man looks
          somewhat retired from life. The little devil I came
          down to see is hopeless. You'd like him—if he comes in
          I'll introduce him."
               As he was speaking the flow into the bar began.
          Nicole's fatigue accepted Dick's ill-advised words and
          mingled with the fantastic Koran that presently
          appeared. She saw the males gathered down at the bar,
          the tall gangling ones, the little pert ones with round
          thin shoulders, the broad ones with the faces of Nero

and Oscar Wilde, or of senators—faces that dissolved suddenly into girlish fatuity, or twisted into leers—the nervous ones who hitched and twitched, jerking open their eyes very wide, and laughed hysterically, the handsome, passive and dumb men who turned their profiles this way and that, the pimply stodgy men with delicate gestures; or the raw ones with very red lips and frail curly bodies, their shrill voluble tones piping their favorite word "treacherous" above the hot volume of talk; the ones over-self-conscious who glared with eager politeness toward every noise; among them were English types with great racial self-control.

Balkan types, one small cooing Siamese. "I think now," Nicole said, "I think I'm going to bed."

"I think so too."

—Goodby, you unfortunates. Goodby, Hotel of Three Worlds.

1497   She began building up a legend. She was a "gun moll" and the whole trip had been a frame to get Mr. Ives into the hands of the mob.

1498   Owning a little of New York by 1815 patent

1499   In a moving automobile sat a southern gentleman accompanied by his body-servant. He was on his way, after a fashion, to New York but he was somewhat hampered by the fact that the upper and lower portions of his automobile were no longer in exact juxtaposition. In fact from time to time the two riders would dismount, shove the body on to the chassis, corner to corner, and then continue onward, vibrating slightly in involuntary unison with the motor.

1500   Only a few apathetic stags gathered one by one in the doorways, and to a close observer it was apparent that the scene did not attain the gayety which was its aspiration. These girls and men had known each other from childhood; and though there were marriages incipient upon the floor tonight, they were marriages of enviornment, of resignation, or even of boredom.

1501   Old woman and lost Atlantis

1502   For drunkard chapter—Variation in rules of courtesy, because people have changed. Bottle not sent out. Can't call. Gerald and I—the Montgomery boy and I. The man dancing with Scottie.

1503   The "Ickle durl" bored him. She admired him; she was used to clasping her hands together in his wake and heaving audible sighs. When the music stopped he gave her an outrageous compliment to atone for his preoccupation and left her at her table.

1504   As he dressed for dinner he realized that he wanted them both. It was an outrage that he couldn't have them both. Wouldn't a girl rather have half of him than all of Harry Whitby, or a whole Spic with a jar of pomade thrown in? Life was so badly arranged—better no women at all than only one woman.

1505   He took them each in one arm, like a man in a musical comedy, and kissed the rouge on their cheeks

1506   The Champ d'asile in Texas 1816 (for Napoleonic veterans)

1507   Zelda and the taxi man's teeth + Dr Davenport

1508   Vidor at the Luxumberg

1509   Two men stalking each other with deer rifles through Bois de Bologne

1510   Almost a whole chapter on the man's attempt to educate his children without knowing where he stands himself—amid difficulties.

1511   Horses behind at Pthodomy Club

1512   Boy carried off Titanic by his mother.

1513   A chapter in which their kid comes to him for homosexuality and a consequent long consideration of homosexuality from some such attitude as a Groton father thinking it's maybe all right for social reasons Use Groton material from Chateau D'Oex

1514   Coat off in theatre

1515   Tremendous American generosity, without comment

1516   In the shadow of the Pope's palace at Avignon our ★ Greek guide, an exile from the butcheries in Smyrna, told us with wild enthusiasm of his cousin, a restaurateur and an Elk of Terre Haute, Indiana.

"He wears a high hat and a blue coat with epaulettes and blue braid and green trousers and carries a gold sword in his hand and marches down the main street once a year behind a big band and—"

1517   "Don't you think that at 104 a man ought to make his will?"

A burst of laughter.

"A hundred and three," they corrected.

"Well almost a hundred and four. Don't you think that at a hundred and four a man ought to get his affairs in order?"

"No we don't," they said.

I was overwhelmed by their callousness—certainly this grey beard, far from being senile, had common sense.

1518   Meeting Cole Porter in Ritz.

1519   ——— abortion on his daughter.

1520   We all went to hear Chaliaplin that night; after the second act he stayed out in the bar talking to the bar maids and then joined us afterwards a tall unsteady figure, pale as the phantom of the opera himself descending the great staircase.

1521   Imagine saying to Bob Cresswell, apropos of his brother's death: "Well, he must have been an awful pig."

1522   About me being in the furnace room and running
        upstairs for Scottie and Andrew

1523   Brawl in lunch room in Charlottesville

1524   Mme. Tussand and girl who did statue (Ask Nora)

1525   "They don't allow us and the other rich boys to go   ★
        to anything except comedies and kidnapping and
        things like that. The comedies are the things I like."
            "Who? Chaplin?"
            "Who?"
            "Charlie Chaplin."
        Obviously the words failed to record.
            "No, the—you know, the comedies."
            "Who do you like?" Bill asked.
            "Oh—" The boy considered, "Well, I like Garbo and
        Dietrich and Constance Bennett."
            "Their things are *comedies*?"
            "They're the funniest ones."
            "Funniest what?"
            "Funniest comedies."
            "Why?"
            "Oh, they try to do this passionate stuff all the time."

1526   "Then somebody told us about 'party girls.' Business
        men with clients from out of town sometimes wanted to
        give them a big time—singing and dancing and
        champagne, all that sort of thing, make them feel like
        regular fellows seeing New York. So they'd hire a room
        in a restaurant and invite a dozen party girls. All it
        required was to have a good evening dress and to sit
        next to some middle-aged man for two hours and
        laugh at his jokes and maybe kiss him goodnight.
        Sometimes you'd find a fifty dollar bill in your napkin
        when you sat down at table."

1527   The engine in the army.

1528   Most Pleasant Trips   Most Unleasant Trips
            Auto Paris Zurich   Auto Zelda and I South
            Auto Zelda and Sap and I   Around Lake Como

Auto Ernest and I North
P.L.M. going north 1925
Cherbourg-Paris
Havre-Paris
South to Norfolk
Around Lake Geneva

Mentone
California
Quebec
North from Norfolk
Tom and Ceci

1529   They got on the children's train and made a tour of the zoo and the woodlands and the playing fields. They sat in single file

1530   Remember the day my little marmoset got loose and chased the two ladies.

1531   Scottie's triumph at the races

1532   The pushing with palms

1533   So horribly (?) unattractive
frightfully (?) unattractive (Sara to Goulding)

1534   "The somewhat nervous little man at the desk" after a long conversation as to whether the celebrity is "just folks"—"just like anybody else," etc. with the nervous little man caustic and resentful, divulges himself suddenly as the celebrity.

1535   She had never done anything for love before. She didn't know what it meant. When her hand struck the bulb she still didn't know it, nor while the shattered glass made a nuisance by the bedside.

1536   The psychology back of this is kidding the matinee idol *without* losing dignity. You give them a rather disappointing moment at first, appearing with long sheaf of papers and beginning to read
　　"In the light of—"
　　　(Stage direction, black down)
Your voice in the dark—*"In the light of recent
　　　　developments—"*
　　　(Lights on again)
Gable—looking rather annoyed—*"In the light of*

> recent—"
> *(Stage direction, black down)*
> Gable—in the darkness, in a rather discouraged voice—"*It was felt that my public should really see me as I am and not—*"
> *(Lights go on—turns to ms.)*

1537 "Pick up the phone and say 'Hello,' " directed Schroeder.

"Don't say who you are."

"Hello," said Hannaford obediantly.

"Who is this?" asked a girl's voice.

Hannaford put his hand over the mouthpiece. "What am I supposed to do?"

Schroeder snickered and Hannaford hesitated, smiling and suspicious.

"Who do you want to speak to?" he temporized into the phone.

"To George Hannaford, I want to speak to. Is this him?"

"Yes."

"Oh, George, it's me."

"Who?"

"Me—Gwen. I had an awful time finding you. They told me—"

"Gwen who?"

"Gwen—can't you hear? From San Francisco—last Thursday night."

"I'm sorry," objected George. "Must be some mistake."

"Is this George Hannaford?"

"Yes."

The voice grew slightly tart: "Well, this is Gwen Becker you spent last Thursday evening with in San Francisco. There's no use pretending you don't know who I am, because you do."

Schroeder took the apparatus from George and hung up the receiver.

1538   *NOSTALGIA OR THE FLIGHT OF THE HEART*

Young St. Paul
Florida
Norfolk
Burgundy
Montgomery as it was
Paris Left Bank
New York 1911, 1917, 1920
Hopkins
Bermuda a little
Chicago
Wheatley Hills
Capri
Old Boarding house or summer hotel
Place across from Niagara
Annecy
The First Ships
First London
Second Paris
Provence
Riviera (Antibes, St. Raphael, St. Tropez, Nice, Monte
         Carlo, Cannes, St. Pol)
Gstaad
Randolph
Placid
Frontenac
Early White Bear
Woodstock
Princeton 1st and 2nd years
Yale
Newman as grad.
Deal Beach
Athens, Georgia
Sorrento
Marseilles

Battle fields
Virginia Beach
Orvietto
Bou Saada
Terr i tet?

Other Playgrounds—Rockville and Charlestown,
                     Montana, Washington
                     Deal, Ellerlie

1539   Little boy of seven:
  "Mister, are you drunk?"
  "No why? What made you think that?"
  "I noticed you had a stick"
  "Does everybody who—" (exit little boy on
    velocepede)

1540   Turning on Mrs. Lyons and Virginia and W. Virginia in reference to Charlestown

1541   Yale Banjo Club men drunk and asleep on stage

1542   Man hides by playing drum in orchestra

1543   A bitch dripping milk over a black dress at a formal party.

1544   Rose Marie's Husband

1545   Man showing some children vanishing coin,   ★
accidentally intercepts coin from passer-by. Serves ice cream cones made out of snow.

1546   Roscoe at the information booth like Chaplin on the street car. Information taps his fingers with a hammer.

1547   Hunts for job in barber shop and is lathered by mistake. Lather is taken off and put back in cup. He lathers customer interminably and latter protests he wants shave instead of scour. Starts to shave but razor shakes.

1548   Becomes barker for Fifth Avenue clothing store. Rival barker pulls clothes over his head. The professor as an act of villainy tips tired mother.

1549   For baggage he has one tooth-brush. While his only shirt is washed in laundry he wears a woman's camisole. Tough boy gives him his business by tearing collar from his neck. He picks up woman on edge of laundry cart.

1550   Burglar uses eating utensils out of his bag. Adds to stock.

1551   Kidnapper gives baby revolver to play with.   ★

1552   Crooks put scrap iron in his pocket to sink him. When   ★
       rescued he has trouble in walking. Kids bob up and
       down around him in final close-up with girl.

1553   Animated illustrations in book.

1554   The mind reader called in to help at a third degree
       shouts out suddenly that the criminal is escaping.
       "No, its all right. Go on," says the chief detective.
       "That was just Inspector Harrigan leaving the room."

1555   Respectful frisking of bellboys at Plaza—nervous
       collapse of head waiter at restaurant where they dined.

1556   Blackstone's man with the gun in Wilmington

1557   Piercing the ear—not the pain but the irreparability of
       it.

1558   Woman who deposited own check in safety deposit

1559   Dean and sedative

1560   Crook in next room—that case in northern New York
       where they carried off three probationers as booty. The
       only one they tortured was the one who took care of
       her.

1561   Dusk along the Boulevard. I'm the King of Sweden.

1562   Duck Notes—Kinds—Mallard, Blackhead, Canvasback,
       smaller kind that makes good eating. —Pintails (?)
       Squeal of the gull, the dog that ate five partridges
       (coveys of three) and the letter—I forgot to tell you.
       The shack at five, the gun, the blinds, the clothes. The
       decoys, sunrise on the Potomac, calm weather and
       south wind, Wash. monument, Alexandria and Mount
       Vernon. The stoves. Geo (Mad Athony Wayne) and
       the sailor (Henry) Mark left circling flight, swarms
       overhead. Aeroplane formation, gulls, buzzards, crowd.
       The three dogs, Chesapeake Bay retrievers. Dogs in and

out of blinds, killing three at once, the poor decoys.
Henry at breakfast, wounded and living ducks, two
triggers at once, Henry on what people will do for you,
the boatman after the ducks, the furry feel of the breast,
gulls eating each other, beautiful sunrise and different
sorts of ducks, pictures, sleep, two triggers, migration,
the line through glasses, the calling, suddenness, my
two lost opportunities, dog had dry coat. Growing
darker (4.30) No results, the white mist, the sunset over
Virginia, the quiet, the sounds far away, waiting, they
fly at you looking large as eagles, the Kentucky
humanitarian, the dog diving for duck, the extreme
cold, dog licking blood of wounded duck, hanging up
duck, cooking duck, the curious mongrel duck, the
its cover. Fish eaters, Indian celery bed.

1563   A Dream: Pariale. Betty Foster at party
                   Her house. Discussion with Asa Bushnell of
                   Football, Oregon, Caulkins, various swells in
                   Empty Toy Store.
                   Downtown, leaving car. Larry Noyes. Losing
                   him, men on bicycles
                   Buying ginger snaps that became trick rings.
                   Deportation. The line of people, struggle in
                   corner. The marine fear. His kick and fall in
                   areaway. (Remember bayonet dream)

1564   His son went down the toilet of the XXXX hotel after
         Dr. X—Pills

1565   During the Indian attack she rushed about in
         the center of a blank cartridge bedlam, waving her arms
         and pointing here and there at the circling redskins as
         if to indicate startling tactical dispositions.

1566   Perhaps a duck scene   ★

1567   *The Sport Roadster*

         When I was a boy I dreamed that I sat always at the
         wheel of a magnificent Stutz—in those days the
         Stutz was the stamp of the romantic life—a Stutz as low as a

snake and as red as an Indiana barn. But in point of
fact, the best I could manage was the intermittent use
of the family car. If I were willing to endure the most
unaristocratic groanings and vibrations I could torture
it up to fifty miles an hour.

But no matter how passionately I slouched down
in the seat, I couldn't make it look like a Stutz. One
day I lowered the top and opened the windshield, and
with the car thus pathetically jazzed up, took my
mother and another lady down town shopping.

It was a scorching day. The sun blazed down upon us,
the molten air blew like the breath of a furnace into our
faces—through the open windshield. I could literally feel
the sunburn deepening on me, block by block. It was
appalling.

The two ladies fanned themselves uneasily. I don't
believe either of them quite realized what the trouble was.
But I, even with the perspiration pouring into my eyes,
found sight to envy the owner of a peagreen cut-down
flivver which oozed by us through the heat.

My passengers visited a series of stores. I waited in the
sun, still slouched down, and with that sort of half-sneer
on my face which I had noted was peculiar to drivers of
racing cars. The heat continued to be terrific.

Finally my mother's friend came out of the store and I
helped her into the car. She sank down into the seat—then
sank quickly up again.

"Ah!" she said wildly.

She had burned herself.

When we reached home I offered—most unusually—to
take them both for a long ride—anywhere they wished to
go. They said politely that they were going for a
little walk to cool off!

1568   As they turned into Crest Avenue the new
cathedral, immense and unfinished in imitation of a
cathedral left unfinished, by accident in some little
Flemish town, squatted just across the way like a
plump white bulldog on its haunches. The ghost of
four moonlit apostles looked down at them wanly from

wall niches still littered with the white dusty trash of
the builders. The cathedral inaugurated Crest Avenue.
After it came the great brownstone mass built by R. R.
Comerford, the flower king, followed by a half mile of
pretentious stone houses built in the gloomy 90's.
These were adorned with monstrous driveways and
porte-cocheres which had once echoed to the hoofs of
good horses and with high circular windows that
corseted the second stories.

The continuity of these mausoleums was broken by
a small park, a triangle of grass where Nathan Hale
stood ten feet tall with his hands bound behind his
back by stone cord and stared over a great bluff at the
slow Mississippi. Crest Avenue ran along the bluff, but
neither faced it nor seemed aware of it, for all the
houses fronted inward toward the street. Beyond the
first half mile it became newer, essayed ventures in
terraced lawns, in concoctions of stucco or in granite
mansions which imitated through a variety of gradual
refinements the marble contours of the Petit Trianon.
The houses of this phase rushed by the roadster for a
succession of minutes; then the way turned and the car
was headed directly into the moonlight which swept
toward it like the lamp of some gigantic motorcycle far
up the avenue.

Past the low Corinthian lines of the Christian
Science Temple, past a block of dark frame horrors, a
deserted row of grim red brick—an unfortunate experiment of the late 90's—then new houses again, bright
binding flowery lawns. These swept by, faded, passed,
enjoying their moment of grandeur; then waiting there in
the moonlight to be outmoded as had the frame, cupoloed
mansions of lower town and the brownstone piles of older
Crest Avenue in their turn.

The roofs lowered suddenly, the lots narrowed, the
houses shrank up in size and shaded off into bungalows.
These held the street for the last mile, to the bend in the
river which terminated the prideful avenue at the statue of
Chelsea Arbuthnot. Arbuthnot was the first governor—
and almost the last of Anglo-Saxon blood.

All the way thus far Yanci had not spoken, absorbed still in the annoyance of the evening, yet soothed somehow by the fresh air of Northern November that rushed by them. She must take he fur coat out of storage next day, she thought.

"Where are we now?"

As they slowed down Scott looked up curiously at the pompous stone figure, clear in the crisp moonlight, with one hand on a book and the forefinger of the other pointing, as though with reproachful symbolism, directly at some construction work going on in the street.

"This is the end of Crest Avenue," said Yanci, turning to him. This is our show street."

"A museum of American architectural failures."

1569   It was a large luxurious boudoir, panelled, like the lower hall, in dark Ebglish oak and bathed by several lamps in a mellow orange glow that blurred its every outline into misty amber. In a great armchair piled high with cushions and draped with a curiously figured cloth of silk reclined a very sturdy old lady with bright hair, heavy features, and an air about her of having been there for many years. She lay somnolently against the cushions, her eyes half closed, her great bust rising and falling under her black negligee.

But it was something else that made the room remarkable and Myra's eyes scarcely rested on the woman, so engrossed was she in another feature of her surroundings. On the carpet, on the chairs and sofas, on the great canopied bed and on the soft Angora rug in front of the fire sat and sprawled and slept a great army of white poodle dogs. There must have been almost two dozen of them with curly hair twisting in front of their wistful eyes and wide yellow bows flaunting from their necks. As Myra and Knowleton entered a stir went over the dogs; they raised one-and twenty cold black noses in the air and from one-and-twnety little throats went up a great clatter of staccato barks until the room was filled with such an uproar that Myra stepped back in alarm.

But at the din the somnolent fat lady's eyes trembled open and in a low husky voice that was in itself oddly like a bark she snapped out: "Hush that racket!" and the clatter instantly ceased. The two or three poodles around the fire turned their silky eyes on each other reproachfully, and lying down with little sighs faded out on the white Angora rug; The tousled ball on the lady's lap dug his nose into the crook of an elbow and went back to sleep, and except for the patches of white wool scattered about the room Myra would have thought it all a dream.

"Child!" she said—and Myra started, for again the voice was like a low sort of growl—"you want to marry my son, Knowleton?"

Myra felt that this was putting the tonneau before the radiator but she nodded.

"Yes, Mrs. Whitney."

"Ah—"

Myra was not certain whether this last ejaculation was conversation or merely a groan, so she did not answer.

"You'll excuse me if I don't appear downstairs," continued Mrs. Whitney, "but when we're in the East I seldom leave this room and my dear little doggies."

"Good night, mother," said Knowleton.

"Night!" barked Mrs. Whitney drowsily, and her eyes sealed gradually up as her head receded back again into the cushions.

Knowleton held open the door and Myra feeling a bit blank left the room. As they walked down the corridor she heard a burst of furious sound behind them, the noise of the closing door had again roused the poodle dogs.

1570   Once upon a time Princeton was a leafy campus where the students went in for understatement and if they had earned a P wore it on the inside of the sweater, displaying only the orange seams as if the letter were only faintly deserved. The professors were patient men who prudently kept their daughters out of contact with the students. Half a dozen great estates ringed the township which was inhabited by townsmen and darkies—these latter the avowed

descendants of body servants brought north by
southerners before the civil war.

Nowadays Princeton is an "advantageous residential
vicinity"—in consequence of which young ladies dressed
in riding habits with fashionable manners may be
encountered lounging in the students' clubs on Prospect
Avenue. The local society no longer has a professional,
almost military homogenuity—it is leavened with many
frivolous people, and has "sets" and antennae extending to
New York and Philadelphia.

1571   "Been looking all over the ship for you for two
days."

The speaker was an ageless Jew, wrapped in a polo
coat, and tied with a belt—his nose was a finger pressing
down his compressed lips which shuffled under it as he
mulled and valued, his eyes were beautiful and mean. The
two men each recapitulated to himself the many dealings
they had had in the past or were likely to have in the future.

"Where did you keep yourself, Lew?" asked the Jew,
Bowman, "I thought I'd see you at the Captain's table."

*"We heard you were on board so we stayed in our
cabin," Lew answered gravely.*

*Bowman's face fell, not at the harshness of pleasantry
but because he usually looked forward to a few minutes of
formal cordiality before people commenced the abuse
which he subconsciously demanded.*

*"That was a wise thing for you to marry a lady.
There's nothing like a lady. I've always been glad I married
a lady myself."* ★

"Do you call that broad of yours a lady?" asked Lew.

"Bowman looked at him.

"You don't feel in a good humor today."

"Yes, I do," said Lew. He had resented the implication
that he and Bowman were upstarts and with sadistic
cruelty he prolonged the moment; then he laughed, "Hell,
George, I'm kidding you. If you had any self-respect you'd
have socked me. Of course Edith's a lady, one of the finest
ladies I know." Anyhow half the word was true, so he'd
heard.

"You're all right, Lew," said Bowman meditatively, "All you need is every-once-in-a-while a good swift kick in the—"

"Sure, that's right, and to make up for that I'll come to your lowsy party."

"You don't need to come to my party. You, a Yale man, talking like that. No one would ever know it." He went Jewish suddenly, "But come to the party."

"Sure I will." He put his hand in a friendly way on Bowman's arm.

He was thinking of her—he knew now that his abstraction had hurt her, for it was always after he had hurt her that she seemed most beautiful, unattainable and serene.

He found her in the cabin, just standing, thinking. He was afraid of her when she thought, knowing that in the part of her most removed from him, there was taking place a tireless ratiocination, the synthesis of which was always a calm sense of the injustice and unsatisfactions of life. He knew with which her mind worked, but he was always surprised that it brought forth in the end protests that were purely abstract, and in which he figured only as an element as driven and succourless as herself. This made him more afraid than if she said, "It was your fault," as she frequently did—for by it she seemed to lift the situation and its interpretation out of his grasp. In that region his mind was more feminine than hers—he felt light, and off his balance—and a little like the Dickens' character who accused his wife of praying against him.

1572   "Well, Cassandra," he said.

Her grey eyes moved over him as if she was checking up on something she had formulated in her mind. But: "Who was Cassandra?" she asked.

"She was a prophetess. Listen, darlo, you thought I didn't want you to walk with me, didn't you?"

She shook her head slowly.

"I was thinking of those curtains. I'd like a room with just stars in it."

He put his arms around her, enclosing her completely as if he didn't want even the intangible to escape, but even as she came close to him he felt something fly off into the salty air of the cabin. Simultaneously he had a sense of change, of a new rhythm that in a moment became a great silence. Far off in it there were voices calling.

He stepped back, shaking his head like a wet dog.

The engine's stopped," he said, "Something's happened."

On the deck people walking, reading, loafing, exercising, were all hurrying toward the stern.

1573   The constant endeavor of trained nurses in a patient's room is to get all moveable articles out before the doctor arrives approximating as closely as possible the stripped look of an operating chamber. The result is like that obtained in the case of a dog baring a bone. It is the burying that matters; not the bone—in the meantime after the nurses' departure, missed or forgotten objects turn up in the corners of strange drawers and escritoires. The hanging of trousers is another matter in which technique must be part of the nurses' course. From the decorums of Hopkins to the casualness of the Pacific they are seized by both cuffs, twisted several times in reverse, placed in the corner of the hanger and left to dangle rather like a man hanged. That same nurse may go home and put away a pair of slacks in perfect shape for future wearing, but no man ever left a hospital with the same crease that he had when he went in.

1574   They had been run into by a school bus which lay, burning from the mouth, half on its side against a tall bank of the road, with the little girls screaming as they stumbled out the back.

1575   "You know", he said to Miss Hapgood, "I was about nine years old when they had that war flu in 1918—and that was the kind of disease to have. We lived near a camp and I got it. That was a real bug. I was playing cops and robbers and one mintue I was behind a tree yelling something and one minute later I was trying to hang on to some garden furniture and asking another boy to tell my father I was sick. When it hit you either you woke up dead or you woke up with somebody bringing in bacon and eggs—and not enough of them. You know—like the Bubonic Plague."

1576   A young man phoned from a city far off, then from a city near by, then from downtown informing me that he was coming to call, though he had never seen me. He arrived eventually with a great ripping up of garden borders, a four ply rip in a new lawn, a watch pointing accurately and unforgivably at three. . But he was prepared to disarm me with the force of his compliment, the intensity of the impulse that had brought him to my door. "Here I am at last," he said teetering triumphantly. "I had to see you. I feel I owe you more than I can say. I feel that you formed my life."

1577   Singer flashing light

1578   Man met Cab Calloway and Eddie Duchin under the impression that they were Yale Football stars.

1579   Hearing Hitler's speech while going down Sunset Blvd. in a car.

1580   The Selwynn-Rothstein mixup.

1581   "You frozen?"
"No—but I will be eventually. So I think I'll get married this spring, when the winds are warm on Long Island and I find someone with an open car."
"That sounds good," he said pensively but in the vista of pungent darkness that stretched suddenly before his mind's eye he saw Jill's hair flying. "Spring—what a big word.. It's almost everything."
"No," she said. "There's summer, if you've planted the proper trees."

Titles

1582   Journal of a Pointless Life.
Wore out his welcome.
"Your cake."
Jack a Dull Boy.
Dark Circles.
Mr. Ridinghood ("Red") ★   for Cutter's name
The Parvenue hat
Talks to a drunk
The firing of Jasbo Merribo. *Sketch*
Tall Woman
Birds in the Bush
Travels of a nation.
Don't You Love It?
All five senses.
Napoleon's coat
Tavern music, Boat Trains
Dated
Thumbs Up
The Bed in the Ball Room
Book of Burlesque entitled "These my betters"
Title for bad novel: God's Convict   ★
Skin of His Teeth
Picture-minded
Love of a Lifetime.
Gwen Barclay in the 20th Century.
Result—Happiness

Murder of my aunt
Police at the Funeral.
The District Eternity

Unclassified

1583   My extraordinary dream about the Crimean war.

1584   The improper number of Life and the William's Purple
Cow cover beginning something.

1585   Time: Henry VIII cut from a halitosis ad.

1586   Husband did everything he wanted himself, so in what
didn't concern him she did what she wanted.

1587   Snubs, Marice, Ruth (Clothes), Toolman and son,
Gerald bull fight.

1588   Just before quarrel had been talking about the best and
what it was founded on.

1589   She and her husband and all their friends had no   ★
principles. They were good or bad accoring to their
natures; often they struck attitudes remembered from
the past, but they were never sure as her father or her
grandfather had been sure. Confusedly she supposed it
was something about religion. But how could you get
principles just by wishing for them?

1590   The war had become second-page news.

1591   Meeting Princetonians in the army as buglers etc.

1592   Diary of the God Within—they got half of it—this is
the other half.

1593   Before breakfast, their horses' hoofs sedately scattered
the dew in sentimental glades, or curtained them with
dust as they raced on dirt roads. They bought a tandem
bicycle and pedaled all over Long Island—which a
contemporary Cato, considered "rather fast" for a
couple not yet married.

1594   Color blind doctor who couldn't tell baby had jaundice.

1595   The brain of Dr. Gantt's dog.

1596   About three pieces of the truth (specific) fitted into one
of the most malicious and troublesome lies she'd ever
told. These latter are permitted this indiscretion within
limits as about the only surcease they will ever find in
this world.

1597   We took a place in the great echoing salon as far away
from the other clients as possible, much as theatrical
managers "'dress a thin house" distributing the crowd
to cover as much ground as possible.

1598   *In Hendersonville*

        I am living very cheaply. Today I am in comparative
affluence, but Monday and Tuesday I had two tins of
potted meat, three oranges and a box of Uneedas and
two cans of beer. For the food that totalled 18 cents a
day—and when I think of the thousand meals I've sent
back untasted in the last two years. It was fun to be
poor—especially you haven't enough liver power for an
appetite. But the air is fine here and I liked what I
had—and there was nothing to do about it anyhow
because I was afraid to cash any checks and I had to
save enough for postage for the story. But it was funny
coming into the hotel and the very deferential clerk not
knowing that I was not only thousands, nay tens of
thousands in debt, but had less than 40 cents cash in
the world and probably a $13. deficit at my bank. I
gallantly gave Scotty my last ten when I left her and of
course, the Flynns etc. had no idea and wondered why I
didn't just jump into a taxi" ($4.00 and tip) and run
over for dinner.

Enough of this bankrupt's comedy—I suppose it has been enacted all over the U. S. in the last four years, plenty times.

Nevertheless, I haven't told you the half of it, i.e. My underwear I started with was a pair of pajama pants—*just that*. It was only today I could replace them with a union suit. I washed my two handkerchiefs and my shirt every night, but the pajama trousers I had to wear all the time and I am presenting it to the Hendersonville Museum. My socks would have been equally notorious save there was not enough of them left for they served double duty as slippers at night. The final irony was when a drunk man in the shop where I bought my can of ale said in a voice obviously intended for me, "These city dudes from the East come down here with their millions. Why don't they support us?"

1599   LIVES OF THE DANCERS

(A Ballet Synopsis)

by

F. Scott Fitzgerald

SUMMARY

I   Some Russians and the dance, before the war. Heartburn in a village.

II   The dancing characters are moved by fate to post-war Paris.
The great days of the ballet seem to end in catastrophe.

III   Again destiny moves the protagonists on—this time to the new world. The deathless art takes root to grow again in fresh soil.

———————

Music for Scene I, Russian folk song and classic composers—pre-war

Music for Scene II, Appropriately blended selection from Diagloff ballets of 1919-1929

Music for Scene III, American music to be composed or

assembled—some use of former
Russian airs. This to be decided later.

Scene I   *A Russian Village*

Lubov, village belle, has received word that
her childhood sweetheart, *Serge*, now
embarked upon a career in the Russian
Imperial Ballet will arrive to see her. The
renewal of his youthful pledge, so thinks she
and her friends.

Serge arrives in a carriage, shows off his
acquired talents, dallies with her but makes it
evident to the audience he is not serious but
has some other purpose.

Serge is followed by *Unknown* (magicians
costume, black mask, black silk stockings and tail
coat, old fashioned stock and opera hat) who
indicates "do what you're here for."

Serge, fascinated by the lure of art, obeys,
using *Lubov* as decoy to find out from *Old
Peasant Woman* (comedy type) secret pagan
festival dance needed by Imperial Ballet.

Serge is by this time drawn to *Lubov* and
wants to marry her and take her away even
though it compromises his career. But before
he has entirely committed himself *Unknown*
appears, fascinates *Serge* with technical tricks
he can still show him. Serge weakens, follows
Unknown while Lubov brokenhearted laments
with peasant girls who try to console her.
Cossachs of village called up for army, depart
and other girls rush to speed them off but
Lubov laments only her lost Serge.

CURTAIN

-3-

Scene II   <u>Theatre de Dance Russe, Paris</u>

Asbestos curtain up disclosing drop curtain painted to
represent exterior theatre, posters, etc. <u>Season of 192-</u> prom-
inently displayed.

Practical portal to theatre. Audience enters from wings
and exits through portal. During this:

(1) Entrance of Lubov now become international high courtesan.

(2) Last to enter--after crowd, the <u>Unknown</u>, unmasked, grey
devilish beard and proprietary air about performance.

<u>Immediately</u> after

Drop curtain rises upon this:

> Partition running front to rear
> to indicate curtain. Later swing-
> ing on its own central axis
> forms middle panel of new
> back drop, other panels being let
> down or run out from wings

Well lit **Dressing Room** *White* *Spots*	*Dark*	*Dark*	Red plush **Opera Box** *Amber & rose* *Spots*

Shallow
to be →
hauled into
wing later

← Shallow
to be
hauled into
wing later

Real audience

<u>In Dressing room</u> - <u>Serge</u>, the star making up adulation, flowers,
last instruction of <u>Unknown</u> who is clearly indicated now as ballet
master and impressario.

<u>Opera Box</u> - Entrance of <u>Lubov</u>, popular, chic, but preoccupied,
indifferent. Leaves box and reappears in <u>Dressing Room</u>. Black out
box and roll out.

<u>Dressing Room</u> - Reunion <u>Serge</u> and <u>Lubov</u>. He tries to attone--too late
she says--she's now hot stuff and well kept in Paris. Sad. He
shrugs shoulders. Obvious both regret. Resignation. Black out
dressing room.

In Dressing room—Serge, the star making up adulation, flowers, last instruction of *Unknown* who is clearly indicated now as ballet master and impressario.

*Opera Box—*Entrance of *Lubov,* popular, chic, but preoccupied, Indifferent. Leaves box and reappears in *Dressing Room.* Black out box and roll out.

*Dressing Room—*Reunion *Serge* and *Lubov.* He tries to attone—too late she says—she's now hot stuff and well kept in Paris. Sad. He shrugs shoulders. Obvious both regret. Resignation. Black out dressing room.

Scene is *Back Stage* as it would be seen looking *toward* the imaginary audience before curtain rise. Prop curtain swings and gives full stage as indicated by diagram. *Unknown* drilling girls in last rehearsal.

Groups of artists, musicians, writers.

Unknown indicates ill health from overwork. Word to clear stage for curtain rise. Girls in wings. Music starts. Unknown takes final look, starts to leave stage, collapses, dies.

General commotion, music continues; played in back of *real* back drop to indicate it's being played in orchestra pit; Serge rushes out horror stricken; *Unknown* placed on bier; they are all stricken but defer to Serge's grief. Music dies away.

Entrance of dancing chorus. Death dance in dimming lights, with singers in muted orchestra; wierd green spot on *Unknown* lying on bier. *Serge* solos alone. Lubov comes in to console him but he drives her fiercely away.

CURTAIN

Scene III   *A Road House on Long Island, 1933.*

Serge poor and dancing at roadhouse (Beer Signs, etc.) conducts a class by permission of owner before opening for business. Bad class, hopeless, one good pupil who is mysterious and always appears masked.

Class goes—*Serge*, overworked and discouraged, dozes—fragments of the past appear. He rises in sleep, gropes toward vision of *Unknown* but when stage blacks out for a moment and former lights come on to indicate reality he finds himself holding *Mystery Pupil*; who, when unveiled, is fifteen-year old girl and who has crept back to practise at bar while he slept.

Lubov appears—widow of rich American; forty, still pretty. She indicates that *Mystery Pupil* is her daughter and has inherited her potential talent.

Serge and *Lubov* reconciled. He will teach her daughter and is absorbed in beginning lessons when road house guests begin to drift in; there is a sort of counterpoint of American and Russian music, ballet of guests upstage taking its tone (but jazzing it) from classic ballet indicated by dancing lesson of three principals in front.

1600   *A Preface:*

Acknowledgements, who have verified references for me or made valuable suggestions, oceanography etc., Garbo, Beebe or mythology, etiquette, lost cooking Mrs. Rorer, exploration, Hemmingway bullfighting, communism, Dos Passos, cannibalism, my own early works for necking (or petting), Amelia Earhart air currents, John J. Pershing military science, the Badaeker guides to Provence, China also curators Smithsonian Cardinal Vatican; also Universities Paris, etc., Guttengen

Hydrogen, Oxygen, Tuskeegee, fresh water and Springfield Y.M.C.A. and college of electors at Washington, use of library, editors of Encyclopedia, Mr. Charles Scribner for the use of a pencil sharpener; proofs Hem., corrections Joyce Shaw. Stravinski scoring of certain passages. To Picasso for etching, Brancusi for wood pulp, Stalin U.S.S.R. Stenography for faithfully and uncomplainingly typing the entire ms. Last and least to my wife, daughter, aunts, who put at my disposal letters, wills, portraits, photographs, documents, stamp books, post card collections, laundry marks, cigar bands, report cards, diplomas, pardons, trials, convictions, accusations, leases and unpaid bills, stamp collections and Confederate money. The idea if I'm going to begin all over again at 37. Buy book if your name in it. Bibliography. I'am indebted by Mayor Walker of Cannes. The book is without index. On England and on the Continent—but enough have shown their friendship, and I feel that they have written this book just as much as I have. (or: they have all been willing collaborators, etc.)

1601   There are many places here and there and up and down the world, which like O'Henry's "Five Stories Cities," suggest that one has only to go there to see something happen, but his illusion persists largely in those without the opportunity to travel. There can be a simply unimaginable dullness in a Montana cow country saloon, in Chinatown or Limehouse—perhaps because we expect so much; this applies also to a glamorous and youthful ball after one has reached a certain age, or a gondola in Venice if one hasn't; or to Hollywood teas if one is invited or to the real haunts of the underworld if one is not; or to a Paris cafe or a lonely road at night, or a park bench at dawn—it is best to stop here and rest a moment on the park bench, using it both for a seat and for an example.

1602   *To begin a chapter*—It is said that the Tartar tribes cooked their meat by slinging it saddle wise across their horses and riding on it all day, producing, I suppose, a sort of pound steak.

1603 The Rocky Mountains still being formed.

1604 All my life I had wanted to meet a big shot—as a matter of fact I met one of the biggest when I was boy, but I was too young to know that he was loaded. They began dying off in the nineteen hundreds and there was no one to replace them except Henry Ford and he was all washed and groomed and the rotogravures showed him in camp with Edison and the other members of the success back-field. By and by Morgan was dead and Harriman was dead and you couldn't scrape enough color of all their successors together to make up a juvenile lead.

1605 My great grandmother visted Dolly Madison

1606 Save Chauffeur from Josphine II

1607 Savings from Grit

1608 It appeared on the page of great names and was illustrated by a pictures of a cross-eyed young lady holding the hand of a savage gentlemen with four rows of teeth. That was how their pictures came out, anyhow, and the public was pleased to know that they were ugly monsters for all their money, and everyone was satisfied all around. The society editor set up a column telling how Mrs. Van Tyne started off in the Aquitania wearing a blue traveling dress of starched felt with a round square hat to match.

1609 An Akbar—Mohammedan name for man with halitosis

1610 From a little distance one can perceive an order in what at the time seemed confusion—the case in point is the society of a three generation middle-western city before the war. There were the two or three enormously rich, nationally known families—outside of them rather than below them the heirachy began. At the top came

those whose grandparents had brought something with
them from the East, a vestige of money and culture;
then came the families of the big self-made merchants,
the "old settlers" of the sixties and seventies, American-
English-Scotch, or German or Irish, looking down upon
each other somewhat in the order named—upon the
Irish less from religious difference—French Catholics
were considered rather distinguished—than from their
taint of political corruption in the East. After this came
certain well-to-do "new people" —mysterious, out of a
cloudy past, possibly unsound. Like so many structures
this one did not survive the cataract of money that came
tumbling down upon it with the war.

This preamble is necessary to explain the delicate
social (relation) so incomprehensible to a European
between Gladys Van Schillinger, aged fourteen, and her
senior by one year, Basil Duke Lee. Basil's father had
been an unsuccessful young Kentuckian of good family
and his mother, Alice Rielly, the daughter of a
"pioneer" wholesale grocer. As Tarkington says
American children belong to their mother's families,
and Basil was "Alice Rielly's son." Gladys Van
Schillinger, on the contrary—

1611   After awhile he lowered his paper slowly until the
bottom part of it crumpled a little in his lap.

"What are you looking at?" he inquired.

The mood and the tone of the question were
impatient—he tried to soften them with a faint smile.

"Do I look funny to you in any way?

No answer. His smile widened—suddenly disappeared. He took up the paper again and began the
cartoon.

—*Where did Skigum go? Drat that man..Scaw
you!* he read. There was a picture of a stout woman
chasing spotted dog from pantry.

—*Hello Gert. Did Skigum—I'll get him out for you*—
He dropped the paper to his lap again.

"Have I done anything?" he demanded, "You've
got that look on your face you always have when I've
done something."

His wife sighed faintly.

"No, you haven't done anything," she said, with the implication that it would have been a hundred times better if he'd done something. "You haven't done anything at all."

He knew that answer. He knew all the answers. If he asked "Why are you looking at me?" she would have the choice of several—"Do you object to my looking at you?" or "I didn't realize I was looking at you."

But confound it she was looking at him! And if there's one thing a woman has no right to do it is to look at her husband with the silent, mysterious persistence of a reproachful sphinx. He called it the "West Point Silence" sometimes. He had read that when a man's conduct was being tacitly criticised at the Military Academy no one spoke to him. So in his more spirited moods he called it "The West Point Silence." He tried another note.

"I love you, dear, and I can't read the paper with any pleasure when I know you've got something against me in your mind."

Lucile got up and regarded herself in a long mirror with solemn interest. There was a white wisp of lint on her long eyelashes which she removed and the pink ghost of a smudge which she erased from the left scallop of her pretty mouth.

1612   Bread and Butter Letter from a Chicago Gentleman:
Dear Marion,
     I certainly enjoyed myself. The chow was all good, mostly, but the butter was rancid. The bed was hard but uncomfortable. The talk was over my head but there was some made sense—that part about my being a great guy for instance.
     I got home sick at the stummuck but I do not blame *you* at all.
     Will you tell the servents next time I like my soup hot and more of a sharp edge when they press my pants.
     You said I only had to pay one buck for board but even that is too much when the service is not good. That

black bean soup was rancid too, and mine had a beetle in it. Besides there wasn't enough blankets and the only good one was stale like it had been used for a baby or something.

I liked all the people I met except that woman I had to slug at dinner. Tell her I hope she found her teeth in the tomato soup when they emptied it out. No gentleman should have done a thing like that but I cannot stand a warm stocking on my ankle under the table.

I'm sorry I shot the horse and dog but they kep me awake ½ the night and I come there for a rest. You will find a lot of cigar stubs in the refrigidaire as I did not know where to put them. I do not want them however so give them to one of the negro servants, you know the colored ones, not your uncle or aunt or anybody like that. The black ones.

I'll tell you when I can come down again and we will have more of that fun in the dumb waiter—hey kid, you know? Only I'm sorry I left you between floors when I went to bed. I thot it would give you more time to cool off so you could get some sleep too.

All right kid and goodby and I know now you are not such a dumb cluck as you look like.

"Tick"

P.S.   If you called that thing a cocktail then listerine is the Holy Grail.

1613   *Songs of 1906*
Way Down in Cotton Town
          Rogers Bros.
Teasing
Coax Me
Kiss Me Good Night Dear Love
Don't Get Married Anymore, Love
Waiting at the Church
Vesta Victoria
Tale of a Kangaroo
Dearie, My Dearie
If It Takes My Whole Week's Pay

Roosevelt and Big Stick
Princeton Glee Club

Nora Bayes and Harvest Moon

Vernacular

1614   Man saying, "This is Jack O'Brien,","this is Florence Fuller."

1615   "Sleep, male cabbage."

1616   " 'Cause I just came from there and they told me one of their mos' celebrated heartbreakers was visiting up here, and meanwhile her suitors were shooting themselves all over the city. That's the truth. I used to help pick 'em up myself sometimes when they got littering the streets."

1617   Freeman: Grease in the transcommission—What are you scused of?

1618   Those dumguards.

1619   The McCoy.

1620   Modern Slang:

Pushover	A Heel
Grand	A Dick
Bag	A Natural
Lay	On the Lose (not loose)
Sugar	A Punk
Life preserver	Kee-ooot

1621   Well you're not exactly in the saoth or the soth or the suth or even the sith.

1622   A prenograstic=stenographer (Freeman)
       A toomer—a tournament

1623   Retire
                      Expectorate
       Ring's friend Wish some potatoes

1624   "Put it down there" for "sit down."

1625   Andrew's coinages (investigate)

1626   Cliche: In spite of them perhaps because of them

1627   Obsolete expression: Confound it!

1628   Unusual—Babbitt's word very, very fine   ★

1629   Unbeknownst   ★

1630   "Ai feel ez if eme being kpt," said the English lady

1631   "Admired mentality" of Mrs. Richards   ★

1632   Slang. Branegan (party) conk (kill) klink (jail)

1633   Too much shiftin of the vessels for the movin of the
       vittles

1634   It burns her up
       She burns up   in movies   ★
       He burns up

1635   No Dice
       No Soap

1636   Sheilah (pouting) All raht. Ah wull.

1637   Comes in a pa-a-akige, so conve-e-n't. (ending all clauses
       and sentences)

Work References

1638   For Shaggy: Dogs are supposed to want to talk but
      that's just one of the phoney ideas people have about us.

1639   Correction of New Yorker Poem:

        Was that each of us got holy
          then got mad
        Trying to give the third one to
          the other.

1640   *For Tender is the Night*
      Book I   Insert 2 words
                at beginning   (To P. 148
       The Prelude

      Book II
       Before the Prelude   (To P. 212
                Insert 3 words on
                P. 149 prelude
      Book III

       After the Prelude   (To P. 306
                Insert 3 words on sep. page. Just don't number
                Chaps. 11 to 23 would be chaps. 1 to 13.
      Book IV
       Suite   (To end
            Insert one word on P. 307
      Renumbering of Chapters.

Youth and Army

1641   Bobby's motorcycle and cigarette case.

1642   Club elections in 1915 were in the worst snow storm in years. Found that out 20 years afterwards, but remember chasing Sap thru the snow.

1643   The forced march.
The rides to see Zelda
The thief at Leavenworth
The missing material
The scene with sergeants.

1644   Once in his youth he had been a boy scout for a month, but all he remembered was the scout call, "Zinga, Zinga Bom-Bom."

1645   I can read faster than almost anybody, much faster than any of those nasty little girls in Vanilla that think they can read so fast, the big smarties! I read "When Patty Went to College," when some girls don't read it till they're ten.

1646   "Don't touch me," she said quickly. "You've been handling money."
"But not in my mouth, mother," he protested humorously.

1647   They sat, as they had so often, in a row on the steps, surrounded, engulfed, drowned in summer.

1648   Now, in the relief, the parents grew angry with Josephine as with a child who has toddled under galloping horses.

1649   There was a flurry of premature snow in the air and the stars looked cold. Staring up at them he saw that they were his stars as always—symbols of ambition, struggle and glory. The wind blew through them, trumpeting that high white note for which he always listened, and the thin-brown clouds, stripped for battle, passed in review. The scene was of an unparalleled brightness and magnificence, and only the practiced eye of the commander saw that one star was no longer there.

1650   Mrs. Perry was a vague lady. She knew that Josephine was going to be in some amateur play and she imagined vaguely that it was under the personal supervision of the University professors with the President himself probably popping in and out at rehearsals.

1651   Mary Pulipitut, Sherba Thene, Jane Refile, Miss Trigor.

1652   Johnson, Pettijohn, Radamacher, Rosenwald, Walker (2) McGovern.

1653   "I always say 'Entre' ", Scotty.

1654   Going down to Carling's restaurant to drink whiskey, wines and beer. Perhaps on her way back to the lake after the dance, Minnie, passing by, would see his face among the wildest of the revelers and understand. "I'm going to Maxim's," he hummed to himself desperately; then he added impatiently, "Oh, to heck with Maxim's!"

1655   Who called me Fitzboomski during Russo-Jap war?

1656   Children's lack of emotion as we know it is healthy.

1657   Six authors in search of a character (Newman School)

1658   Sir Tonsidor.

1659   Dressing in Curtain.

1660   Aunt Clara scrubbing my feet

1661   Candle grease, Alley's room, Grandma and dog, lettuce,
        Revue de Deux Mondes

1662   Sap and national debt

1663   Shame at the inequality by Hooker and Scarlett covered
        by deep seriousness and lowering of eyes.
        Innocence—appreciated by outsiders and unconsciously
        exploited—Byles etc.
        Faint Homosexuality unconscious hero worship involved.

1664   Scotty—When I was four years old and you were in the
        habit of spanking for me.

1665   Chemical Experiences (Scotty's word)

1666   Eating Garlic

1667   Great Big Fat Dumbbell

1668   The Mome

1669   I kiss the two parents

1670   Scotty preoccupied

1671   Playing movie actress

1672   Freak of nature

1673   The days of blazers and two sorts of telephones

1674   Scott Fitzgerald so they say
            Goes a-courting night and day

1675   Playing with yo-yos in the drug store walking the dog
        ditto

1676   Presently Iris told them a joke.
            "In the bus," she said, "there was a man who wanted

to get up. Well, thinking himself intelligent, he asked the conducteur, 'Your Noel's arch, is it complete?! and the conducteur said, 'Yes, now we have the donkey, will you climb?' "

Morgan and Frieda looked at each other frankly. It was less intelligible than it would have been in its native French though certain words sounded familiar. Noel's arch for instance.

"Don't you see," explained Iris, "the Noel's arch would be complete because he was a donkey."

This was more confusing than before.

"Could she mean Noah's Arc?"

"Of course. And the conductor said that with the addition of the donkey it would be complete. Very good, Iris—tell me another."

"They don't sound as funny in French as in English."

"No," Morgan agreed, "perhaps not."

1677   Excursion to Concarnneau, a beautiful seaport. Is famous for its blue fishing nets when all the brilliant of the colours are gathered together under the sunbeams it is magnificent. (Scotty)

1678   ...the essential is that it doesn't rain...Pouah!

1679   The sea blue with green nightgowns and white nightcaps. Mlle. is waiting for the water to get warmer to go in. I think she can wait a whole century for that miracle.

1680   And the socks were long because the dress was short—it simply wasn't becoming to show so much flesh. If the dress were longer the socks could be shorter, did Madame see?

1681   Dearie
        Stay in your own back yard
        Waiting at the church
        Tropic color
        Kiss me good night

I'm Romeo
Oh moonbeam light and airy
Bamboo tree

1682   McKibben, Driscoll and Dorsey. French, Van Slyke McConville.

1683   My buckboard

1684   Alley's razor

1685   Banjo lessons

1686   The Mormon who came to see me at Aunt A's in St. Paul

1687   "Everybody works" and "I'm the guy"

1688   "Dear old fellow
      I may inform you that I received your note. But can also inform you that the place where I stay is Le Poildu and not La Poildu. Amen. I play every afternoon in the garden with a little girl who lives in the hotel. When we climbed on the top of a toll sort of thing we had a magnificent view of the country all around. Brittany is a really very pretty place. Very many laboureurs, workers, farmers with their wives, farmers and washers. You can see rocks and rocks with the night-capped waves attaching them. I hope you have the same exquisite site. I am learning tennis with a very good teacher at the Union sportive de la poel.
      Oug! Aie! there is the cat Dicky who is putting his claws into my innocent skin of my delicious self."

      There followed a portrait of Dickie "seen of face and of side" and the letter bore the signature "Iris, your delicious daughter"
      P.S. I just left this note on Mile's bureau "Puisque vous me faites le supplice de Pruneaux delivrey-moi des gouttes dan le nez. I hope she will have pity."
                                                                    (Scotty)
      Morgan opened one of the "weekly newspapers" that Iris had made for him when she was away en Brittainy last summer:

The loo Pieces of New News

India is in a bad case

Yesterday the english king spoke of a complete defeat among the indians the defeat of Calicut is terrible for us

We will sadly announce that Mrs. Iris Parklings' reverend daughter, Miss Marie-Antoinette Parkling who came from Bellagio, Italy, had to go yesterday to the doll hospital. Her arm came straight off during her school recess while she was tumbling over a pile of comrades.

Fine Arts

The new fantasy of Miss Iris Parkling.

The well-known actress has had a fantasy these last days and has wanted to by clay to undertake schulpture. She wants to model a head of Mlle. her most complaisant poser.

1689   Fitzgerald's livery stable

1690   Jimmie and me kissing Marie and Elizabeth, and the sprained ankle.

1691   Gave up spinach for Lent

1692   "Idioglossea" what Driscoll twins had.

1693   May I take the key

1694   Sing Song at Yacht Club

1695   Candy being distributed in youth—"Oh come on you know me."

1696   You're liable to get a bullet the side of the head.

1697   Foxy Grampa

1698   Sis Hopkins

1699   Mrs. Wiggs

1700   My lady sips from her satin shoe

1701 Since he rode into Brussels in a staff car in October 1918

1702 It all seemed very familiar to me, probably it was like some hay ride of my youth.

1703 *Thirteen*
Me: What? Did they separate the sexes at the play?
Scotty: Daddy—don't be vulgar!

1704 Curious nostalgia about Pam, Anne of Green Gables, ets.

1705 Her eyes, dark and intimate, seemed to have wakened at the growing brilliance of the illuminations overhead; there was the promise of excitement in them now, like the promise of the cooling night.

1706 with a bad complexion brooding behind a mask of cheap pink powder

1707 As the car rose, following the imagined curve of the sky, it occured to Basil how much he would have enjoyed it in other company, or even alone, the fair twinkling beneath him with new variety, the velvet quality of the darkness that is on the edge of light and is barely permeated by its last attenuations. Again they reached the top of the wheel and the sky stretched out overhead, again they lapsed down through gusts of music from remote calliopes

1708 When I was young the boys in my street still thought that Catholics drilled in the cellar every night with the idea of making Pius the ninth autocrat of this republic.

1709 She and I used to sit at the piano and sing. We were eighteen so whenever we came to the embarrassing words "lovey-dovey" or "tootsie-wootsie" or "passion" in the lyric, we would obliterate the indelicacy by hurried humming.

1710 Among the more Jazzy of the Themes in Annabel's convent composition book, I found "Earthquakes,"

"Italy," "St. Francis Xavier." The subjects had a familiar ring.

1711   Father Barrow told me of a pious nun who opened the regents examinations in advance and showed it to her class so that Catholic children might make a good showing to the glory of God.

1712   Young Alec Seymore wrote a story and read it to me. It was about a murderer who after the crime was "greatly abashed at what he had done."

1713   Notes of Childhood:
  Make a noise like a hoop and roll away
  She's neat ha ha
  Grandfather's whiskers
  Aha, she laughed
  Annex rough house
  Hume against Lock
  Changing Voice
  Snow
  Hot dogs
  Hair oily and pumps from notes
  Miss Sweet's school
  Folwell Paulson
  Each Bath
  Writing in class
  Debates
  It's one thing to call a man
  Story of dirty shirt
  Trick show lemonade stand

1714   Baby's Arms   Buttercup
  Tulip Time   Rose of No Man's Land
  Dardenella   How You Going to Keep 'em
  Hindustan   Long Long Trail
  After You've Gone Mlle from Armentieres
  I'm Glad I could Make My Buddy
  Smiles   Home Fires
  Down to Meet You in a Taxi Want to go home
  Shimmee   Madelon

Wait Till the Cows Come Home   Joan of Arc
Shimmee Shake or Tea   Over There
So Long Letty   We Don't Want the Melon
Why do they call them babies   God Help Kaiser Bill
Goodbye Alexander   Belguim Rose
Nobody Knows   All around the Barnyad Rag
Bubbles
Dear Heart
Pretty girl like melody (1920)

1715   *Poem*
Une fois
ma mere a moi
habitait pres de Java
mais je ne suis pas
une javanaise. Reflechissey—y tout a votre. Elle vivait
dans une cabane
aise reconverte de feuilles de banane
une fois j'allais la voir
avec un petit chien noir
car la bas il n'e ont que des blancs
avec des poils vert a leur flancs.
Une Maison de ler arrondissement est a vendre a la mairee
au bas prix
de 12 louis Ainsi disont une petite bonhomme du ler
seizieme siecles (Scottie)

1716   Italian woman who stole my boat at Placid

Supplementary Notes*

*Seventeen numbered pages typed on yellow paper inserted at the back of the second binder.

1717   Note: The little fish at Malibu. Ask me.

1718   Note: New novel note at top of p. 10. Put in section
where Stahr is ill in N. Y.

1719   *1865*   S
Down Pennsyvania avenue, past the gibbering dinges
on the sidewalks and the fat profiteers in the stands,
marched the sweated labor of farm and factory, now
entilted "The Army of the Potomac".
In his raw grave, Lincoln shifted his position wearily,
glad at any rate to be away from his horrible wife. It was all
pretty lousy.

1720   The 20th Century reached New York an hour late, and   E
the station master made it back all the way to Chicago to   ★
get an excuse.

1721   *Syndicate idea*   I
Erroneous news paragraph contributed by Miss Inform-
ation.

1722   Names for the Bowes House—Easy Payment   N
                                    Down Payment
                                    Empty Larders
                                    Termite's Rest
                                    Little Casino
                                    Old Panneling
                                    Conway Tearle

1723   Note about smudges in orange grove (ask me   ★

1724   Novel Index
                            For Post
                         My Successful Year.

            It is impossible to tell this story without gloating. If I   I
        attempted to tell it with the exquisite modesty, the taste of
        Joseph Conrad, it would be a falsification, for this story is
        bumptious and gluttinous—call it crude, coarse, and be
        done with it.

1725   Miss Cuba at Rhodadendron Festival.   S

1726   Car description on quiet night, padded hush of tires,   D
         quiet tick of a motor running idle at curb.   ★

1727   There was a bright sun and a wind, and the woods   D
         were singing.   ★

1728   Pershing shot for cowardice in 1918.   E

1729   Man, by subterfuge, gets his own natural children   S
         adopted and brought up by childless wife.

1730   You could paint Lenin's face inside every backhouse in   O
         Iowa and not make him any more important than the
         phallic quatrain of the Chromo Christ. You might just
         manage to make him as important to the young as
         Santa Clause.

1731   "Nigger" name: "Brunell Massey".   P

1732   The aristocracy can remake their manners overnight—if   E
         it were not for the philosophy of his story, the world
         would be governed by Louis-Phillipes (and Mary
         Harrimans)

1733   *Conversation*: "Do you know what I've come to the   V
         conclusion of etc."

1734   "Nigger" talk: Illegiterate = ⎡ Illigitimate
                                          ⎣ Illiterate   V

1735   Idea of play in which dolls grow older.   I

               I Dolls new
               II Dolls crisis
               III Dolls older than humans.

1736   Not like the travel folders—not enough Gables and   O
Powells to go around. For romance, the patrons of the
1,000 Rivieras went to the movies.

1737   Slang (collegiate)   V
    A Jeep.............................Orchid Consumer
    Floating ....Long Dress
    Drag ....Main Street   ★
    Jelly.............................Small Date
    Joe College ....Collegiate
    A drip ....Bird
    " of the pt. water.................Bird
    Clapping ....Cutting in.
    Trucking ....Walking like that.
    Smooch   )
    Perch   ) ———— Necking
    Pitch and Fling Woo)

1738   Of a man: It never entered his head that he was   E
somewhat of a liability.   ★

1739   When Zelda Sayre and I were young, the war was in the   J
sky.

1740   For she has a good forgetting apparatus. That's why   G
she's so popular, why she can have a heart like a hotel.   ★
If she couldn't forget, there wouldn't be any room.

1741   Story of Leland Hayward   I

1742   Story of Marion Davies   I

1743   For story contrast, the Magazine types.   I

1744   She'll never meet a stranger.   G

1745   "Shall I save him for another five minutes?" says Nora.   M

1746   *To Carter + Marion*

What wonder if the poet   J
          wants to rave
That the bells within the
          washer start to ring,
That the banners in the flagstone
          start to wave,
For at seven-forty-five tonight,
          it's spring.

The crackers in the cracker box
          explode,
The very shoes I wear are get-
          ting tight.
Why this modest, unassuming
          little ode,
Is careening around the paper as
          I write.

I must go and pull a strip tease
          in the park,
But remember, dears, this most
          important thing.
Though I'm fined by Misseldine
          for being stark,
Still at seven-forty-five tonight,
          it's spring.

1747   That wiley old Kiss-puss, Mr So-and-so.   H

1748   Paralyzed troups of beggars like the Salvation Army can O
         beat the Y.M.C.A.

1749   Three outside phones)
)—In Scottie's house.   Y
         Three inside phones   )

1750   A story—
              The arrival at the chateau. (Rich family arriving. Poor I
         family in contrast.) Suggested by Gt. Amer. Fortunes.

1751   Oh, I can cover paper like you do till I'm ninety.   E

1752   Girl in green transparent rain-coat, looking like   **G**
        something from the florist.   ★

1753   The mechanical sound of pingpong balls on a rainy   **D**
        afternoon.   ★

1754   *Nora's Day*   **S**
        Engaged to two. The Band of Four arrive—
        Mumble-de-peg.
        The proposals. The father.
        All night. The hammock. The freezer—Bump
        heels—hands. Sent to Europe.

1755   Gurrodge and Mussodge for Garage and Massage.   **V**

1756   Opera plot: A youth, unjustly imprisoned and   **I**
        embittered, joins big mobster. Idealistically
        disillusioned, he is redeemed.

1757   One man only felt suffering as with his fingers felt its   **O**
        rough shape. Another seemed to hold it against his   ★
        cheek.

1758   The episodic book, (Dos P. + Romaine etc.) may be   **L**
        wonderful, but the fact remains that it is episodic, and   ★
        and such definition implies a limitation. You are with
        the character until the author gets tired of him—then
        you leave him for a while. In the true novel, you have
        to stay with the character all the time, and you acquire
        a sort of second wind about him, a depth of realization.

1759   The Barber's too slick,   **J**
            The maid's too clean.
        The boy's too quick,
            The clerk's too keen.
        The music too gay,
            The tunes too mad.
        I'm leaving today,
            And that's too bad.

                            Compliments of a contented guest.
                            F.S.F.

1760   At M.I.T., he studied birth control, flood control, self control and remote control.

1761   Story—A hole or bag in which someone finds all the things he's ever lost.

1762   Part of the wall gives way at the pressure of a button and a bar slides into view. A muted radio begins to whisper Star Dust into the room,] and Mr. Deere orders things on the phone. It is girls he is ordering—three—four—

"—and if you can't get her get Miss Lindsay. But Miss Crane sure, if you've got to trace her all around town..."

It is five now and the room seems full of girls, all very young and new under an alternate set of shaded lights. From behind another panel rolls a little piano with four octaves and a tall thin man goes ravenously to work on it while the smoke thickens and white coated waiters serve hors d'oevres and champagne and a young woman melodiously confronts the monied men with the enigma of why she was born. Hopkins from Topeka will have a tale to tell back home.

1763   Early dark of a December afternoon in 1929. Lower New York and all the great blocks still gleaming with light, and after five going out row by row but with many tiers still gleaming out into the crisp dusk.

1764   In Spring when there was no leaf dry enough to crackle and the loudest sound was a dog barking in the next county.

1765   In a short story, you have only so much money to buy just one costume. Not the parts of many. One mistake in the shoes or tie, and you're gone.

1766   Of course, these boys are more serious—this is the generation that saw their mothers drunk.

1767   There was only spring whispering in the air, faint as the flutter of last year's leaf.

1768   Barbara's coat that the moths ate except buttons.   ★ S

1769   It is the custom now to look back ourselves of the   O
boom days with a disapproval that approaches horror.   ★
But it had its virtues, that old boom: Life was a great
deal larger and gayer for most people, and the stampede
to the spartan virtues in times of war and famine
shouldn't make us too dizzy to remember its hilarious
glory. There were so many good things. These eyes
have been hallowed by watching a man order
champagne for his two thousand guests, by listening
while a woman ordered a whole staircase from the
greatest sculptor in the world, by seeing a man tear up
a good check for eight hundred thousand dollars.

1770   The Woman's Times.   I

1771   The suit beginning in 1000 about land in Naples given   I
away by mistake for the millenium.

1772   A woman who smelled of gooseflesh.   H

1773   Swallowy air, velvet texture of the air on the   D
Spartansburg road.

1774   The Bowes children were excited to ride in a train—   Y
plane commonplace.

1775   Loretta Young—nigger pretty.   G

1776   My story of self conscious woman who said son-of-a-   M
bitch instead bitch at hunt dinner.

1777   One of those mysteries like why Southerners have big   E
ears, and why chess is listed in the sporting news.

1778   Man playing harp as piano.   I

1779   Trees resting gold green bosoms on the water of Lake   D
Lanier.

1780   Zelda picking pink flowers from the sedge.   D

1781   Man who got radio by hooking ear phones to bed   A
springs.

1782   Zelda says of the Cevennes——chestnut trees, ghosts and a   I
       lone cow.

1783   Play—For Act II. Something happens that to audience,   I
       changes entire situation, such as significant suitcase to
       country, or old terror apparently buried in Act I.

1784   The kind of man who stamps just before he laughs or   D
       shoves forward your chair with each change of emotion.   ★

1785   In front of lazy group Animay-*shun*!   N

1786   "They're two of us"
           "Oh, there are? So *that's* it. I noticed things were   C
       costing, and I thought I saw something, but I thought
       it was one of the work relief projects."

1787   No connection at all between being right and being   O
       attractive. The French, the Communists, etc. The
       answer, of course, is "bread alone".

1788   Invention of two-end cork tip cigs.   E

1789   Mimi McLeish on "Little Masters & Little Monsters".   Y

1790   At Groton they have to sleep in gold cubicles and wash   E
       at an old platinum pump. This toughens them up so
       they can refuse to help the poor.

1791   Houses of 1925 overflowing with the first editions of   D
       Joseph Hergersheimer and colored toilet paper.

1792   The value of culture. Ecclesiastes, the freethinker of the   O
       bible, said one of the most erroneous remarks that there
       was no new thing under the sun, because he hadn't
       traveled to Athens in space or Kitty Hawk in time.

1793   "Right away—high" sang the central in a mad cheer.   N
       He laughed.   ★

1794   Russell Woolcott's turtle that grew and diminished   I

1795   From the room where Mandy lay,   J
       And the toilet flushed like thunder
       Out of China cross the way.

1796   *Ages 1700—1967*   I

Monarchs	Louis XIV
Philos.	Voltaire
Nations	Washington
Tyrants	Napoleon
Peace	Victoria
Science	Darwin
Empire	Wilson
Revolution	Lenin

1797   "Wealth, wit and beauty of two continents." "What's   E
the other continent?" "Africa. Starks is from Africa."

1798   In Train. "Here's where we're going—" And then as   C
they looked hastily out the window at a graveyard, "But
not now".

1799   "When I go to bed at night, I put on so many blankets   E
that I have to put a book-mark in to tell me where to
get out."
                            Nora Flynn.

1800   Misty, enchanted arbors of light   D

1801   The deep South from the air—a mosaic of baseball   D
diamonds set between dark little woods.

1802   A movie wedding. Ushers were Harold Lloyd, Victor   E
Varconi, Ronald Coleman, and Donald Duck.

1803   Story idea about prison. Girl hates town. Meets convict   I
released. Helps him and when he goes back, she does,
too.

1804   I've got a cancer. What cancer
Tomato can, sir.

1805   I'm Sick. How sick? Sick of one—half a dozen of the other

1806   I've got a pane   N
Pane of glass in my eye.
Spectacles to you.

1807　Smelt Pot—Small box of candy

1808　A pen—appenditius

1809　Sinus—of the declaration

1810　　　　TO CARTER, A FRIENDLY FINGER

My name is Death. You may remember me.
　　We met some days ago, but you refused
The introduction, and with such snobbery
　　That I felt temporarily confused.

I'd thought to meet you on some great day
　　When you were drowsing in the oldsters' land.
On silent feet, I'd come to where you lay,
　　Before you knew it, I'd have touched your hand.

But since you have the art of driving well,
　　You've quite forgot that you might meet another
Who drives as fast but clumsily as hell.
　　So I may see you soon. Step on it, brother!

———————————

Listen, my children, and you shall hear
　　Of the midnight ride of Paul Revere.
But the story of Carter's is not on sale.
　　Dead men generally tell no tale.

———————————

Ye Scott ha' *not* wi' Carter bled
　　By road sign "Dangerous Curve Ahead".

———————————

Gather ye Carter while ye may
　　From all the points of the Zodiac.
This is the tie that he wore that day,
　　Here is a tooth and part of his back.

———————————

Not a drum was heard, not a funeral note
　　As we dropped the bits into the rumble.
We wrapped his spleen in his overcoat,
　　But we lost his ears in the jumble.

All the Kings horses and all the King's men,
   That are not at the Coronation,
Managed to gather up Carter again,
   But couldn't restore animation.

The splendor falls
   On Carter's gall.
Stones scattered o'er.
   Route one-six-seven,
The convicts crush them into mush
   While Carter Brown looks down from Heaven.

We've just replaced the car, cash down.
   But how we miss you, dear old pal, you
We've no new model Carter Brown.
   Your chasis had no trade-in value.

1811   *PRIZEFIGHTER'S WIFE*

My love is down
   I saw the blow
Only my love for him
   Makes me know
God give me pity
   That doesn't frown
Stand away—stand aside
   My love is down!

I had a room once
   Brush and a comb
When things were tough
   I could run home
Now there's the ring and ?
   Purse—and a town—
But stand away—stand aside
   My love is down!

My love's a rough neck
   My love's a pug

All of the family
    Think I'm a mug
I was just born this way
    Somebody's clown—
Stand away! *Stand aside!*
    My love is down!

F. Scott Fitzgerald

Appendix: Loose Notes*

*General notes with the material for *The Last Tycoon*.

1812   My remark about 2 beautiful girls is a drama—fifty is only a chorus.

1813   Something a little sad about it like woman of fifty in flesh colored stockings.

1814   Most women would rather hope I think—they are good hopers.

1815   It was midsummer, summer in the dangerous age, when there is nothing more to expect from it and people try to live in the present—or if there is no present to invent one. (used?)

1816   Early August is for imprudent loves and impulsive and unmotivated crimes. (used?)

1817   Career—a story about John Bishop.

1818   Story idea. Joe-Kiki-Ruth girl has loads of old letters, is all set, needs old neglected beau, vamps him (she thinks). He takes her to country + excuses himself.
　　　　Follow him to her house, keys, letters, plane ect
　　　　Her discovery.

1819   Ernest would always give a helping hand to a man on a ledge a little higher up.

1820   For a Bishop Story

x was so far down now that almost anything you said of him was liable to be true. Just like when he was way up nothing that anyone said against him was liable to be true. Even if it were true it sounded like jealousy. He was always a little afraid that x might be good after all and they might dig him up. There would be a picture of x green and jabbering in a corner of the gallery. It was not a picture he would like his boys to see.

I sat there with blue hair and one eye—that was the night King called up + let me down.

1821   The body gets down and crouches in a corner of itself and says 'You're doing this to me. I'll make you pay' and you say never mind—stay down there.

1822   Two people go away—and they take it along with them. Silence falls—nobody has any lines. Silence and trying not to guess behind the silence—imitating how it was before, and more silence—and big wrinkles in the heart.

1823   Come in! Come in!
And have a Micky Finn.

1824   Dick Scheyer and the sword.

1825   Ernest Hemingway and Ernest Lubitsch—Dotty "We're all shits."

1826   In thirty-four and thirty-five the party line crept into everything except the Sears Roebuck Catalogue.

1827   Drinking gives a sort of steely completion.

1828   The cleverly expressed opposite of any generally accepted human idea is worth a fortune to somebody.

1829   Max Perkins didn't want to leave himself lying around.

1830   A cadence started in his head like a motor warming up. That was one way—to get something to it—the word, the name, the shape of the sky get it quickly. The other way was to start with the thing, to be profoundly affected by it, until it stretched elongated, stood up and walked.

1831   When you once get to the point where you don't care whether you live or die—as I did—it's hard to come back to life. Compton McKenzie for instance. It's hard to believe in yourself again—you have slain part of yourself.

1832   My blue dream of being in a basket like a kite held by a rope against the wind.

1833   The trained nurse stood gazing into the medicine closet. "I wonder what the hell medicine to give him," she muttered to herself. "They all look like the same old horse poison to me." She wishes the labels were written in American so she could tell what the drugs were for. She considered shutting her eyes and picking one at random with a pointing finger but some might be poison and she did not dare.

1834   Before death thoughts from crack-up. Do I look like death (in mirror at 6 p.m.)

1835   Prayers are punctuations and reminders.

1836   But he never forgot—he was forever haunted by the picture of the girl floating slowly out over the city at dusk, buoyed up by delicious air, by a quintessence of golden hope, like a soaring and unstable stock issue.

1837   The two young men quit jobs as hotel clerks and lay around the beach all summer on nine dollars a week unemployment insurance. One of them turned down a job at forty but he had fun. But the old barber who had mental troubles and physical troubles and financial troubles oh and everything in hell the matter with him—they told him to scram out of there quick.

1838   Walk her from the room by the seat of her sea-green slacks.

1839   A miraculous little stranger from the stratosphere—so apt at spreading the infection of whatever she loved or laughed at—that he suddenly understood why the world forgave her for not being a really great beauty.

1840   Listening to a stealthy treacherous purr creep into his voice.

1841   People here seemed to want to get out in the country and cling, instead of really going places.

1842   Shipping out the papers in her possession by means of the little granddaughter who innocently lights a stuffed candle at church every Sunday evening.

1843   Somebody repeats: Baby, I tore him in two.
        A bored man: (later) Did you partition him?

1844   The pulp writer—that superficial hysteria which he substitutes for emotion.

1845   And you so beautiful with your hair in clasp on clasp of gold.

1846   The people of Hollywood are not very nice outwardly—there is too much unwelcome familiarity, too much casual snootiness. (the agent who picked up paper in the office).

1847   It's fun to stretch and see the blue heavens spreading once more, spreading azure thighs for adventure.

1848   That spoonful of magic which is allowed us once or twice in life.

1849   I wouldn't go to a war—unless it was in Morocco—or the Khyber Pass.

1850   It was all small change, incessant nickles and dimes of conversation.

1851   A feeling of having had life pass virtually and endlessly before their eyes like a motion picture reel and give it that much attention.

1852   If their souls are alive they no longer speak or perhaps it is that I have grown deaf.

1853   Malibu: A bunch of dressing cabins for people who can't swim. (look up and see if it's mine or DeMille's)

1854   The man in the taxi with his single hand gesturing.

1855   Something like a drunk's "I just want to tell you one thing."

1856   She's a one-girl jazz age.

1857   Virginia has lovely puffed straw hair and the grey eyes of home—she was a late developer, an awkward duckling at twenty-one, but learning a whole series of things that unmarried women don't. At twenty-seven her charm was in full flower.

1858   Mrs. Whitney phoning Virginia about her thoroughbreds—twenty thousand dollars a day.

1859   Organizing the thoughtless.

1860   If you have an inconvenient opinion they name it like a disease and quarantine you.—"I'm a *what?*"

1861   For Mankiewicz—the ten days that shook down the world.

1862   The writers at Ted Paramore's were all in low gear, temporarily or permanently.

1863   Scottie: "mousing around" (in regard to a quiet couple.)

1864   You drew people right up close to you and held them there, not able to move either way.

1865   The flickering patches of white on the jockeys made it look like a flight of birds.

1866   And went down to the lake for a dip, swimming on an unreal surface that existed between a world of water like mist and a drizzling firmament of air.

1867   Tragedy of these men was that nothing in their lives had really bitten deep at all.

1868   Bald Hemingway characters.

1869   He was so old, so wise that he looked forward only to his anticipations. Oh God give me good anticipations.

1870   Strong women wept into their vichysoisse.

1871   In life too much luck, in drama too much destiny.

1872   Dolly had done her worst suffering on the boat in an economical way she had, it was weeks before George saw her eyes silvery clear in the morning.

1873   Which Vanderbilt—the one with the boat mouth, the horse and the scrambled teeth.

1874   Turkey Burger (Gerald)

1875   He had met the two Lindbergs and thought them dazed and tragic spooks. and. . . and. .

1876   He's got four-legged caviar in his pantry.

1877   She wore a little summer number from Saks, about $18.98 and a pink and blue hat that had been stepped on on one side.

1878   You're all the songs

1879   Most of us could be photographed from the day of our birth to the day of our death and the film shown without producing any emotion except boredom and disgust. It would all just look like monkeys scratching. How do you feel about your friends' home movies of their baby or their trip. Isn't it a God awful bore?

1880   Behaviorism—the only guide to the validity of emotion.

1881   Like many men he did not like flowers except a few weedy ones—they were too highly evolved and self conscious. But he liked leaves and horse chestnuts and peeled twigs and even acorns, unripe, ripe and wormy fruit.

1882   I always like the horse chestnuts and leaves better than flowers.

1883   A howling dog outside made sound effects for her nightmares—whatever she heard in her dreams it turned out to be the dog (unfunny ghoulish ones—invert and rewrite).

1884   There is no book for beautiful women.

1885   Peter Powdirblugh.

1886   When I saw Scottie and the boy with the pimply face in the launch and realized to my dismay (and jealously) that she liked him. He was alive to her.

1887   Don't ever go Dalton. This is an Idea for Princeton Alumni Weekly

1888   Hope of Heaven. He didn't bite off anything to chew on. He just began chewing with nothing in his mouth.

1889   My plan about the reissue of Paradise with changed names. (For those under Thirty Six.)

1890   Expected a great beauty—saw a billious little chippie.

1891   One of those mysterious people like "that lady" to whom her mother took the little squares she had crocheted every month and "that woman" told her how to put them together.

1892   The shorts of the men carving. The short of the Boston college Dressing room. "You think you can stick it out o'Rourke? I think I can coach."

1893   Fastest typist isn't best secretary. Swinburne. Trick golfer with watch, lightening calculator, kicker, et. Faulkner and Wolfe are those.

1894   Indian's Names: Extended Tail feather—Sweet Corn— John Other Day.

1895   Bloody Pope and Bradley britches full of exploded guts lying over the battlefied of the Dardenelles.

1896   Tough producer about taking you. "Whatsa matter with the guy—I had my first dose at fifteen."

1897   It was rather like the autumn page from the kitchen calendars of thirty years ago with blue instead of brown October eyes.

1898   He sat in his office writing a long letter to Jill and then set fire to it in the cold stove, but the flue was closed and the smoke curled into the room. He listened to the milkman's hour on the radio and when his window turned grey went out into a soft crowing country morning.

1899   Eddie Mayer hates women—funny I didn't notice it before. Like Tom Wolfe. But for different reasons. He goes to them for sexual satisfaction, but he likes men emotionally more. I don't know how far back it reaches but certainly women play a very mean and unstable role in his plays. He admired his father excessively, I gather. He sticks with the gang. You feel that he values his conquests so that he can brag about them. Talking is his vice. He would rather confide in men though than in women. He is a gent and all this is modified by that fact. He is extremely likeable and liked. His talent is not exactly thin, like Dotty's and so many Jewish and Irish talents—it is simply infrequent. He needs years to dream. I do not know him well. I surprised myself by the regurgitation of the idea that he was a physical coward. I don't know at all.

1900   Sid Perleman is effete—new style. He has the manners of Gerald Murphy and almost always an exquisite tact in prose that borders on the precieuse. I feel that he and I (as with John O'Hara and the football-glamor-confession complex) have some early undisclosed experience in common so that at this point in our lives we find each other peculiarly sympathetic. We do not need to talk.

Sheilah noted his strange grace doing his interpretation of "Slythy" in the Charade the other night.

I like his brother-in-law West. I wonder if he's long-winded as a defense mechanism. I think that when I am that's why. I don't want to be liked or to teach or to interest. That is my way of saying "Don't like me—I want to go back into my dream."

I know Nat through his books which are morbid as hell, doomed to the underworld of literature. But literature. He reminds me of someone. That heaviness. But in the other person it could be got used to—in Nat it has no flashes except what I see in his eyes, in his foolish passion for that tough and stupid child Mc———. Sid knows what I know so well that it would be blasphemy to put it in conversation.

1901   John O'Hara is in a perpetual state of just having discovered that it's a lousy world. Medium is always as if the blow had struck him half an hour before and he's still dulled by the effect. Nunally J--- says that he's like an idiot to whom someone has given a wonderful graflex camera and he goes around with it not knowing what to snap.

1902   The big statue of Eleayer, wondering whether he'd squash down by the end of the carnival and give a funny effect with his face.

1903   They made love. For a moment they made love as no one ever dares to do after. Their glance was closer than an embrace, more urgent than a call. There were no words for it. Had there been, and had Mae heard them, she would have fled to the darkest corner of the ladies' washroom and hid her face in a paper towel. What was it they said? Did you hear it? Can you remember?

1904   The English will never make snappy pictures until they stop breaking off football games to have tea.

1905   Kiki's remark about "being one of us".

1906   Witty but faintly intoxicated with herself in her old role of disturber of the peace.

1907   Our pathetic childish vanity that we share with actors.

1908   I wish he'd get run over by a school bus.

1909   Her brown legs stayed tentaviely hoveringly on the brown doorstrip. She rocked suddenly on her heels as if about to throw a forward pass.

1910   I think the level of novelty and entertainment is so low that I don't think adults go when they feel good—they go when they feel bad. They go as for an anaesthesia as to the speakeasy—expecting bad liquor and not able to care. I saw a John Garfield picture last night that was a tenth carbon copy of his old ones. They can't tell me that feebs who will swallow that have funds enough for first run movie houses.

1911   After Margaret B. talks Sarah says "There *can't* be that many words."

1912   Title: The One About the Farmer's Daughter.

1913   Axel plot for movie

1914   Death of de Martel.

1915   I talk with the authority of failure—Ernest with the authority of success. We could never sit across the table again.

1916   She didn't understand when she used the word "ruthless" about me, that the word means something else to those Finance-Jews. They must have sneered in their hearts.

1917   Once when you were strong, you gave me the luxury of loving you most, of even being cruel in a small little vain or impartial way. When you were weak, you came to me, nosing into my arms like a puppy. But later it was different. You used your strong times to edge away

from me—break out a new world of your own where I
was excluded. Your weak times belonged to me, but
you had forgotten all the words that had melted me.

1918   People like Ernest and me were very sensitive once and
saw so much that it agonized us to give pain. People
like Ernest and me love to make people very happy,
caring desperately about their happiness. And then
people like Ernest and me had reactions and punished
people for being stupid, etc., etc. People like Ernest and
me----

1919   That moment I felt from time to time with Zelda that
she has unravelled the whole skien—that I am speaking
with the lightly rolled skien before me, not wanting to
disturb it. That even in my most alone and savage and
atavistic moment I am doing so. Note Rousseau went a
little crazy after finishing the Contract Sociale.

1920   I wasn't precocious, I was merely impatient (or
hurried?)

1921   Arthur Kober type of Jew without softness. Certainly a
Jewish character of that type. Trying to realize himself
outside of Jewry.

1922   Longfellow—his best line stolen from a lapland song.

1923   Scottie and I pupils at same school.

1924   Tom Fast's story of Ernest.

1925   The smell in the Woolworth article.

1926   "Dear Lester: —I just love to write you letters. I have
fun. How are you? My grandmother sent me a new
pencil and paper today so I thought I would write you
a letter.
        To put it snappily, etc., etc.
        Is this not a sweet letter? My grandma was good to
send the pencil and paper.
                                        The Punk."

1927   Although earlier in the day she had spoken sympathetically of her father, later, she said scornfully: "He's nuts". Her statement to police was salted with schoolgirl slang—such as "Mother started to 'conk' me."

Almost absentmindedly, when she revisited the house of death, Chloe strummed the keys of the small organ Davis had bought for his children: she called attention to the three pairs of roller skates on the porch, to the dolls of the slain younger children and to the books in her own room.

"I'm a bookworm," she confided. "I read all the time." She admitted that neither of her parents ever had been cruel to her: she insisted that she loved her sisters and he~ brother deeply.

1928   Another world war victim (wooden leg) went crooked after a successful career today, shot himself. Innocent and worthy as Warren Groat.

1929   Young married misery.

1930   My latest medico-legal monograph. The Corpse with the Floating Kidney.

1931   Miss Foodstuffs.

1932   How to Read is the biggest fake since Van Loon Art. Now that Mencken has retired the boys who really hate books and pictures are creeping out of their sinecures again and trying to make them into specimens for dissection.

1933   Moradino Juice
Clery, lettuche, Radmishes
Mardinos oglivies
Can of Fishy Gue   From New Yorker
Edges
Chuckmes for dessert
Syvapi
Szlami

1934   You don't have to know much if you're ignorant because you're very content with what you know.

1935   *Fragment*

Now is the time for all good men to come to the aid of the
     party
But I shall not come to the aid of the party—
           any party.
For we and the Jews are going to be butchered
We the liberals because we were too kind, the Jews because
     they were too wise.
Wisdom and kindness are crimes against the spirit of life
We should know that who were raised in the school of
     scrapping.

1936   You'll be reckless if you
           Do-do-do
You'll be reckless if you don't
You'll be happy if you
           Woo-woo-woo
You won't be happy if you won't.

1937   Kyle Forsite in Concrete.

1938   Sweden is going to give the Nobel Peace prize to
Russia—and they better do it damn quick

1939   Titles:—My Own Race Prejudices
     The Position of the Political Nance during the
     World Crisis.

1940   The day it tipped over (le Seizieme)

1941   Today is Friday and in the back of Epictetus.

1942   March Family, Hat Family, Halegen Family

1943   False build-up of stimulants. They endure from 11:30
p.m. to 11:30 a.m. correspondingly.

1944   Behind him a one man epedemic coughed, sneezed and
rocked the seats ahead in his agony.

1945   Story Idea: Find a drug good for two things and you
have a climax. For instance: if pareldehyde or chloral
were also ink eradicators.

1946   Story Idea: (New Yorker) Scientist tells family his theory that deprived for X days of salt or sunshine or water (McSweeney) or forced to eat, would turn people black—they quarrel. So they turn. Top is tails (?)

1947   Advice to young writers—Read Tolstoi, Marx and D. H. Lawrence and then read Tolstoi Marx and D.H. Lawrence.

1948   Play laid in a publisher's office.

1949   Money in bonds. Finale Welles' broadcast.

1950   Tell the story of the Alex Haine study hall disturbance. *But* as if it were a riot. Call it controll. Only disclose at end that they were boys.

1951   To describe an apparently dastardly character like the turn coat in Janice Meredith and then show he is the real hero of the whole thing, the most politically progressive and class conscious. This is really a grand idea; a series including this and Philippe might be built around it. It is the recalitrant peasant in Phillipe who splits from him in disgust + is the father of peasants.

1952   Changing my channels of avidity s.g.

1953   In the haut bourgoise or feudal it's called cruelty—
In the petit or middle: bad taste
In the proletariat: vulgarity?
But it's the same thing
Tommy's cruelty—me and Joe McKibbey
S's talk of Z and of human functions.
This is interesting too because it shows classes in movement. Why and where I caught a petit bourgoise attitude I don't know. But it's not like Dot's and Don's who revolted from being eternal poor relations.

1954   A story to show how a person of the 16th century had to look up things—by kindness and friendliness, by travel and effort—and, since Diderot—

1955   For Pat: Vacuum bomb—His sister.

1956   Paderewsky Sees—Paderewski Sees
All right now! All right now! You better take a look
yourself. Ignace Jan Paderewski the celebrated pianist
and president of the Assembly of the Polish Parliament
in exile, declared today in a broadcast to "my American
friends" that the war will "end in the ultimate victory
of right and justice." —Paris, Jan 29.

1957   Anatomy research was interrupted by Alexander the
Great

1958   English political history—Peterloo 1819-1885.

1959   Play about Woodrow Wilson Title "I suppose".

1960   You're going to hit somebody with that teething ring.
You're going to stick your rattle in somebody's eye.

1961   Don't lose your temper or your nose will get as red as
your eyes.

1962   The trouble is you can take it but you can't hand it out
anymore.

1963   Call waiter and the Germans will come running.

1964   Don't kid yourself—you're so bougeoise you smell of
cheap caviar.

1965   Masterpieces of American Poetry by Mark Van Doren.
He opened it to his astonishment upon a group of
eight poems by Mark Van Doren. Rising from his
couch he scissored these out and put them in the
Johnny but finding Mr. Van Doren's selections as
uninspired as the impertinence, he laid the book away.
Life was difficult. Thsi ubiquitous feeb or was it his
brother actually influenced American sales through the
Book of the Month Club.

1966   Miss X who gets around a lot says all the good writers
think that Van Doren—the one who put his own

poems in an anthology—is an ignorant man. And that the artists spit blood about Van Loon's History of the Arts with his own illustrations. The Dutch are condescending. He does not think much of the Book of the Month., etc.

1967   I have decided to buy in all my outstanding books.

1968   D.P.—The only girl so mean she had to hire a male nurse.

1969   Those comics going—without emphasis.

1970   She was dead but she ran around the room for ten or fifteen seconds, skidding in her own blood but managing to keep her feet while some sound kept trying to come through her blood choked throat. Then she crashed down flat as if she had fallen a thousand feet.

1971   You were—too good to be true. That was—the matter with you.

1972   Idea about composition of a squad. Average bravery and tenacity of men.

1973   As a novelist I reach out to the end of all man's variance, all man's villainy—as a man I do not go that far. I cannot claim honor—but even the knights of the Holy Grail were only striving for it, as I remember.

1974   Native Son—A well written penny dreadful with the apparent moral that it is good thing for the cause when a feeble minded negro runs amuck.

1975   Let Richard Whitney out
New Republic Anthology

1976   What we have given Europe.

1977   Film called Nice People to include baby talk idea and child's day. A grave but not a tragic thing happens—he hits a cop, almost by accident.

1978   Play like "L'apprenti sorcerer". Young lawyer blunders in on corporation deal. Using Arnold.

1979   Ideas on Fear as being removed as well as profit motive. We know the latter can—but the former. Some day when the psycho-an are forgotten E.H. will be read for his great studies into fear.

1980   Against Free Speech.

1981   Story note: Trunk of clothes sent to France creating an era.

1982   Biography is the falsest of the arts. That is because there were no Keatzians before Keats, no Lincolnians before Lincoln.

1983   That eternal Ghetto that we love.

1984   Nun with a floating kidney.

1985   A fag—his ups and downs like Amorous (Martin) and others—humility and fatalism.

1986   The psychoanalysts again and Herman M—.

1987   As soon as a man is made a producer he gets to be two things—a son-of-a-bitch and Bernard Shaw.

1988   A man who's been drunk and wakes up at 40 looking at things through new eyes, meeting same people and scenes and contrasting them with what they were.

1989   Inside my Plaster Cast—how it became a home to me. I can't tell you what went on inside that cast—(no wise cracks, please; no form of dry land insect could possibly have lived there, although a small tropical minnow might have carried on at a subsistence level.)

1990   On Charlie Mac—He's my grandfather—I'm his. All right, we're not brothers anymore. Let's leave it at that. No diminution of affection, simply a diminution of communicability.

1991   Nathan and dirty movie in France.

1992   We have 3 feet of snow and the place looks like Sun Valley with girls in mink coats and slacks and dark glasses.

1993   In a vague way seemed to have been to "Parus" but never in any country that approximated France.

1994   That cruel old man's mouth refined down to a girl's— sweet and filled out just a little toward conventional beauty.

1995   Ernest and "Farewell to Arms"—producer story.

1996   An inferiority complex comes simply from not feeling you're doing the best you can—Ernest's "drink" was simply a form of this.

1997   Gag with cork tip cigarette.

1998   Communists asks you to accept a simplification that is itself a distortion—a mystical belief in a line. I believe that you could build right up through Lenin including only heretics. Just as in the Christian church you could do the same.

1999   The enemy of men is Fear—the enemy of women is pity. That was settled thousands of years before our era, so—continue about trained nurses and into situation. Men train their sons in games and women in hard guile.

2000   Story idea—Navajoes.

2001   I am the last of the novelists for a long time now.

2002   PROBLEMS: Most problems can be settled in their simpler stages and a whole lot of your problems are still in that stage. Not so suddenly that you have no pause for breath. Life becomes complex with marriage, money or something and when it gets really complex, it is absolutely insoluble except in the simplicity of the grave.

2003 Right behind the eight ball. Give. For my dough. What'll we use for money.

2004 "Word instructive strikes horror in soul stop please not too instructive".

2005 Develop this: Difference in conversation between Gerald Murphy and Tommy Hitchcock. Tommy doesn't answer foolish questions or trivial questions—Gerald on the contrary, in spite of what he says about the omnipresence of bores, contrives always a little arpeggio of grace which he uses as a bridge so that no matter what is said to him he fills in the gap between the graciousness and his own talents of wit and delicacy. Trace a character who once was like Gerald and who now tends toward Tommy Hitchcock's impatience with fools.

2006 I gotta see a hog about a plan.

2007 Dog's name: Miss Alliance!

2008 With each lunge of the mouse she shrank back against the bedroom door.

2009 Black Scotties with heads like clowns' hats.

2010 Jewish people are Continental, whether they think so or not.

2011 He would offer to the nation ghastly bits of conversation—dialect thinly masked as dialogue.

2012 A lady whose past was booked solid with men.

2013 He was what I think of as the Judd Grey sort of man, spectacles which made him look more than ever like any salesman—a cheap product often in a position above his capacities. A good fellow—one of the boys wearing underneath the heart of a turrp. Something that made him always carry his chin a little too high with his "inferiors" and little too low when on the spot. The alignment of features just out of focus so that "nice looking" was the best to be said of him.

2014   Girl looked like angel cake cut this morning. Clearer than Virginia Bruce.

2015   In his reign as the first citizen of Chicago, Insull was the president of eleven corporations, chairman of the boards of 65 companies and sat on the boards of 85 corporations.

2016   The flappers and the Japanese sex book.

2017   A FABLE FOR TED PARAMORE
by
F. Scott Fitzgerald

A great city set in a valley, desired a cathedral. They sent for an eminent architect who designed one distinguished by a great central tower. No sooner was it begun, however, than critics arose who objected to the tower calling it useless, ornamental, illogical, and what not—destroyed his plan and commissioning another architect to build a cathedral of great blocks and masses. It was very beautiful and Grecian in its purity but no one ever loved the cathedral of that city as they did those of Rome and Sienna and the great Duomo of Florence.

After thirty years wondering why, the citizens dug up the plans of the first architect (since grown famous) and built from it. From the first Mass the cathedral seized the imagination of the multitude and fools said it was because the tower pointed heavenward, etc., but one young realist decided to dig up the artist, now an old man, and ask him why.

The artist was too old to remember, he said—and he added "I doubt if I ever knew. But I knew I was right."

"How did you know if you don't know your reasons?"

"Because I felt good that day", answered the architect, "and if I feel good I have a reason for what I do even if I don't know the reason". So the realist went away unanswered.

On that same day a young boy going to Mass with his mother quickened his step as he crossed the cathedral square.

> "Oh I like our new cathedral so much better than the old", he said.
> "But the academy thinks it's not nearly so beautiful".
> "But it's because of the mountains", said the little boy. "Before we had the tower I could see the mountains and they made everything seem little when you went inside the Church. Now you can't see the mountains so God inside is more important".

That was what the architect had envisioned without thinking when he accidentally raised his forfinger against the sky fifty years before.

2018   Burlesque on Christina Rosetti—Rover Boy Communist

2019   I wouldn't trade her for a Sunday roll
With the best strip-teaser in the gallup poll.

2020   A.   You bastard.
          B.   I bet you never saw a bastard. I bet you wouldn't know a bastard if you saw one.

2021   Idea: You didn't fool anybody.

2022   You Can't Organize Feebs

Sure you can organize the feebs. Look you can organize anything. Look at the cults in Los Angeles.

But I mean how can you keep them organized if they're feebs.

"Keep your shirt on, said Standing. "They stay organized because you can give them a new directive every twenty four hours. They can return for twenty four hours."

"No, they can't. Look, I was a guard in Bloomingdale—"

"Say, listen we're not talking about nuts—we're talking about feebs. Were you around during the last war—well, I was. And the average mental age of the draftees was thirteen and a half wasn't it. So there must have been a lot age nine or ten."

"My kid's ten said X and he comes back from the movies complaining they're not self-conscious. If his brain never grew up another year you couldn't sell him a bill he didn't believe in. Not that easy."

"Sure—but he reads the paper doesn't he?"

"He reads the worker."

"Well, my idea's dames. They don't read any paper except the movie page. I say we can organize the feeb dames."

"All right try it. You got nothing to do. You got to lie low till they wash up your case. I bet you five smackers you don't have a chance. You can't organize Feebs."

2023   Story Ideas: Tom, Julian and the two Swiss girls.
Kill no more pigeons than you can eat. (Franklin)
The muses love the morning. (Franklin)
He is not well bred that cannot bear ill-breeding mothers. (Franklin)

2024   A sub-reptile: I don't feel you have the brains of a bat, the sensibility of a mouse or the moral standards of a rat.

2025   Man chooses his own form of execution—chooses that the executioner be blindfolded at forty paces.

2026   CAPTIONS FOR NEW YORKER
Nothing is as old as last year's new.)
) `Born 1806.
IT SEEMS LIKE YESTERDAY   )

2027   Without the brains of a bat but with a double load of intuition.

2028   Mr. Flynn is not behind the times but ahead of it—he isn't about 350 A.D., just pre-Constantine according to the Spenglerian calendar. Another quarter century of cheap movies, radio and professional sport will undoubtedly soften up the helots even more so that we can accept his fatalism. But the time is not yet.

2029

Marlbourough	Clive
Walpole	Hastings
Chatham	Washington
Pitt	Jefferson
Dr. Johnston	Franklin
Fox or Burke?	Payne

2030   Plutarch of the 18th Century. The Islanders vs. the Colonials (leaving out, of course, philosophers, scientists, artist, literary men of whom the colonists had none.

2031   There's no such thing as a "minor" character in Dostoevski.

2032   The girl must be humble; there is a lack of humility in Wolfe, Saroyan, Schlessinger that I find as depressing as O'Hara's glooms.

2033   Look what the cat brought in. Honey little funny little. It looks like love.

2034   Magic Leg!
Opens up like a Harp
Veterans! Throw your crotch away.
Miss S. Beanquest of Beanquest Dorm. writes. So do all the other girls in Beanquest Dorm except Fanny the Feeb.
Sincerely
Mrs. S.O.B.
(name on request)

2035   Special Inducement
Piccolo Juice

2036   Man who pays bill long after to pesthouse is rewarded with guard job and goes wrong.

2037   I look out at it—and I think it is the most beautiful history in the world. It is the history of me and of my people. And if I came here yesterday like Sheilah I should still think so. It is the history of all aspiration—not just the American dream but the human dream and if I came at the end of it that too is a place in the line of the pioneers.

2038   The purpose of a fiction story is to create passionate curiosity and then to gratify it unexpectedly, orgasmically. Isn't that what we expect from all contacts?

2039   Tender is less interesting toward the climax because of the absence of conversation. The eye flies for it and skips essential stuff for they don't want their characters resolved in dessication and analysis but like me in action that results from the previous. All the more reason for *emotional* planning.

2040   Congratulations on your brilliant display of human nature.

2041   Actresses have to be show offs and not look like show offs.

2042   One room slum.

2043   There is a time in the life of all great conquerors when they would gladly settle in for a safe colonelcy—but they can't; for them it's Victory or elimination.

2044   Child: What would you like for Xmas.
        Papa: Nothing I'd rather have the money.

2045   It must be wonderful to be able to make people so happy just by leaving them.

2046   At twilight on September 3rd, 1923, a girl jumped from the 53rd story window of a New York office building. She wore a patent inflatable suit of rubber composition which had just been put on the novelty market for fun purposes—the wearer by a mere jump or push could supposedly sail over fences or street intersections. It was fully blown up when she jumped. The building was a set-back and she landed on the projecting roof of the 50th floor. She was bruised and badly shaken but not seriously hurt.

2047   Hell, the best friend I have in Hollywood is a Jew— another of my best dozen friends is a Jew. Two of the half dozen men I admire most in America are Jews and two of my half dozen best men in History are Jews. But why do they have to be so damned conceited. That minority conceit—like fairies. They go ostrich about their faults—magnify their virtues which anyone is willing to grant in the first place. They point at Benny Leonard or this war hero here and say we got pugnacity. When the nurses in the hospital admit that a Jewish patient groans at the sight of a needle. Our Mommas—God bless them.---have been saying too long, Go out David—but don't use your slingshot—we are in lands of peace and plenty. What she might have said had she been a seer is: "Go David—like the Celts in America—leave your "cleverness" your slingshot behind. In 1910 the Catholic nuns secretly wrote the Regents Examination on the blackboards so that their pupils would pass first. The first evangelist was a Priest who said: "Sister, you must start with personal honor. . . . . When you hear Louis B. M----. --Jesus.

2048   Mary J. groping along beside him---(for description)

2049   Each year there is always one line worked to ad nauseum limits by scenario hacks. Last year it was "right behind the eight ball". This year it is "boil some hot water—lots of it". This is used in all accident scenes. I snicker now when I hear it—it occurred in Stanley and Livingston.

2050   Gentle trickling complaint behind the scarlett dress. Scenery from Petrouchka. The endless seats of the bowl, the scattered drape on the platform.

2051   Heritage—Isn't he dead—he was alive the last time I saw him.

2052   Perfect people have no rhythm. The shy type, the religious type. That's why I don't like them. It is a rhythmic question.

2053   When there is a reunion of two people who have once meant a lot to each other—first comes a fine recapitulation of the past and then each thinks "we'll go on" and the time of readjustment has come. They have remembered only the best, forgetting it was picked out from a time of ordinariness, forgetting that the ordinariness was pleasant expecting the ball to roll of itself as it once did—and miserable in a vast human silence.

2054   The great homosexual theses—that all great pansies were pansies.

2055   The earth was not marvelous enough so people listened to Eliza and Joseph Smith. But the universe, discovered thru science is *too* marvelous—so we listen to them again. Truth—with your old black widows weeds from the death of illusion—truth must we avoid you always. (Answer: Yes!)

2056   To start her weary rounds between the divorce court, the abortionist and the sanitarium. What a pity—for any smart person with a little money and a little luck ought to have a keen time till they're thirty. After that——

2057   List of people, classes I've quarrelled with.

2058   In Fisher's Mormon Book there are interesting questions of tempo *contrary* to the dramatic assumptions or at least uneasy to answer in dramatic terms. For example: at the end we get the brave men yeilding—how does Fisher show the background of that to unbelievers. I *know* it is true—but there is lack of art. On the other hand, in dramatic inevitability such as a Kauffman scenario or an expert picture there is too much inevitability.

2059   Remember Dave S's Algier book and utterly sincere advice to Bud S.

2060   As I grow older I become increasingly a devotee of the "Mandiean Heresey" which was to regard humanity as a two-faced creation—and to give God and the Devil opposite if not equal attributes. That is to say: to give good and evil as a proportionate sway in every man. This feeling plays, of course, into the hands of the determinists into the cheating fingers of luck.

2061   The state of Metro.

2062   Her letters are tragically brilliant on all matters except those of central importance. How strange to have failed as a social creature—even criminals do not fail that way—they are the laws "Loyal Opposition", so to speak. But the insane are always mere guests on earth, eternal strangers carrying around broken dialogues that they cannot read.

2063   Ten books not to be cast away on a Desert Island with: How to repair a Linotype machine—Emerson on Friendship.

2064   Mr. Harry Haukinspit.

2065   The gay nineties, the yellow nineties were really the empty nineties.

2066   It is so to speak Ernest's 'Tale of Two Cities' though the comparison isn't apt. I mean it is a thoroughly superficial book which has all the profundity of Rebecca.

2067   When Dotty took the veil.

2068   I want to write scenes that are frightening and inimitable. I don't want to be as intelligible to my contemporaries as Ernest who as Gertrude Stein said, is bound for the Museums. I am sure I am far enough ahead to have some small immortality if I can keep well.

2069   It was a pale, even spiritual face lit reverently with great brown eyes, but the pointed ears and the corners of the mouth were puckish and grotesque and the smile with which he greeted Josephine said plainly enough that they were all three characters in a ghastly joke, and that he was glad she understood it from the beginning. "One of those crazy men," she thought to herself—"

2070   Action is character.

2071   Fitzgerald you keep on as if that class still existed, etc.. *From a Review* and Auden quotation.

2072   Brought up on a life of leisurely crime.

2073   Hoped I look like   )
         Trying to look like)   A Petty drawing.

2074   When better women are made I will make them.

2075   Man takes cocktail ranch at the Beverly Wilshire.

2076   Feel a girl's skull and she becomes a human being.

2077   They're Swell people—an essay on softness.

2078   She first discovered love in her throat.

Editorial and Explanatory Notes

1. "On Schedule," *Saturday Evening Post*, CCV (18 March 1933).
9. "Indecision," *Saturday Evening Post*, CCIII (16 May 1931).
22. John Keats to Benjamin Bailey, 22 November 1817.
24. "Indecision."
25. "A Snobbish Story," *Saturday Evening Post*, CCIII (29 November 1930).
26. "A Snobbish Story."
27. From the drafts of *Tender Is the Night*; the comment about scratching is also in "The Swimmers," *Saturday Evening Post*, CCII (19 October 1929).
28. "Magnetism," *Saturday Evening Post*, CC (3 March 1928).
29. "The Love Boat," *Saturday Evening Post*, CC (8 October 1927).
30. Zelda Fitzgerald's sister, Rosalind Smith. See 606, 965, 981.
31. "What a Handsome Pair!" *Saturday Evening Post*, CCV (27 August 1932).
32. *The Last Tycoon*, Chapter IV.
38. "Diagnosis," *Saturday Evening Post*, CCIV (20 February 1932).
39. "Diagnosis."
40. "On Your Own," unpublished 1931 short story. Also titled "Home to Maryland."
41. "On Your Own."
42. From the drafts of *Tender Is the Night*.
43. From the drafts of *Tender Is the Night*.
50. "One Hundred False Starts," *Saturday Evening Post*, CCV (4 March 1933).
53. From the drafts of *Tender Is the Night*.
56. From the drafts of *Tender Is the Night*.
60. From the drafts of *Tender Is the Night*.
62. Possibly a reference to Fitzgerald's friendship with Hemingway.
71. Bijou O'Connor, an Englishwoman Fitzgerald knew in Switzerland. See 550 and 749.
77. From Fitzgerald's letter to Beatrice Dance, September 1935.

81. From the drafts of *Tender Is the Night*.
85. *The Last Tycoon*, Chapter I.
89. From the drafts of *Tender Is the Night*.
102. "The Bridal Party," *Saturday Evening Post*, CCIII (9 August 1930).
105. "Dice, Brassknuckles & Guitar," *Hearst's International*, XLIII (May 1923).
111. "On Your Own."
112. Probably from a draft of "The Rubber Check," *Saturday Evening Post*, CCV (6 August 1932). See 907.
114. "What To Do About It," unpublished 1933 short story.
115. "What To Do About It."
116. "On Your Own."
117. Sara Murphy.
118. Possibly Archibald MacLeish.
120. "On Your Own."
121. "Dice, Brassknuckles & Guitar."
122. "Dice, Brassknuckles & Guitar."
123. "Dice, Brassknuckles & Guitar."
124. "Dice, Brassknuckles & Guitar."
142. "Magnetism."
143. "A Freeze-Out," *Saturday Evening Post*, CCIV (19 December 1931).
151. "New Types," *Saturday Evening Post*, CCVII (22 September 1934).
153. "On Schedule."
154. "On Schedule."
155. "On Schedule."
156. "On Schedule"; also *The Last Tycoon*, Chapter V.
157. "Diagnosis."
158. "Diagnosis."
159. "The Love Boat."
160. "The Love Boat."
161. "A Night at the Fair," *Saturday Evening Post*, CCI (21 July 1928).
162. "A Night at the Fair."
166. "Love in the Night," *Saturday Evening Post*, CXCVII (14 March 1925). Fitzgerald's imitation of "The hare limp'd trembling through the frozen grass" from Keats's "The Eve of St. Agnes."
167. "Love in the Night."
168. "Love in the Night."
169. "Basil and Cleopatra," *Saturday Evening Post*, CCI (27 April 1929).
173. Maxwell Perkins to Ann Chidester, 6 January 1947: "When Scott was writing 'Tender Is the Night'—he didn't think he ought to talk about the books he was doing, and so put it this way—he said the whole motif was taken from Ludendorf's memoirs. They were moving up the guns for the great Spring offensive in 1918, and Ludendorf said, 'The song of the frogs on the river

drowned the rumble of our artillery.' When he told me this, it puzzled me, but when I read the book I realized that there was all this beautiful veneer, and rottenness and horror underneath.''

184. ''Diagnosis.''
185. ''Diagnosis.''
186. ''Diagnosis.''
187. ''Flight and Pursuit,'' *Saturday Evening Post*, CCIV (14 May 1932).
188. ''Flight and Pursuit.''
189. ''Flight and Pursuit.''
190. ''Flight and Pursuit.''
191. ''The Swimmers.''
192. Adapted for *The Last Tycoon*, Chapter IV. Also in ''Travel Together,'' unpublished 1935 short story.
194. ''Travel Together.''
195. ''Travel Together.''
198. ''The Bridal Party.''
199. ''The Bridal Party.''
200. ''The Bridal Party.''
201. ''A Snobbish Story''; adapted for *The Last Tycoon*, Chapter V.
202. ''Indecision.''
203. ''A Snobbish Story.''
204. ''A Snobbish Story.''
205. ''The Hotel Child,'' *Saturday Evening Post*, CCIII (31 January 1931).
206. ''Love in the Night.''
207. ''Dice, Brassknuckles & Guitar.''
209. ''The Popular Girl,'' *Saturday Evening Post*, CXCIV (11 February and 18 February 1922).
212. Biltmore mansion.
218. ''The Popular Girl.''
219. Adapted from ''The Love Boat.''
221. ''Indecision.''
222. ''Indecision.''
226. Fitzgerald lived in a furnished room on Claremont Avenue in Manhattan while working for the Barron Collier advertising agency in 1919.
231. .''A Snobbish Story.''
232. ''Magnetism.''
234. ''A Freeze-Out.''
235. ''A New Leaf,'' *Saturday Evening Post*, CCIV (4 July 1931).
242. See 479.
244. ''Diagnosis.''
245. Paris nightclub.
246. ''Indecision.''

254. "What To Do About It."

256. "On Your Own."

257. "On Your Own."

258. "On Your Own."

262. "A Penny Spent," *Saturday Evening Post*, CXCVIII (10 October 1925).

264. Baltimore.

270. "A Penny Spent."

274. "What To Do About It."

276. "The Bridal Party."

277. "John Jackson's Arcady," *Saturday Evening Post*, CXCVII (26 July 1924).

278. "John Jackson's Arcady."

281. "On Your Own."

282. "On Your Own."

283. "On Your Own."

284. "Dice, Brassknuckles & Guitar."

285. "Dice, Brassknuckles & Guitar."

287. "The Unspeakable Egg," *Saturday Evening Post*, CXCVII (12 July 1924).

288. "John Jackson's Arcady."

289. "Myra Meets His Family," *Saturday Evening Post*, CXCII (20 March 1920).

290. "The Popular Girl."

291. "Not in the Guidebook," *Woman's Home Companion*, LII (November 1925).

295. "John Jackson's Arcady."

302. "Dice, Brassknuckles & Guitar."

308. Fitzgerald went on location at Dartmouth in February 1939 to work on *Winter Carnival*.

311. " 'Trouble,' " *Saturday Evening Post*, CCIX (6 March 1937).

314. Dorothy Parker.

317. Giuseppe Zangara attempted to assassinate Franklin Delano Roosevelt in 1933.

321. A wealthy American who moved to Paris in 1912.

325. "Indecision."

327. William Jennings Bryan and Clarence Darrow, opposing lawyers in the 1925 Scopes "monkey trial" which tested the Tennessee law prohibiting teaching the theory of evolution. See 1174.

335. "One Trip Abroad," *Saturday Evening Post*, CCIII (11 October 1930).

348. See 1179.

350. "One Interne," *Saturday Evening Post*, CCV (5 November 1932).

370. In "The Snows of Kilimanjaro," Hemingway wrote: "He remembered poor Scott Fitzgerald and his romantic awe of them and how he had started a story once that began, 'The very rich are different from you and me.' And how someone had said to Scott, Yes they have more money." This rejoinder was

in fact made to Hemingway by Mary Colum. See Bruccoli, *Scott and Ernest* (New York: Random House, 1978).

373. Gerald and Sara Murphy, the Fitzgeralds' close friends.

383. A health camp for men.

388. From the drafts of *Tender Is the Night*; Fitzgerald had originally used this joke in Book III, Chapter 7 when Dick Diver fails at the aquaplane stunt.

389. ". . . the test of a first-rate intelligence is the ability to hold two opposed ideas in the mind at the same time, and still retain the ability to function" ("The Crack-Up," *Esquire*, V [February 1936]). This idea may have derived from Keats's concept of negative capability.

390. Quirt was a character in the play *What Price Glory* by Maxwell Anderson and Laurence Stallings.

394. Fitzgerald lived at The Cambridge Arms on Charles Street in Baltimore in 1935-1936.

396. Kyle Crichton wrote for *New Masses* under the pseudonym Robert Forsythe. See 1038, 1040.

398. A play on Cheyne-Stokes breathing: respiration characterized by rhythmic waxing and waning with periods at which breathing ceases.

408. The motto of the Order of the Garter: "Honi soit qui mal y pense." Fitzgerald rented a house at Malibu beach in 1938.

409. Georges Clemenceau was elected to the National Assembly after the French Revolution of 1870, which was precipitated by the German victory in the Franco-Prussian War; Hitler became Chancellor of Germany in 1933.

419. "What To Do About It."

422. "The Popular Girl."

426. Gerald Murphy's sister.

427. Friends of the Murphys on the Riviera.

430. "The Rubber Check."

437. "Six of One—" *Redbook*, LVIII (February 1932).

438. Possibly T. S. Matthews who wrote for *New Republic*. Michael Gold, author of *Jews Without Money* and columnist in the *Daily Worker*.

442. "What a Handsome Pair!"

445. In 1932-1933 Fitzgerald rented "La Paix" on the Turnbull estate.

450. "Diagnosis."

451. "What a Handsome Pair!"

454. From the drafts of *Tender Is the Night*.

456. From a draft of "On Your Own."

458. "Babylon Revisited," *Saturday Evening Post*, CCIII (21 February 1931).

460. "Diamond Dick and the First Law of Woman," *Hearst's International*, LXV (April 1924).

464. "On Your Own."

466. See 765.

467. "More than Just a House," *Saturday Evening Post*, CCV (24 June 1933).
468. "More than Just a House."
469. "More than Just a House."
470. "The Family Bus," *Saturday Evening Post*, CCVI (4 November 1933).
471. "The Family Bus."
472. "The Rough Crossing," *Saturday Evening Post*, CCI (8 June 1929).
473. "On Schedule."
475. "On Schedule."
476. "The Hotel Child."
477. "The Bowl," *Saturday Evening Post*, CC (21 January 1928).
478. "Magnetism."
479. "Indecision."
480. "The Rubber Check."
481. "What a Handsome Pair!"
482. "The Hotel Child."
483. "New Types."
484. "New Types."
485. "Forging Ahead," *Saturday Evening Post*, CCI (30 March 1929).
486. "Forging Ahead."
488. "The Popular Girl."
491. "What To Do About It."
492. "What To Do About It."
496. "On Your Own."
497. "On Your Own."
498. "What To Do About It."
505. The Vagabonds was a Baltimore little theatre group.
508. "No Flowers," *Saturday Evening Post*, CCVII (21 July 1934). Partly used in *The Last Tycoon*, Chapter V. Also in "What To Do About It."
509. "Basil and Cleopatra."
510. "Basil and Cleopatra."
511. "The Love Boat." Adapted for *The Last Tycoon*, Chapter IV.
512. "The Love Boat." See 1903.
513. "The Love Boat."
514. "Forging Ahead."
516. "The Love Boat."
517. "Travel Together."
518. "Travel Together."
519. "I Got Shoes," *Saturday Evening Post*, CCVI (23 September 1933).
521. "Magnetism."
522. "A Penny Spent."

523. "The Third Casket," *Saturday Evening Post*, CXCVI (31 May 1924).
525. "Magnetism."
526. From the drafts of *Tender Is the Night*.
531. "New Types."
532. "A Freeze-Out."
533. "A Freeze-Out."
534. "A Freeze-Out."
536. "One Interne."
537. "Indecision."
538. "Indecision."
539. "Indecision."
540. "A Snobbish Story."
541. Nora Flynn, a friend of Fitzgerald's in Tryon, N.C. See 552 and 928.
547. "Gods of Darkness," *Redbook*, LXXVIII (November 1941).
549. Probably cut from " 'I'd Die for You,' " unpublished 1935-1936 short story.
550. Bijou O'Connor and Beatrice Dance. Fitzgerald had a brief affair with Beatrice Dance at Asheville in 1935.
552. *The Last Tycoon*, Chapter V.
553. Possibly a reference to Frances Turnbull.
554. The Dartmouth Winter Carnival.
556. Hollywood agent.
564. "A New Leaf."
565. "The Popular Girl."
566. "Flight and Pursuit."
567. From Fitzgerald's letter to Beatrice Dance, summer 1935.
570. Partly used in *Tender Is the Night*, Book I, Chapter 24.
571. "Magnetism."
572. "Indecision."
574. "A Snobbish Story."
576. "A Snobbish Story."
577. "A Snobbish Story."
578. "A Snobbish Story."
579. "The Bridal Party."
582. "The Bridal Party."
584. "Travel Together."
585. "Travel Together."
589. "The Love Boat."
592. "Flight and Pursuit." Also in "Offside Play," unpublished short story.
593. "Flight and Pursuit."
594. "I Got Shoes."
595. "I Got Shoes."

596. "What a Handsome Pair!"
597. "The Rubber Check."
598. "On Schedule."
599. "Basil and Cleopatra."
602. Secretary of State, 1933-1944.
603. Erskine Gwynne, publisher of the Paris *Boulevardier*. William Rhinelander Stewart, philanthropist.
612. Ernest Hemingway. See 728, 757, 1002, 1019, 1021, 1034, 1237, 1246, 1277, 1437, 1528, 1819, 1825, 1868, 1915, 1918, 1924, 1979, 1995, 1996, 2066, 2068.
616. Critic and editor.
622. "Basil and Cleopatra."
623. Katherine Littlefield, Philadelphia ballet teacher.
624. "Indecision."
625. "A Snobbish Story."
626. "A Snobbish Story."
630. Possibly a note on Francis Melarky for the early drafts of *Tender Is the Night*.
632. "The Love Boat."
633. "The Love Boat."
634. "Travel Together."
635. Probably Johns Hopkins Hospital in Baltimore. The oyster barrel note was used in "Zone of Accident," *Saturday Evening Post*, CCVIII (13 July 1935).
636. "First Blood," *Saturday Evening Post*, CCII (17 May 1930).
644. Screenwriter Herman Mankiewicz.
646. H. L. Mencken.
647. "A Penny Spent."
657. "Dice, Brassknuckles & Guitar."
658. "The Unspeakable Egg."
659. "Not in the Guidebook."
662. Servant at "La Paix." Fitzgerald used this name in "On Schedule."
664. Adapted from "A New Leaf."
665. "Our Own Movie Queen," *Chicago Sunday Tribune* (7 June 1925). This story was written by F. Scott and Zelda Fitzgerald, but was published under his by-line.
670. "Six of One—"
671. "What a Handsome Pair!"
673. "On Schedule."
676. "Forging Ahead."
678. "A New Leaf."
680. "A Snobbish Story."
682. "What To Do About It."
685. "On Your Own."

686. "The Popular Girl."

697. Possibly actress Lois Moran. See *The Last Tycoon*, Chapter I.

725. English lesbian, member of Natalie Barney's Amazon circle in Paris.

738. Jackson Budd, *Gallows Waits* (1932); Hugh Walpole, *Fortitude* (1913).

744. The Fitzgeralds rented "Ellerslie," near Wilmington, Del., in 1927-1929. Lois Moran.

754. Brown was a diplomat and professor of international law at Princeton. Buchmanism, also known as Moral Re-armament and the Oxford Group, was a revivalist movement founded by Frank N. D. Buchman in 1922. Until 1926 the center of operations was at Princeton University.

764. Highlands, N.C.

765. Recollections from the Fitzgeralds' 1924 residence on the Riviera.

790. Movie actress Constance Bennett.

792. Carter Brown, proprietor of the Pinecrest Inn in Tryon, N.C. See 863.

796. Chief of the Arveni who led rebellion against the Romans in 52 B.C.

800. Ring Lardner.

801. Fitzgerald attended the Newman School in 1911-1913.

803. Hymn by Reginald Heber: "From Greenland's icy mountains. . . ."

805. Possibly an idea for a sequel to "John Jackson's Arcady."

808. Possibly an idea for a Basil Duke Lee story.

809. Possibly an idea for a Josephine Perry story.

814. Movie director Rex Ingram had a studio on the Riviera.

817. "A Smile for Sylvo" was the original title for "The Smilers" (1920); Hemingway's "A Canary for One" (1927); *Dinner at Eight* (1932), a play by George S. Kaufman and Edna Ferber.

821. See 1179.

823. *Scarface* was a 1932 gangster movie.

827. In 1937 the yacht owned by the Hon. Mrs. Reginald Fellowes was fired upon by a Greek warship.

830. Refers to a scene in the second draft version of *Tender Is the Night*, in which the Kellys walk the decks of a liner.

832. Gerald Murphy's older brother.

834. Monsignor Sigourney Fay, headmaster at Newman who was Fitzgerald's mentor.

835. Dorothy King, a model, was murdered in 1923; the case involved blackmail.

837. Father Joseph Thomas Barron of St. Paul.

839. A reference to Zelda Fitzgerald's involvement with Edouard Jozan in 1924.

840. Movie director who had made his reputation as Greta Garbo's director.

842. Novel by Joseph Hergesheimer.

845. These movie stories—if they were written—are unlocated.

848. " 'I'd Die for You.' "

861. *Nassau Literary Magazine*, LXXIV (February 1919).
862. *Nassau Literary Magazine*, LXXIV (February 1919).
863. Brown was active in steeplechasing and fox-hunting.
884. "The Boy That Killed His Mother," which Fitzgerald performed as a party stunt. This poem provided the working title for the first version of *Tender Is the Night*.
896. Written for a proposed musical for the Vagabonds. Other lyrics in this section were probably also intended for this project.
902. Character analysis of Zelda Fitzgerald.
904. English playwright Frederick Lonsdale.
907. "The Rubber Check."
908. "The Rubber Check."
909. "What a Handsome Pair!"
910. "Forging Ahead."
911. Crowninshield was editor of *Vanity Fair*; the Coffee House is a New York club for writers and publishers.
913. "Magnetism."
917. "Minnie the Moocher," song popularized by Cab Calloway. See "Zone of Accident."
920. From the drafts of *Tender Is the Night*.
922. Philip McQuillan.
923. From the drafts of *Tender Is the Night*.
924. From the drafts of *Tender Is the Night*.
925. "The Smilers," *Smart Set*, LXII (June 1920).
926. "The Popular Girl."
927. Peggy Hopkins Joyce, much-married showgirl.
928. Nora Langhorne was one of the beautiful Langhorne sisters who were referred to as "the Gibson girls." She married Paul Phipps in 1909. In 1931 she married M. B. (Lefty) Flynn, Yale football star and cowboy actor. The Flynns lived in Tryon, N.C. where they were friendly with Fitzgerald during the "crack-up" period.
931. Novelist James Boyd; polo player Tommy Hitchcock.
935. From the draft of "On Schedule."
936. From the draft of "On Schedule."
937. From the draft of "On Schedule."
949. Yale Senior Society.
950. "Magnetism."
952. Sandra Kalman of St. Paul; Fitzgerald's sister Annabel.
954. "A New Leaf."
955. From the drafts of *Tender Is the Night*.
956. "A Penny Spent."

957. From the drafts of *Tender Is the Night*.

959. Professional party-giver Elsa Maxwell. See 966.

962. Movie actress Constance Talmadge; musical comedy star Fannie Brice.

964. Possibly Ruth Obre Goldbeck de Vallombrosa, an American who had married into French society.

966. Humorist Donald Ogden Stewart. See 1007-1008.

971. From the drafts of *Tender Is the Night*.

974. Probably a reference to movie producer Irving Thalberg. See 1312.

975. Princeton classmate of Fitzgerald's.

976. From the drafts of *Tender Is the Night*.

982. "Diagnosis."

1003. Cody was a silent movie star and producer.

1010. By Richard Harding Davis, 1897.

1011. Author of *The Counsel of the Ungodly* (1920), *Week-end* (1925), *The Last Infirmity* (1926), *American Colony* (1929), and *Entirely Surrounded* (1934). See 1053.

1013. Wallace was a prolific author of mysteries and thrillers; Henty wrote fictionalized history for boys.

1014. Servants at "La Paix."

1018. Franz Werfel, *The Forty Days of Musa Dagh* (1934).

1022. See Keats's comments on the disinterested mind in his letter to George and Georgiana Keats, 19 February 1819. Rita Swann was a Baltimore friend of Fitzgerald's. See 1063.

1026. Le Grand Guignol, Paris horror theatre.

1030. The last line of Shakespeare's Sonnet 94: "Lilies that fester smell far worse than weeds."

1031. Possibly "Then Back to Ancient France Again." "Mediaval" refers to the Count of Darkness stories, in which Philippe was modeled on Hemingway.

1042. Dorothea Brande, *Wake Up and Live!* (1936); also *Becoming a Writer* (1934), *Most Beautiful Lady* (1935), *Letters to Philippa* (1937), and *My Invincible Aunt* (1938).

1047. William Ernest Henley's poem "Invictus."

1051. Popular novelist, author of *Freckles* (1904), *A Girl of the Limberlost* (1909), *The Harvester* (1911), and *Laddie* (1913).

1057. Series of juvenile books by Annie Fellows Johnston, published 1895-1920.

1061. Booth Tarkington was a reformed alcoholic.

1062. John O'Hara, Edmund Wilson, and John Peale Bishop.

1063. Article by Fitzgerald; *Ladies' Home Journal*, XL (June 1923).

1064. Novelist and editor.

1068. "Thank You So Much, Missus Lowsborough-Goodby" (1934).

1070. Actor Horton owned the "Belly Acres" estate at Encino, Cal., where Fitzgerald rented a cottage in 1938-1939.

1072. Ginevra King, Fitzgerald's first love while he was at Princeton; Joseph L. Mankiewicz, the producer of *Three Comrades* (1938) at MGM with whom Fitzgerald fought over script changes.

1074. Ernest Renan's *The Life of Christ* (1863), which treated Christ as an historical figure.

1077. "Shaggy's Morning," *Esquire*, III (May 1935).

1081. Writer Margaret Case Harriman.

1091. "On Your Own."

1096. "New Types."

1100. "Love in the Night."

1101. "A Snobbish Story."

1102. "A Freeze-Out."

1103. "Magnetism."

1104. "The Swimmers."

1105. "On Your Own."

1106. "A Snobbish Story."

1108. "Forging Ahead."

1109. "Forging Ahead."

1110. "A Night at the Fair."

1112. "Travel Together."

1114. "What a Handsome Pair!"

1115. "What a Handsome Pair!"

1116. "On Schedule."

1118. Novelist and critic Carl Van Vechten.

1119. "The Love Boat."

1120. "What a Handsome Pair!"

1128. Marcel De Sano, Fitzgerald's collaborator on the unproduced screenplay for *Red-Headed Woman* (1931).

1143. "The Grand Canyon Suite" (1931) by Ferde Grofe; "Horses, Horses, Horses," a 1926 novelty song popularized by the George Olsen orchestra.

1144. "On Your Own."

1148. "On Your Own."

1151. From the drafts of *Tender Is the Night*.

1152. Sheilah Graham.

1157. Playwright; *Babes in Arms*, a musical comedy by Rodgers and Hart.

1164. "The Rubber Check."

1166. "The Rubber Check."

1167. "The Rubber Check."

1169. "The Swimmers."

1174. Clarence Darrow defended Leopold and Loeb in their trial for kidnapping and murder in 1924.

1175. Parody of the biographies in John Dos Passos's *U.S.A.*

1179. Fitzgerald was unimpressed by the back-to-the-soil school of fiction which dealt with simple rural character types. Norwegian novelist Knut Hamson and R. W. Chambers. See 348.

1186. Adapted from "A Short Trip Home," *Saturday Evening Post*, CC (17 December 1927).

1188. From the drafts of *Tender Is the Night.*

1194. "John Jackson's Arcady."

1209. From the drafts of *Tender Is the Night.*

1211. From the drafts of *Tender Is the Night.*

1216. Double-talk.

1221. Fitzgerald's version of Shelley's "Ode to the West Wind": "O Wild West Wind, thou breath of Autumn's being. . . ."

1223. The Goldwyn Studio was originally named for the partnership of Samuel Goldfish and Edgar Selwyn. It was later merged with the Metro and Mayer Studios. Goldfish took the name Goldwyn for himself.

1227. An adaptation of Kipling's line, "Beaches of Lukanon before the sealers came."

1235. Henry H. Strater, Princeton '19—the model for Burne Halliday in *This Side of Paradise.*

1239. "A Freeze-Out."

1244. "A Snobbish Story."

1246. "The Bridal Party."

1247. "Forging Ahead."

1248. "Forging Ahead."

1250. "Magnetism."

1252. "The Swimmers."

1254. "A Snobbish Story."

1257. "Six of One—"

1259. "What a Handsome Pair!"

1261. "Babylon Revisited."

1281. "Magnetism."

1292. Stone played the Scarecrow in the 1903 production of *The Wizard of Oz.*

1293. Lubov Egorova, Zelda Fitzgerald's ballet teacher in Paris.

1295. "Two Wrongs," *Saturday Evening Post*, CCII (18 January 1930).

1300. From the drafts of *Tender Is the Night.*

1305. From the drafts of *Tender Is the Night.*

1307. "More than Just a House."

1312. Irving Thalberg of MGM, the model for Monroe Stahr in *The Last Tycoon.*

1314. Dr. Oscar Forel, the psychiatrist who treated Zelda Fitzgerald at Prangins Clinic in Switzerland.

1332. "The Popular Girl."

1340. John Spargo, American socialist leader; Giovanni Papini, Italian philosopher who converted to Catholicism; G. K. Chesterton, English Catholic writer; Sir Henry Arthur Jones, English social-problem dramatist.

1350. Isabel Owens, Fitzgerald's secretary at "La Paix."

1365. Massachusetts preparatory school.

1370. Princeton undergraduate club favored by athletes.

1373. Becky Sharp and Amelia Sedley in *Vanity Fair*.

1376. Textbook by Philip Van Ness Myers, which went through several editions between 1888 and 1916.

1381. "Jimber-jawed Serge" was used in "Love in the Night." Spurgeon and Flieshhacker were used in *The Last Tycoon*. Beauty Boy was used in "Dearly Beloved," *Fitzgerald/Hemingway Annual 1969*.

1389. "Discard," *Harper's Bazaar*, LXXXII (January 1948).

1397. A discarded episode from *Tender Is the Night*.

1398. "New Types."

1399. Francis Eliot (1756-1818), writer on finance.

1400. "Love in the Night."

1404. "The Rubber Check."

1405. "Flight and Pursuit."

1406. "Flight and Pursuit."

1407. "Flight and Pursuit."

1409. In July 1931 Zelda Fitzgerald was allowed a furlough from Prangins Clinic.

1415. A Baby Gar was a motorboat; this reference may connect with the aquaplaning episode in *Tender Is the Night*. Probably Marise Hamilton, an acquaintance of the Fitzgeralds and many of their friends on the Riviera. Arno was a cartoonist for the *New Yorker*. Probably Walker Ellis, with whom Fitzgerald had collaborated on the Princeton Triangle Club show *Fie! Fie! Fi-Fi!* Probably Archibald MacLeish.

1416. Probably Lefty Flynn.

1417. "Gods of Darkness."

1418. "The Hotel Child."

1420. "A Freeze-Out."

1421. American Negro who was a musical star in Paris. "Babylon Revisited."

1422. "The Bridal Party."

1423. "The Bridal Party."

1424. "A Snobbish Story."

1427. "Indecision."

1428. "A Night at the Fair."

1429. "A Night at the Fair."

1430. "A Night at the Fair."

1432. From the drafts of *Tender Is the Night*.

1435. "The Rubber Check."

1439. The Don Ce-Sar hotel in St. Petersburg, Florida, where the Fitzgeralds vacationed in 1932.

1449. After quarrels with Fitzgerald, Zelda had burned her clothes and thrown away her diamond watch.

1459. Long Island polo club.

1461. From the drafts of *Tender Is the Night.*

1470. Wife of Fitzgerald's college friend, Judge John Biggs.

1474. From the drafts of *Tender Is the Night.*

1475. "Magnetism."

1476. "Magnetism."

1477. "Magnetism."

1478. Jim Powell is a character in "Dice, Brassknuckles & Guitar"; this material was possibly salvaged from a projected sequel to that story.

1480. From the drafts of *Tender Is the Night.*

1481. "The Bridal Party" was based on the wedding of Powell Fowler.

1484. Probably Percy Pyne, Jr., Princeton '18—member of a wealthy family of Princetonians; but possibly Percy Pyne II, Princeton '03.

1486. From the drafts of *Tender Is the Night.*

1488. From the drafts of *Tender Is the Night.*

1493. "John Jackson's Arcady."

1494. Fitzgerald visited Charlottesville on 24-25 May 1933. Laurence Lee was on the University of Virginia faculty. Possibly John W. Thomason, author of Civil War fiction.

1496. From the drafts of *Tender Is the Night.*

1497. "On Your Own."

1499. "Dice, Brassknuckles & Guitar."

1500. "The Popular Girl."

1503. "Indecision."

1504. "Indecision."

1505. "Indecision."

1508. Movie director King Vidor.

1513. Groton is a Massachusetts preparatory school. See 1790.

1520. From the drafts of *Tender Is the Night.*

1521. Robert Cresswell, Princeton '19.

1522. Andrew Turnbull.

1523. See 1494.

1524. Madame Tussaud's London waxworks.

1525. "What To Do About It."

1526. "On Your Own."

1528. Charles (Sap) Donahoe, Princeton '17. Father Thomas Delihant and Cecilia Delihant Taylor, Fitzgerald's cousins.

1536. Fitzgerald revised Clark Gable's act when Gable was making a personal appearance at a Baltimore movie theatre in February 1934.

1537. "Magnetism."

1563. Asa Bushnell, Princeton Athletic Manager; possibly architect Lawrence Noyes.

1565. "Our Own Movie Queen."

1568. "The Popular Girl."

1569. "Myra Meets His Family."

1571. From the drafts of *Tender Is the Night*. The Dickens character is Jerry Cruncher in *A Tale of Two Cities*.

1572. From the drafts of *Tender Is the Night*.

1574. "Cyclone in Silent Land," unpublished 1936 short story.

1576. The visitor was Charles Jackson, author of *Lost Weekend* (1944).

1578. Bandleaders Calloway and Duchin.

1580. Theatre producer Edgar Selwyn; gambler Arnold Rothstein, the model for Wolfshiem in *The Great Gatsby*.

1582. Red Ridingwood is a character in *The Last Tycoon*; "Thumbs Up" was a rejected title for "The End of Hate," *Collier's*, CV (22 June 1940).

1584. The February 1910 issue of the original *Life* when it was a humor magazine. *The Purple Cow* was the Williams College humor magazine.

1587. Marice Hamilton; possibly Ruth Obre Goldbeck de Vallombrosa.

1589. "A Freeze-Out."

1590. "A Snobbish Story."

1592. Possibly Robert S. Hichens's *The God Within Him* (1926).

1593. "What a Handsome Pair!"

1598. Hendersonville, N.C. where Fitzgerald began writing "The Crack-Up" in November 1935.

1601. In "A Municipal Report" O. Henry disagreed with Frank Norris's claim that there were only three "story cities" in America.

1607. Fitzgerald wrote the unproduced screenplay for *Grit* (Film Guild, 1924).

1608. "The Unspeakable Egg."

1610. From a draft of "A Night at the Fair."

1615. "The Swimmers."

1616. "Basil and Cleopatra."

1617. The Fitzgeralds' handyman in Montgomery 1931-1932. See 1622.

1625. Probably Andrew Turnbull.

1636. Sheilah Graham.

1638. "Shaggy's Morning."

1639. "Lamp in a Window," *New Yorker*, XI (23 March 1935).

1642. The Princeton club elections in Fitzgerald's sophomore year.

1646. "Love in the Night."

1647. "A Snobbish Story."

1648. "A Snobbish Story."

1649. "Basil and Cleopatra."

1650. From a draft for "A Snobbish Story."

1654. "Forging Ahead."

1658. See 18.

1660. Clara McQuillan.

1681. Song titles.

1686. Annabel McQuillan.

1687. Song titles.

1688. Based on the news-letters Scottie sent Fitzgerald in 1931.

1696. "Diamond Dick and the First Law of Woman."

1697. Syndicated comic strip by Charles E. "Bunny" Schultze, 1900-1918.

1699. Alice Hegan Rice, *Mrs. Wiggs of the Cabbage Patch* (1901).

1703. Partly used in "Too Cute for Words," *Saturday Evening Post*, CCVIII (18 April 1936).

1704. Bettina von Hutten, *Pam* (1905); Lucy Maud Montgomery, *Anne of Green Gables* (1908).

1706. "A Night at the Fair."

1707. "A Night at the Fair."

1710. Fitzgerald's sister Annabel.

1714. Song titles.

1717. The grunion scene in *The Last Tycoon*, Chapter V.

1718. For *The Last Tycoon*; this scene was not written.

1732. Mary Harriman, wife of financier E. H. Harriman.

1741. Hollywood agent.

1742. Actress, mistress of William Randolph Hearst.

1746. Carter and Marion Brown.

1750. Gustavus Myers, *History of Great American Fortunes* (1910).

1758. John Dos Passos; Jules Romains, author of *Men of Good Will* (1932-1946).

1773. Spartanburg, S.C.

1779. Lake in Polk County, N.C. and Greenville County, S.C.

1782. Highlands in southern France, west of Provence.

1789. Archibald MacLeish's daughter, Mary.

1790. From Fitzgerald's letter to his daughter Scottie, c. 1937.

1810. Carter Brown had been in a car wreck, fall 1936.

1811. Possibly a lyric written for the Baltimore Vagabonds.

1820. King Vidor.

1825. Movie director Ernst Lubitsch; Dorothy Parker.

1829. Fitzgerald's editor at Scribners.

1831. English novelist, author of *Sinister Street* (1913-1914), which had influenced *This Side of Paradise*.

1838. "Discard."

1849. "Discard."

1853. Probably movie director Cecil B. DeMille.

1858. Mrs. Payne Whitney.

1861. Movie producer Joseph Mankiewicz.

1862. E. E. Paramore, Fitzgerald's collaborator on the screenplay for *Three Comrades*.

1866. " 'I'd Die for You.' "

1870. "The Last Kiss," *Collier's*, CXXIII (16 April 1949).

1872. "Discard."

1887. Private school in New York City.

1888. Novel by John O'Hara, 1938.

1889. This plan for *This Side of Paradise* was not acted on.

1895. English military tailors.

1897. " 'Trouble.' "

1899. Screenwriter Edwin Justus Mayer.

1900. Humorist S. J. Perelman married Nathanael West's sister. West married Eileen McKenney.

1901. Screenwriter and producer Nunally Johnson.

1902. Eleazer Whitlock, founder of Dartmouth College; Fitzgerald went on location at Dartmouth for *Winter Carnival* in 1939.

1903. "The Love Boat." See 512. The phrase "closer than an embrace" was used in *The Last Tycoon*.

1911. John Peale Bishop's wife; Sara Murphy.

1914. Frankish ruler; grandfather of Charlemagne.

1921. Humorist and screenwriter.

1922. "A boy's will is the wind's will, / And the thoughts of youth are long, long thoughts." —"My Lost Youth." Adapted by Longfellow from a poem in John Scheffer's *History of Lapland* (1674).

1926. Lester Cowan, movie producer for whom Fitzgerald adapted "Babylon Revisited" in 1940.

1931. *The Last Tycoon*, Chapter IV.

1932. Mortimer Adler, *How to Read a Book* (1940); Hendrik Wilem Van Loon, *The Arts* (1937).

1937. See 396. Pietro Di Donato, *Christ in Concrete* (1939).

1941. "Today Is Friday," a short story by Ernest Hemingway.

1949. Possible reference to Orson Welles's 1938 radio dramatization of *The War of the Worlds*.

1951. Paul Leicester Ford, *Janice Meredith: A Story of the Revolution* (1899).

1952. Sheilah Graham.

1968. Dorothy Parker.

1974. Novel by Richard Wright, 1940.

1975. Stockbroker Whitney was imprisoned for embezzlement.

1979. Ernest Hemingway.

1985. Fitzgerald had gone to the Newman School with Martin Amorous.

1986. Herman Mankiewicz.

1988. "The Lost Decade," *Esquire*, XII (December 1939).

1989. Fitzgerald had been placed in a body cast after injuring his shoulder in a 1936 diving accident.

1990. Playwright and screenwriter Charles MacArthur.

1991. Possibly drama critic George Jean Nathan.

2013. Grey and his mistress Ruth Snyder had murdered her husband in 1927.

2014. Movie actress.

2015. Utilities tycoon whose financial empire collapsed in the Depression.

2017. Paramore had revised Fitzgerald's screenplay for *Three Comrades*.

2032. Novelist Tess Schlessinger.

2047. Louis B. Mayer, head of MGM.

2049. Fitzgerald used "Boil Some Water—Lots of It" for a Pat Hobby story (*Esquire*, XIII [March 1940]). *Stanley and Livingston* was a 1939 movie.

2050. *Petrouchka*, ballet with score by Igor Stravinsky.

2058. Vardis Fisher, *Children of God: An American Epic* (1939); playwright George S. Kaufman.

2059. Movie producer David O. Selznick; Budd Schulberg, Fitzgerald's collaborator on *Winter Carnival*; "Algier" was probably a typing error for "Alger."

2060. The Manichean doctrine held that "man's soul, sprung from the Kingdom of Light, seeks escape from the Kingdom of Darkness, the body."

2062. Zelda Fitzgerald.

2066. *For Whom the Bell Tolls* (1940).